THE POLITICS OF CANADIAN-JAPANESE
ECONOMIC RELATIONS, 1952–1983

THE POLITICS OF
CANADIAN-JAPANESE
ECONOMIC RELATIONS, 1952–1983

Frank Langdon

UNIVERSITY OF BRITISH COLUMBIA PRESS
VANCOUVER

THE POLITICS OF CANADIAN-JAPANESE
ECONOMIC RELATIONS, 1952–1983

This book has been published with the help of a grant from the
Social Science Federation of Canada, using funds provided by
the Social Sciences and Humanities Research Council of Canada,
and was also financially assisted by the Government of British Columbia
through British Columbia Cultural Fund and Lottery revenues.

Canadian Cataloguing in Publication Data

Langdon, Frank, 1919–
    The politics of Canadian-Japanese economic
relations, 1952–1983

    Includes index.
    ISBN 0-7748-0188-3

    1. Canada — Foreign economic relations —
Japan. 2. Japan — Foreign economic relations —
Canada. I. Title.
HF1480.15.J3L35 1983   337.71052   C83-091429-3

This book is printed on acid-free paper.

ISBN 0-7748-0188-3

Printed in Canada

Contents

List of Tables

Preface

Before spelling out the aim of this book, it might be useful to clarify what it is not. This is not a book about all the phases of Canada's relations with Japan. Nor is it a historical account which attempts to detail principal events, one by one, as they occur. What the book does attempt to do is to deal with major issues in the economic sphere as they have affected the two countries since the Second World War in their relations with each other. Economic issues and objectives have dominated the bilateral relationship. Therefore, this treatment aims at explaining those issues and objectives.

Perhaps because official and formal contacts require that governments, groups, firms, and individuals gloss over disagreements in public and present an often excessively rosy view of bilateral ties, I have tried to outline clearly where genuine disagreements or disappointed hopes exist. However, I hope I have not overemphasized negative aspects, and I do not deny that coopera- tion and goodwill are the dominant themes in postwar relations. On the contrary, I believe that Canada-Japan ties are largely harmonious and charac- terized by goodwill on both sides, perhaps too much so. I believe it is better if both sides have a healthy understanding of their best interests and avoid illusions which can only produce confusion or frustration.

Cultural ties are very important, too. It is highly desirable to bring about more person-to-person or people-to-people contacts between Canada and Japan. Still, I do have doubts about the extent to which these contacts will bring any greater response from the government of Japan to Canada's trade or investment hopes. It would certainly help Canada, in its aim of greater entrée to the Japanese market-place, for Canadian businessmen to have a better command of Japanese language, customs, and tastes. However, cultural understanding is no substitute for financial, political, or military influence when Canada is in competition with the United States or Western Europe. Even the businessmen of those countries have not been very successful in regaining the foothold in the Japanese market that they once enjoyed. Further penetration requires great personal and organizational commitment, as well as vast sums of money—something Canadians have not been willing to invest in the way that the Japanese have in our markets. The close ties in Japanese business between firms have often taken generations to establish. To go further, Canadians will have to build some of the same sort of bonds in Japan, unless Japan's economy and society change even more than they have.

Japan is Canada's most important overseas trading partner. Yet the character of our relations with each other is comparatively unknown to the majority of Canadians, while in Japan, knowledge of Canada is even more rudimentary. As the world's most dynamic economy, Japan has become extremely important to Canada; but it is almost impossible to find anything of a broad coverage about our policies and experiences with each other in the current period in English, French, or Japanese in our bookshops. Recent books which deal with Japan tend to be special studies which are not always readily available or include important accounts such as those dealing with the suffering of Japanese-Canadians during the Second World War.[1] Zavis Zeman's monograph which speculates on the possible future impact of Japan's remarkable trade and investment expansion has aroused considerable comment.[2]

A small but dedicated group of academics can be found in Japan concerned with Canadian trade, diplomacy, history, and literature, but their works are usually limited to professional journals and conferences which reach only a few of the well-informed.[3] Similarly, in Canada there are a few economists writing about trade and investment and some political scientists interested in government policy and foreign affairs concerning Japan.[4] They, too, are apt to be restricted to publications with limited circulation which are not as readily available as one could wish. Even in much of that frequently high quality study there is still a major gap, a lack of accounts of recent relations, both governmental and private, between Canada and Japan. It is the hope of beginning to fill that gap which has inspired the present work. A valuable contribution can be found in the excellent chapter by Gérard Hervouet on the Trudeau government's foreign policy toward Japan.[5]

In my treatment I have concentrated on the period since 1952 when Japan regained its independence after the Allied occupation which followed the war. At that time Japan became able to carry on full diplomatic and commercial relations once more. In Chapter 1, I sketch the character of the earlier trade with Japan and outline conflicts that arose in connection with it. Many of the basic aspects of our relationship were established in the period before the Second World War.

The early wholly Canadian commercial agreement with Japan, which set the framework of our commercial relations, is described in Chapter 2. This agreement attempted to ensure a market for Canadian natural resource products, the area of greatest success for Canadian foreign economic policy toward Japan. It was less successful in checking the sudden influxes of manufactured exports that were to prove so upsetting to the central provinces where Canada's manufacturing is concentrated. Canada's role in sponsoring Japan's entry into postwar trading privileges under the General Agreement on Tariffs and Trade (GATT) was undertaken partly to encourage Japan to side with the North Atlantic Treaty Organization (NATO) allies at the time of the Cold War and the Korean War in which Canada participated.

In Chapter 3, the struggle to limit the inroads of manufactured imports from Japan is brought closer to the present, with an examination of the informal restraints and voluntary quotas on textiles, television sets, and automobiles. Chapter 4 deals with Canada's participation in the North Pacific Fisheries Convention with the United States and Japan in order to limit Japanese access to eastern Pacific fishing. Japan's attempts to improve its entrée to those resources of the sea were frustrated by the exclusive economic zones established throughout the Pacific in 1977.

Chapter 5 takes up the problem of obtaining a greater Japanese market for Canadian manufactured and high technology exports, which has become almost an obsession with federal policymakers in Ottawa under Prime Minister Trudeau. This concern antedates the more recent efforts of the United States and the European Economic Community (EEC) to accomplish the same thing. Rather surprisingly, they have fared little better than Canada in this difficult enterprise, which may turn out to have some of the same difficulties as those experienced by Japan when it turned to free itself from foreign economic domination at the end of the nineteenth century and enter the markets of Europe and America. On this point, Canada has followed in Japan's footsteps in seeking to shake loose from what is often felt to be the smothering embraces of the United States and Europe. The federal "third option" policy of 1973 aimed at greatly increasing trade and other relations with Japan and the EEC to reduce dependence on the United States. It was crowned by a Framework for Economic Cooperation signed by Trudeau himself in Tokyo in 1976. However, the hoped-for breakthroughs in sales of the Canadian nuclear reactor (CANDU) or Short Takeoff and Landing (STOL) aircraft have not ensued. Resort to a Japanese-style trading company was considered by the Liberal government which was returned to power in 1980.

Chapter 6 deals with uranium exports and safeguards, as well as the attempt to sell the CANDU reactor. The concern aroused in Canada by the Indian nuclear explosion of 1975 (with which it was to some extent involved) produced a stringent safeguards policy in Ottawa greatly affecting the sale of uranium and reactors, especially to Japan. To resolve the problem of adherence to the new safeguards, the Canadian government resorted to a uranium embargo before the policy was settled. This action probably helped steel the Japanese resolve to seek greater nuclear independence in rejecting the purchase of a Canadian reactor.

In Chapter 7, the activities of Japanese firms in investing in Canada are surveyed. The investment is mainly in the extracting or processing of resources, usually in joint ventures and rarely with more than minor Japanese ownership participation. These ventures have often been of particular economic importance in the western provinces; but all the provinces, as well as the federal government, have proved eager to attract Japanese investment and the transfer of Japanese technology. Chapter 8 reviews those Canadian objectives and government policies that were presented in a less comprehensive way in the preceding chapters. It tries to predict likely trends in the near future, in the light of current conditions and developments. At the end of this final chapter, a brief assessment of the bilateral relationship between Canada and Japan is treated in terms of cooperation and conflict.

It is difficult to thank adequately all those who have helped me in both Canada and Japan. I am grateful for the financial help received from the Donner Canadian Foundation and the Social Sciences and Humanities Research Council of Canada. Encouragement and support from the director of the Institute of International Relations of the University of British Columbia, Mark Zacher, and the assistant director, David Haglund, as well as my colleagues in the Canada International Trade project, is gratefully acknowledged. The comments of Michael Donnelly, William Wray, and William Holland who read my manuscript were of enormous help. I also benefited greatly from association on this project with Michael Fry, director of the School of International Relations of the University of Southern California. The helpfulness of officials in Ottawa in the Department of External Affairs, and of Trade and Commerce, as well as those posted in Tokyo, was overwhelming; that applies particularly to Genji Okubo, John Tennant, Margaret Huber, and Joseph MacDowell of the Canadian embassy staff. I am indebted to the valuable comments of my colleagues Keith Hay, Douglas Johnston, Takashi Konami, and Klaus Pringsheim, who participated in the project and conference on Canadian Perspectives on Economic Relations with Japan, sponsored by the University of Toronto–York Joint Centre on Modern East Asia, the Institute for Research on Public Policy of Montréal, and the Canada-Japan Trade Council.

I am equally beholden to the numerous officials in the Japanese foreign office and the Ministry of International Trade and Commerce who discussed patiently with me the many questions which I raised. Among Japanese businessmen, Takeshi Sakurauchi of Amax, Japan and Mikio Hasegawa of Nippon Kokan were always generous with their time, as was Don Logan of Cyprus Anvil Mining Company in Tokyo. Thanks are owed, too, to Yoshi-yuki Hagiwara of the Institute of Developing Economies, Tadashi Yama-moto of the Japan Center for International Exchange, Jörn Keck of the delegation of the Commission of the European Communities in Japan, and Yasushi Hara of the Asahi Shimbun. My good friend Natsuaki Fusano from the Federation of Economic Organizations (Keidanren) opened many doors in the business community of Japan. The chairman of the International House of Japan, Shigeharu Matsumoto, and its associate managing director, Tatsuro Tanabe, very kindly sponsored my stays as an academic visitor to Japan. Finally, I am deeply grateful to my Japanese friends and colleagues, such as Nobuya Bamba, Yuko Ohara, and Tadayuki Okuma of the Japanese Association of Canadian Studies, and especially to Glenn and Kenko Hook of Okuyama and Tokyo for their support and encouragement.

1

Early Patterns of Trade

PREWAR RELATIONS WITH JAPAN

Canada's relations with Japan since the Pacific War have been mainly of a commercial nature, centering on trade. These have been relatively uncontentious, contrasting with the prewar era when they were involved in a brief trade war in 1935 and later economic sanctions leading up to the world war. In addition to the Canadian opposition to Japanese imperialist expansion in Asia and the Pacific, attempts by British Columbia to restrict immigration of Japanese laborers in the early years of the century became entwined with early commercial negotiations with Japan.

Nevertheless, the normal postwar trade pattern was first established as long ago as the 1920s, when the export of Canadian resource products, originating mainly in the western provinces, made up the largest part of the trade even before the establishment of direct Canadian diplomatic representation in Japan. A brief look at some of the trade developments in the prewar period is helpful in assessing the more recent commercial ties and government policies, which have their forerunners or counterparts in that early period when Canadian hopes were disappointed. Although the postwar world is very different from the prewar, it is surprising the extent to which the same difficulties recurred that Canada experienced before in dealing with Japan. Canada is now more successful in winning entrée to the Japanese market for resource products, but even among those some difficulties of access persist. Seeking a foothold for Canadian manufacturers was less of a problem in the 1930s, when Canadian manufactured products constituted nearly a quarter of the exports rather than the tiny percentage they now are.[1]

In those days, central Canada shared more equally in the benefits of the trade and even exported automobiles and parts to Japan. Now the difficulty is restraining the Japanese competition, to help auto manufacturers in Ontario who would dearly love to sell parts to Japanese makers once again.

EARLY TRADE AND TRANSPORTATION

Gaining a market for Canadian resource products in the traditional sectors of forest products, grain, and fish was an important motive of the small traders, often themselves Japanese immigrants, in Canada from the earliest days.[2] Rather surprisingly, a shipment recorded in 1878 from Canada to Japan consisted of manufactured goods.[3] In 1886 when direct bilateral trade began with regular Canadian shipping lines, lumber and wooden ships' masts were important in the small export total. A limited amount of coal was sent to Japan in 1891, according to the parliamentary sessional papers, and the first wheat shipment was exported by a Japanese businessman in Vancouver in 1892. Salted herring was exported by Japanese immigrants in the same year, and salted salmon in 1896; Douglas fir lumber followed in 1903. The most successful of these early Japanese traders in Canadian resource products was Shinkichi Tamura who emigrated to Victoria and moved to Vancouver in 1888. He was later decorated by the Emperor for his achievement in trade with North America; he served a term in the Japanese House of Representatives for Kobe where his firm, Tamura Shokai, is still in business in the 1980s.[4]

In 1879, the Mitsubishi Shipping Company proposed to the Canadian government that it should subsidize a Pacific steamship service. Prime Minister John A. Macdonald preferred to wait for the completion of the Canadian Pacific Railway; however, he suggested to George Stephen, president of the railway, that the railway and Mitsubishi jointly operate a shipping line with a government subsidy.[5] Nothing came of this idea. But on 27 July 1886, just three weeks after the first transcontinental Canadian train reached the West Coast, the eight-hundred-ton barque *W. B. Flint* brought a million pounds of tea from Yokohama to Port Moody, the original terminus of the Canadian Pacific. It was chartered by the railway and was the first ship carrying the Canadian flag to have entered a Japanese port. In that year tea made up most of the total imports from Japan. Exports to Japan were only about thirty thousand dollars in the same year.[6]

The Canadian Pacific chartered the former Cunard liners, *Abyssinia*, *Parthia*, and *Batavia*, to inaugurate the regular Canadian shipping and passenger service from Vancouver and Victoria to Yokohama and Hong Kong. The *Abyssinia* arrived in Vancouver, the new terminus of the railway, on 14

Table 1–1
Trade of Canada with Japan, 1886–1940
($000)

Fiscal Years	Imports	Exports	Fiscal Years	Imports	Exports
1886	1,486	2	1915	2,783	964
1887	1,554	30	1916	4,015	997
1888	1,225	56	1917	8,123	1,205
1889	1,197	11	1918	12,255	4,861
1890	1,259	27	1919	13,618	12,245
1891	1,254	17	1920	13,637	7,733
1892	1,947	27	1921	11,361	6,415
1893	1,498	34	1922	8,195	14,832
1894			1923	7,211	14,510
1895	1,573	10	1924	6,298	26,992
1896	1,648	8	1925	6,985	22,046
1897	1,330	142	1926	9,564	34,695
1898	1,458	149	1927	11,170	29,929
1899	2,010	135	1928	12,505	32,968
1900	1,763	112	1929	12,921	42,100
1901	1,621	189	1930	12,537	30,476
1902	1,504	293	1931	9,343	18,959
1903	1,487	325	1932	5,990	16,556
1904	1,999	342	1933	3,861	10,327
1905	1,929	509	1934	3,312	13,803
1906	1,674	492	1935	4,425	16,936
1907	1,638	536	1936	3,466	14,844
1908	2,176	735	1937	4,797	21,630
1909	1,984	756	1938	5,782	26,640
1910	2,180	659	1939	4,467	21,045
1911	2,422	616	1940	4,055	26,000
1912	2,512	486			
1913	3,504	1,138			
1914	2,604	1,587			

Canada, Department of Agriculture, General Statistics Office, *Statistical Abstract and Record of Canada/Statistical Year Book of Canada/The Canada Year Book*, various years. From 1918 issued by Dominion Bureau of Statistics.

June 1887 with the pioneer shipment of silk from Japan. By 1900 silk was earning forty per cent of Japan's foreign exchange and, together with tea, was for long the principal export on which Japan relied to finance essential imports of foreign products and technology for its early industrialization.[7] In 1927 silk constituted sixty-two per cent of Canada's imports from Japan. For more than forty years the crack "silk expresses" of the Canadian Pacific carried it to New York mills, largely to manufacture ladies' stockings, and were an important element in the development of the port of Vancouver and the railway system in Canada.

Thus, in the early days it was Japan's agricultural resource products rather than those of Canada that largely made up the Japan trade and provided lucrative items for the Canadian transportation system. The Canadian Pacific shipping service carried the cargo of silk for North America, while American shipping lines carried most of the other freight at that time. It was not until the First World War that the trade pattern would take on its present form in which Canadian resource products make up most of the two-way trade with Japan.

ENTRÉE TO THE JAPANESE MARKET

Real enthusiasm among Canadians for trade with Japan and access to the Japanese market for Canadian resources did not begin until 1903 under Prime Minister Sir Wilfrid Laurier, who became an ardent promoter of the trade, as so ably chronicled by Robert Gowen.[8] Both he and the governor-general, Lord Grey, were carried away by the vision of forty million Japanese changing their eating habits from rice to bread and providing a market for Canadian wheat and other primary products. But the British Columbia legislature had been engaged in passing restrictive acts excluding the Japanese from many occupations in the province and attempting to prevent them from landing there. The federal government had to disallow these British Columbian statutes in view of the imperial policy of Britain which had contracted an alliance with Japan and did not want to offend the Japanese, and in 1903 Laurier justified the disallowance on the basis of the desire for trade with Japan and consequent friendly relations.

When Britain had concluded a treaty of commerce and navigation with Japan in 1894, the federal government had shown no desire to be included, fearing it might prevent a system of imperial preferences. This attitude began to change in 1903, at the time of the Osaka National Industrial Exhibition. Tamura, at that time a wholesale merchant in Vancouver, proposed that Canada participate. As a result he was asked to manage the display of Canadian products which was so successful that the emperor visited it and it won a prize. One of the most highly acclaimed exhibits was the bread baked from Canadian wheat. It was supplied not only to visitors to the exhibition but to local restaurants in Osaka where it proved to be very popular.[9]

Sydney Fisher, the Canadian agriculture minister, led a group of officials to represent the country at the exhibition. He was swamped with requests for information and was asked why Canada did not sell more to Japan. The minister was quite taken with the trade possibilities. The evidence of his own eyes seemed to confirm the belief that the Japanese could be induced to become bread-eaters instead of rice-eaters. In addition, the rapid development of Japanese newspapers suggested a market for Canadian pulp and paper, and Fisher also thought there were opportunities for exports of fresh and canned fruit, and preserved beef, pork, butter, cheese, and fish. His enthusiasm was not altogether misplaced as these foods did become part of the Japanese diet, but much later on. Wheat, a major export now, and flour faced strong competition from American and Australian producers as well as from the Japanese themselves who began to raise wheat for their own consumption and even became exporters of flour.

The Canadian prime minister asked Fisher to contact the Japanese government on the possibility of a separate treaty of commerce. The Japanese foreign minister, Jutaro Komura, rejected the Canadian proposal, suggesting that Canada adhere to the Anglo-Japanese commercial treaty instead. Fisher then cabled Laurier in Ottawa to consider it, thinking that the special low duties on certain British exports might apply to Canada. This turned out not to be the case. The low duties could not be applied to the commodities Canada had to export. The Anglo-Japanese treaty also provided for unrestricted residence for Japanese subjects, and British Columbia, with which the federal government was already embroiled over immigration, would have objected to this. Laurier instructed the minister to drop negotiations and return to Canada. Fisher returned with the impression that Japanese officials were willing to restrict the movement of laborers to Canada; he even thought he had a document to that effect.[10]

Both Prime Minister Laurier and Governor-General Lord Grey became converts to the idea of Canadian wheat as the staple food of Japan and the Orient. They even spoke of wheat as the future "tea of the Orient," meaning that it would become as common as tea was in East Asia. But although trade did not increase, the Canadian leaders began to reconsider joining the Anglo-Japanese treaty in the hope that it would reduce the *ad valorem* duty from fifteen to ten per cent in the Japanese market, thus breaking through the obstacles to entry. The poorly substantiated hope of the Liberals in Ottawa at that time resembles that of the Trudeau Liberals' effort to gain entrée to the Japanese market today for manufactured and high technology exports.

Probably unintentionally misled by the Japanese consul general in Canada, Tatsugoro Nosse, who thought the government in Tokyo would not issue passports to laborers wanting to come to Canada, the Liberal cabinet went ahead to ask Britain to gain adherence for Canada to the existing commercial treaty.[11] The Canadians thought the Japanese would restrict emigration of laborers, so they did not ask for reservations to their adherence to the treaty. Having dealt only with British diplomats, Tokyo officials thought that the Canadians had abandoned their insistence on restricted immigration, which was disliked by the Japanese in any event.

Thus, in 1907 the Japanese government did issue passports to nine hundred contract laborers who arrived in British Columbia together with about seven thousand other Japanese, many of whom were on their way to the United States.[12] Over eleven thousand Asians arrived in the first ten months, including Chinese and immigrants from India.[13] Provincial opposition and racial antagonism rose to a peak in September, when mobs attacked Japanese and Chinese shops in Vancouver. There were no deaths or serious injuries, but the incident had serious implications. William Lyon Mackenzie King, then deputy minister of labor and later prime minister, went as royal commissioner to Vancouver to investigate and fix compensation for claims arising from damage to Japanese shop owners. The alliance which Britain had effected with Japan was threatened and the racial problem in British Columbia was deeply troubling to all three national governments. Now almost universal Canadian condemnation was launched at the treaty.

Despite the unfavorable political fallout from the explosion engendered by the Liberal trade policy, the prime minister persisted in his belief in the future growth of the Japanese market for Canadian resource products. He defended the treaty and trade policy as well as supporting the alliance between Britain and Japan. Laurier did, however, try to defuse both the domestic and international tension built up over the problems of immigration by a direct approach to Japan.

The prime minister sent Rodolphe Lemieux, the minister of labor, to Japan to negotiate with the Japanese government with the help of the British ambassador, Sir Claude Macdonald. Lemieux was received by the emperor and conferred with Count Hayashi, the foreign minister. To Sir Claude's surprise, Lemieux was successful in obtaining a "gentlemen's agreement" from Hayashi to restrict emigration despite the most-favored-nation treatment specified in the commercial treaty which provided for full freedom of residence by Japanese in Canada. However, it was such a delicate domestic political situation for the Liberals that the prime minister did not divulge his arrangement with Japan for nearly five years.[14]

The Lemieux mission was one of the most important Canadian initiatives in foreign affairs, before the establishment of the Department of External Affairs and at a time when Canada had no diplomatic representation in

Japan. That did not occur until 1929. The problem over immigration was eased, for the time being at least. Canada took a serious interest in trade with Japan at the government level, which gave it an important motive for cooperation with Japan and this in turn encouraged support for British imperial defence policy. The Lemieux agreement also made the commercial treaty more acceptable.

Unfortunately, trade did not quite respond to Canadian hopes. In 1908 the trade commissioner in Tokyo, William T. R. Preston, warned that the Japanese were not turning to bread-eating on a scale significant enough to benefit Canadian wheat exports.[15] Only small amounts were sold in 1910 when total trade actually shrank. When Japan gave notice of the desire to terminate the 1894 treaty, it negotiated a new commercial treaty with Britain in 1911. Canada took the opportunity to ask for a separate treaty again, in hopes of favoring entry for its commodity exports, but the request was turned down because the trade was too small to warrant a special treaty with Canada. The Conservative government of Sir Robert Borden did adhere to the new Anglo-Japanese commercial treaty in 1913, but only reluctantly—not having the Liberals' faith in the opening up of the Japanese market through that type of treaty.

Preston believed that the monopolistic position of the Canadian Pacific Steamship line and the cartel of foreign merchants and commission agents tended to hamper Canadian trade with Japan. He accused the Canadian Pacific of an arrangement with American firms whereby it could handle most of the silk and tea destined for New York as well as for Canada and Britain. American shipping lines handled all the other freight to North America, including that to Canada. Tamura reported that Canadian wheat cost ten per cent more than American wheat in Japan because of the unfavorable freight rates.[16]

Transportation arrangements were not the only difficulty to plague the trade. Richard Cartwright, minister of trade and commerce under Laurier, told the prime minister that he could not understand how Canadian merchants could be expected to capture the Japanese market when they were forever complaining that they would lose even the home market without a high protective tariff. He said, "Canadian manufacturers are exceedingly indifferent to the facilities offered them" for expanding trade, and "so occupied in attending to the home market that they have little time and very little means to spare to push trade in other directions."[17] Consul General Nosse said Japanese importers were often unable to find Canadian companies interested in their orders—a charge repeated by later Japanese buying missions brought here at the behest of Trade Minister Pépin in 1972.

Nevertheless, belief in a great trade expansion with Japan and other Asian markets under Laurier did lead to considerable development in British Columbia. The extension of the Grand Trunk Pacific Railway to Prince

Rupert (which is five hundred miles closer than Vancouver to Asia) and harbor construction were carried out in anticipation of greatly increased commerce across the Pacific. Laurier even encouraged a Grand Trunk Pacific shipping line to compete with the Canadian Pacific.[18] In 1981 it was the Japanese who insisted on a separate coal port at Prince Rupert in addition to Vancouver and Roberts Bank in anticipation of the increased coal exports from the new mines being created in the northeast of British Columbia. Although today grain is seldom shipped fast enough to meet the demand for exports from the West Coast, the large grain elevator built in Vancouver in 1913–1914 stood almost empty until after the First World War.

ESTABLISHMENT OF NORMAL TRADE PATTERN

The early trade with Japan favored that country while Canadian exports remained small. In 1885, the year in which regular Canadian rail and shipping connections were established, imports from Japan topped one million dollars.[19] Until 1900 Canadian exports to Japan were even less than a hundred thousand dollars per year, a small amount even in those days, and they languished without reaching a million dollars until the First World War. It was not until 1922 that the current pattern of trade was well in place. Since then, the trade has been characterized by a large excess of Canadian exports, chiefly resource products, over the imports which are chiefly Japanese manufactured goods.

Canadian exports made a huge advance from about one million dollars in 1917 to nearly five million in 1918, and there was an even bigger gain to twelve million in 1919. They then dropped back to around seven million, until 1922 when exports rose to almost fifteen million. In 1924 they doubled again to nearly twenty-seven million and held in that range until the onset of the Depression in the 1930s. Thus it was only in 1922 that Canadian exports to Japan surpassed the previously much more important import trade, mainly the distinctive traditional Asian products of silk and tea. It was a historic turning-point when the predominant pattern of trade between Canada and Japan shifted in favor of Canadian resource products where it has remained ever since. Silk continued to be imported, mainly for the manufacture of women's stockings in New York, until 1939 when it was replaced by synthetic fibres and the last silk train left Vancouver.

In 1914, Canada's trade with Japan was only one-thirtieth that of the United States with Japan.[20] With the changed pattern after the First World War and a substantial increase in volume, the Canadian-Japanese trade had grown to one-tenth of the American, a proportion much closer to the comparative sizes of their economies.

Table 1–2
Canada's Chief Trading Partners Compared
(% Canada's Exports or Imports)

Partner	1929				1979			
	Exp. Rank		*Imp. Rank*		*Exp. Rank*		*Imp. Rank*	
U.S.	36.7%	1	68.6%	1	67.7%	1	72.4%	1
U.K.	31.5%	2	15.3%	2	4.0%	3	3.0%	3
France	1.2%	11	2.1%	3	0.97%	10	1.24%	7
Germany	3.4%	3	1.6%	4	2.1%	4	2.5%	4
Japan	3.1%	5	1.0%	5	6.4%	2	3.4%	2
Netherlands	3.3%	4	0.7%	9	1.7%	5	0.4%	17
Venezuela	–	–	–	–	1.05%	8	2.0%	5

Dominion Bureau of Statistics, General Statistics Branch, *The Canada Year Book* (Ottawa: King's Printer). Various years.

External Affairs, Policy Planning Secretariat, *Canada's Bilateral Relations: Some Key Statistics*, Dec. 1980.

In 1929, when direct diplomatic relations were established, Japan had become Canada's fifth most important trading partner, taking 3.1 per cent of Canada's exports and sending one per cent of its imports (see Table 1–2, "Canada's Chief Trading Partners Compared"). The bulk of Canada's trade was with the United States and the United Kingdom; all other partners taking comparatively small amounts of either imports or exports. Thus, in terms of trade at least, Canada remained predominantly a continental and European or British trader. Since then, Britain has lost the substantial position it held (with nearly a third of Canada's exports and a substantial share in imports) when it joined the European Economic Community (EEC) which protects its market with high tariffs against Canadian and other exports, especially of grain and agricultural products. Even though Japan has become the second most important trading partner of Canada and has doubled the share of Canada's exports and imports (6.4 per cent and 3.4 per cent respectively), in 1979 only the United States had a substantial proportion of Canadian trade as its single overwhelming market and source of imports. What is surprising is the extent to which Canada's overall global trading pattern is so similar after fifty years, except that it is now even more exclusively continental. Apart from the United States, the other trading partners continue to take fairly small proportions of the trade, just as they did before.

It is important to understand the implications of this pattern, because it is an indication of the difficulty Canada has had as its ties with Europe have weakened and those with the United States have strengthened. The Pacific trade is now larger than that with Western Europe, but it is not large enough.[21] The almost desperate attempts of the Trudeau government to diversify the trade to the EEC and Japan, and now increasingly toward Southeast Asia and Australia, are attempts to reverse the pressures toward continentalism. The battle for access to the Japanese market for manufactured and high technology products, begun by Canada in the early 1970s, has been joined by both the United States and EEC countries, although these have great difficulties too, despite their much larger production base and many other advantages.

If the composition of the trade is examined, the export of Canadian wheat to Japan began to increase in 1914 when Japan's domestic supply proved inadequate. Sales ranged from three million dollars in 1922 and 1923, to twenty million by 1929,[22] when wheat and flour constituted fifty-one per cent of total exports to Japan. Canada's first minister to Japan, Sir Herbert Marler, went as far as China soon after his arrival in an effort to dispose of some of Canada's surplus wheat. Although he was not successful in disposing of it there, China has now become Canada's largest market for wheat.

Lumber was exported to Japan as early as the 1890s, but in 1906 forest products only amounted to $100,000. However, by 1922, lumber exports reached $2,000,000, largely Douglas fir and cedar from the coastal rain forest. The great Tokyo and Yokohama earthquake of 1923 created a huge demand for Canadian logs and lumber, and in 1924 cedar logs, Douglas fir, hemlock, spruce and other timber reached $5,700,000 in value.[23] By 1929 forest products reached $6,800,000, representing sixteen per cent of all exports to Japan. Wood pulp was exported as early as 1899, but in 1914 it was still only $253,000. Between the two world wars it rose from $2,500,000 to $5,000,000 a year, until 1938 when the Japanese government curtailed it as non-essential to the Japanese war effort in China.

Fish was exported early in the form of canned salmon, beginning in 1890 and reaching one-fifth of exports to Japan by 1914. Pickled herring as well as salmon became an important export, but after 1930 it declined in importance, as Japanese fishermen became increasingly successful in their operations in the north Pacific and offshore from Siberia in meeting most of their needs for this major staple of the Japanese diet. Recently Japan has again become a major market for Canadian fish exports. A large contingent of Canada's west coast industry was made up of Japanese immigrants who manned many of the boats in early days or worked in the canneries.

The industrial expansion during the First World War resulted in the export of non-ferrous metals on a large scale and included lead, nickel, zinc, and aluminum. Japan became heavily dependent upon Canada for several of these items. The makeup of the export trade shifted somewhat from the emphasis in the 1920s on grain, fish, and wood products to an increasing importance of non-ferrous metals, pulp, and paper in the 1930s. The only really new exports after the Second World War were fuels such as metallurgical coal and uranium, the latter going first to the United States for processing before being shipped to Japan to operate the American-type light-water reactors. Liquefied natural gas is another potential fuel export.

The early Canadian export of a substantial proportion of manufactured items such as rubber goods in the form of shoes and tires, automobiles and parts, and electrical equipment dropped from a high of 24.5 per cent of Canadian exports in 1935, the year of the trade war with Canada, to less than two per cent in 1939. American motor-car manufacturing companies, which operated in Japan and had the lion's share of the Japanese market, were driven out in the 1930s. In the attempt today of Canada and the United States to compete with Japan in the North American market for similar products, the loss of the earlier foothold in Japan can only be regretted.

If Canada lost its market in manufactured exports to Japan, its imports from Japan continued to be mainly manufactured items, with cotton, rayon, and flax textiles taking the place of the declining silk. There was a large variety of household and novelty goods such as chinaware, glassware, toys, dolls, and fancy goods but these tended to be low in value, and volume to the small Canadian market was not great. Imports from Japan never really recovered from the Depression and hovered at a low figure from 1931. Thus, the trade pattern of the period before the Second World War reversed to a point where exports to Canada languished, in contrast to their comparative vigour in the early years. Exports to Japan, which were negligible in the early years of the trade, became vigorous when Canada was establishing a reputation in Japan as a foremost supplier of food and industrial materials.

TRADE WAR AND SANCTIONS

Canada's record as a reliable supplier and market was challenged in the 1930s first by the Depression and later by the war in the Pacific which resulted in protectionism and finally embargoes in Canada directed at Japan. The conflict over trade protectionism became sufficiently severe to be characterized as a "trade war."[24] It began in September 1930, when the Bennett Conservative government in Ottawa increased tariffs and then raised them higher in June of 1931, the impact falling heavily on certain Japanese exports to Canada. Japan went off the gold standard to permit the yen to float at sixty per cent of its previous value. The Exchange Dumping Duty in October 1931 levied special duties on imports of a kind comparable to those produced in Canada and coming from a country whose currency was depreciated more than five per cent relative to the Canadian dollar. British Empire products were exempted, so the duty fell upon Japan alone. Section 43 of the Customs Act also enabled the arbitrary fixing of values for duty purposes. The difference between those values and the actual selling price was collected as a dumping duty. Trade declined sharply with those measures, some Japanese merchants in Canada even going out of business and returning home.

As lengthy negotiations proved fruitless, the Japanese government levied an added duty of fifty per cent *ad valorem* on Canadian wheat, flour, lumber, wood pulp, and wrapping paper. The Canadian government retaliated with a supplementary duty of 33⅓ *ad valorem* on all Japanese imports including raw silk imported via New York. The most important Canadian export after lumber, which constituted about twenty per cent of the total, was wheat—now doubled in cost to the Japanese importer. Japanese milling companies had increased supplies in anticipation of the new duties, but only sufficient to last to the year's end. It was speculated in Tokyo that Japan would have to raise hard red wheat itself unless it could be obtained from Argentina, the Soviet Union, or Manchuria.[25]

The defeat of the Bennett Conservatives in the 1935 election brought back as Liberal prime minister Mackenzie King, who favored a conciliatory foreign policy. Canada then agreed to limit the duty on goods of a class or kind made in Canada to imports that constituted over ten per cent of the normal Canadian consumption. This eliminated some of the new duties on Japanese exports. For those of a kind not made in Canada, the yen would be valued at the current exchange rate. The value of the yen for ordinary and special duties was to be the average value during the five preceding calendar years. An extensive list of valuations under Section 43 of the Customs Act was cancelled, with appeal to the Tariff Board on new valuations. The surtaxes were withdrawn by both countries in December.

Those severe protectionist and retaliatory measures were in effect too briefly to interrupt trade seriously in 1935, thanks to the timely change of government in Ottawa. Also, exports to Japan were only about three per cent of Canada's total exports and a smaller proportion of its imports. In the case of lumber and pulp, again only three per cent of exports was involved.[26] Compare this with the recent uranium embargo of 1977, which lasted much longer, over a year, and involved about forty per cent of Japan's supply of this critical fuel, there being virtually no domestic sources; however, thanks to stockpiling and lengthy through-put due to processing in the United States, the Japanese power reactors did not have to be shut down. In 1934, as at present, the relatively modest proportion of Canada's global trade which that with Japan represents does not mean the Japanese trade is insignificant to either country.

At that time Canada provided nearly half of Japan's lead and zinc imports and over eighty per cent of its newsprint (see Table 1–3). In British Colum-

Table 1–3
Japanese Reliance on Imports from Canada*
(1934)

Japan Import	Value	Canada Share	Principal Suppliers
Lumber	¥9.5 m.	25%	U.S.
Wheat	¥8.1 m.	20%	U.S. (23%), Aus. (55%)
Lead	¥7.4 m.	40%	Canada
Pulp	¥7.2 m.	15%	U.S. (36%), Nor. (31%) Sweden (16%)
Newsprint	¥5.7 m.	82%	Canada
Zinc	¥3.4 m.	47%	Aus. (32%), U.S. (18%) Canada

*Source: *Far Eastern Survey*, "Japan Considering Retaliation Against Canada," vol. 4, no. 12 (19 June 1935), pp. 93–94.

Note: In 1973 the Canadian share of Japanese imports of the following items was: lead 71%, zinc 30%, copper 38% (Canada principal supplier), asbestos 42%; of Japanese imports of non-ferrous metals Canada's share was 32%. Keizai Dantai Rengokai, *Ni-Ka Keizai Kankei no Sho-Mondai* (Tokyo: 1974), p. 54.

bia, the source or recipient of about half the Canadian trade with Japan, the employment of at least three thousand depended on it. In particular, the forest industry in the province expressed its dismay at the trade war with Japan, while in contrast, the Ontario and Québec cotton and rayon textile producers were firmly behind the Bennett Conservatives' protectionist measures against Japan.[27]

The Canadian textile, rubber, and footwear manufacturers in the central provinces were also in complete sympathy with the intransigence of the Conservatives. Then as now, protection of producers and workers in the politically dominant central provinces was a continuing source of tension in the conflict of economic interests with the outer provinces. At the conclusion of the affair, one Canadian rayon mill closed down, protesting the change of policy in reopening the Canadian market to Japan.[28] But Mackenzie King hoped that the removal of economic grievances with Japan would encourage it to adopt more peaceful policies and that disarmament might make some headway.

Unfortunately, after having detached Manchuria from China in 1931, Japan invaded it again in 1937, starting a war that lasted until 1945. Canada attended the Brussels Nine-Power Conference called to deal with the China

War, but Japan could not be persuaded to attend. As neither Britain nor the United States would take any punitive action or sanctions, Canada saw little it could do to deter Japan from its headlong course of imperialism and also declined to take retaliatory action.[29] As the war progressed, there was damage to Canadian property in China and harassment of Canadian missionaries in both China and Japan. Considerable pressure arose in Canada for embargoes on war materials to Japan, but Canadian leaders doubted the efficacy of embargoes and even permitted trade to increase in the raw materials needed by Japan. Indeed, it could obtain most of these from other sources if the Canadian supply was interrupted; Japan was, and is, much more successful in diversifying its trade than Canada.

Japan began to impose restrictions on commodity imports not essential to the war effort in October of 1937. Consequently some trade to Japan declined in 1938, although the export of minerals and scrap-iron used for war production rose sharply, to increase greatly total exports from Canada. In 1939 Ottawa raised duties on cotton goods to protect Canadian producers and retaliate for Japan's restrictions on non-mineral items.[30]

The United States cancelled its commercial treaty in 1939, and at the same time Britain decided to abrogate the 1911 commercial treaty. The attempt to raise tariffs was judged too damaging by Ottawa, so selective embargoes on specific exports were adopted. The export of scrap-iron and steel was suspended in October 1939. In February 1940 zinc and nickel were held up. These were followed by aluminum in April, cobalt in August, and in October a revised permit system was applied to copper.[31] In July 1941 Canada followed Britain and the United States by freezing Japanese assets and gave notice of termination of adherence to the Anglo-Japanese commercial treaty of 1911. The outbreak of war with Japan finally halted what was left of the trade, until it could recommence in about 1947 under the Allied occupation of Japan.

ASSESSMENT OF EARLY TRADE PATTERNS

To summarize some of the characteristics of Canada's early trade with Japan, it was modest in comparison with the trade with the United States and Britain which were the only large trading partners Canada had. Japan's share of Canada's trade resembled that with other countries such as France and Germany. Even now, as the number two partner of Canada, Japan's trade remains in this category. From the beginning, exports of raw or processed resources tended to predominate, since they complemented Japan's needs as an industrializing country with few domestic resources of its own. The principal sources of these materials were and still are the western provinces, particularly British Columbia. Even for these provinces, their trade with the United States is much larger than that with Japan.

Despite the modest character of the trade, Japan obtained a very substantial portion of various key raw materials from Canada. Japan also found it useful to diversify for the sake of security and competition among other suppliers such as the United States and Australia.

The general trade pattern between Canada and Japan shifted massively after the First World War, when the big surplus in imports from Japan over exports to Japan was reversed in 1922. The 1923 earthquake accelerated Japan's reliance upon Canadian commodity exports of food, minerals, and forest products, and from then on, with few exceptions, Canadian exports have greatly surpassed imports. In the earliest part of the period, from 1870 to 1914, Canadian exports were very small—under a million dollars. This resembles the reversal at the end of the period from 1930 to 1941, when imports from Japan shrank to a very low volume compared with exports from Canada.

From the beginning, imports from Japan were dominated by silk and tea. Even in the 1930s, Canada was the best customer for Japanese rice, and its second best customer for tea—small though the volume was. If the silk from the United States originating in Japan is considered the largest import, pottery was next in the mid-1930s. Thus, the traditional specialized products of East Asian culture were most prominent on the import side. The contrast with the current pattern could not be greater: the most technically advanced and stylish automobiles, cameras, and electronic consumer products now dominate imports from Japan. With this comes a new influence, an eagerness to learn Japanese techniques of industrial organization as well as to understand the traditional culture that lies behind it to some extent. Thus, trade and economic relations are bringing a broader economic, social, and cultural influence to Canada that builds on the economic ties started a hundred years ago.

The early era also contrasts with respect to manufactured goods. In the mid-thirties a quarter of Canadian exports to Japan were manufactured goods, including even automobiles at a time when Japanese entrepreneurs had only a tiny foothold in their own domestic market for these. It has now become Canadian policy to attempt to regain some of that lost market for manufactured items in the high technology category. Even in the early period, the manufacturers of central Canada felt the competition from low-cost textiles and some consumer goods, but now the winds of Japanese competition blow very strongly in that region in connection with products like automobiles and electronic goods.

The greatest difference is in the way the problems of immigration and Japanese expansionism have virtually vanished since the Pacific War, whereas prior to that time they frequently erupted in the attempts to foster trade. Nevertheless, there is a surprising continuity in major characteristics of the trade, in both its size and makeup, which persist from early times into the present. Despite the predominant harmony and economic benefit of economic relations with Japan in recent years, conflicts of interest have sometimes arisen, and disappointed hopes have been held that give considerable variation to the economic ties with Japan.

2

Entrée to Japanese Market for Canadian Resources

Trade between Canada and Japan began to revive even before the occupation ended on 26 April 1952 when the San Francisco Peace Treaty went into effect. In 1950 imports from Japan amounted to about twelve million dollars and exports were about twenty-one million dollars. They showed the historical pattern of an excess of exports, usually raw materials, over imports, chiefly of manufactured goods such as textiles, clothing, pottery, toys, and electrical goods. By 1952 imports were only thirteen million dollars, but exports had leaped to over a hundred million dollars, almost eight times the level of imports.

The extreme trade imbalance reflected Japan's acute need of raw materials for its reviving industries at a time of relative scarcity and when Japan was cut off from many of its usual suppliers in Asia. Particularly important was grain from the prairies and minerals and forest products from British Columbia. This represented a valuable market of great importance to the western provinces. Japan was also running a trade deficit with the United States, on whom it depended for economic aid and American procurement of supplies in Japan for the Korean War to obtain the foreign exchange it desperately needed to finance its purchases in the dollar countries such as Canada.

Japan had to ration its foreign exchange carefully, and was therefore reluctant to continue such large allocations for buying Canadian food and raw materials when it was able to sell so little. Canadian businessmen, officials, and politicians were well aware that they needed to allow greater imports from Japan if they were to continue the profitable trade building up there.

Of course, consumers in Canada benefited greatly from the inexpensive Japanese manufactured goods such as textiles and clothing. However, these

Table 2–1
Canada's Early Postwar Trade with Japan, 1946–1956
($000)

Year	Exports	Rank[1]	Imports	Rank[1]
1946	1,027		3	
1947	559		350	
1948	8,001		3,144	
1949	5,860		5,551	
1950	20,533	9	12,087	20
1951	72,976	4	12,577	25
1952	102,603	4	13,162	19
1953	118,568	3	13,629	19
1954	96,474[2]	3	19,197	15
1955	90,893[2]	3	36,718[2]	5
1956	127,870	5	60,826	5

1. Japan's rank order among countries to which Canadian exports go or from which Canadian imports come.
2. The sudden drop in exports and increase in imports in 1954 seems to reflect the ratification of the commercial treaty when Japan may have reduced export demand and increased its own exports to Canada to resume its place as a major source of Canadian imports in 1955.

Source: Dominion Bureau of Statistics, External Trade Branch/ Section, *Review of Foreign Trade*, Calendar Years 1947–1957. Catalogue no. 65–205.

were sold mainly in the central provinces where most of the Canadian population was located together with one of the largest employers of labor, the Canadian textile industry. Before the war, inexpensive Japanese textiles had been strong competitors of the local industry, which paid much higher wages and had higher costs because of smaller runs.

Britain and other Commonwealth countries also feared the adverse impact on their industries of a revival of Japanese manufacturing and trade. Earlier they had hoped to impose some restrictions on Japan to prevent the competition in connection with the peace settlement. Britain had also placed restrictions on the entry of Japanese goods into her colonies in Asia through exchange controls to protect the pound sterling.

The Canadian industry was already suffering from competition in textiles from both Britain and the United States, which were gaining an ever larger share of the Canadian market. In Britain costs were lower, partly the result of wages lower than those in Canada. In the United States, where wages were higher, runs ten times as long as those of Canadian mills were produced at much smaller cost. Consequently, from 1950 the Canadian textile industry was undergoing an acute falloff in demand, with resulting closures, layoffs, and business failures. The prospect of renewed Japanese competition was thus hardly encouraging for the mills in Ontario and Québec.[1]

Under Article 12 of the peace treaty, Japan was ready to negotiate commercial agreements with the Allied Powers to give most-favored-nation treatment or national treatment to any of them who accorded it such treatment.[2] The Japanese government approached Canada on 19 April 1952, just before the peace treaty went into effect, to propose commercial negotiations.[3] It was not until 19 November 1952 that the Canadian cabinet decision was made on the general lines of its position for the negotiations which were to take place, chiefly in Ottawa, during 1953.

At this time Canada, like most of the major trading countries outside the Soviet bloc, belonged to the General Agreement on Tariffs and Trade (GATT) which provided for more open and unrestricted world trade in the postwar period. Its chief feature was the negotiation of a low tariff schedule and its application, together with other liberal measures, by most-favored-nation treatment to all the other adherents of the agreement. The participating countries were prepared to renegotiate new tariffs on a multilateral basis, which would greatly advance a relatively liberal and expanding world trade in the subsequent thirty years.

Japan was eager to join GATT to enjoy the favorable tariffs and access to trade with the members. In July 1952 it proposed entering, and applied to the headquarters in Geneva in August. Britain and other Commonwealth members such as Australia and South Africa were reluctant to face the Japanese competition, but the Intersessional Committee decided it should be considered at the annual general meeting in October. The October meeting unanimously agreed to refer it to the Intersessional Committee again as to the timing and conditions of Japan's entry and to report back the following year. Opponents from the Commonwealth asked that committee to look into Japanese trade practices and labor conditions, some of which involved unfair competition such as dumping or copying foreign trade marks.

After the Canadian cabinet approved the general lines of its discussion with the Japanese in November 1952, the Japanese submitted a draft of a most-favored-nation trade agreement. The Interdepartmental Committee on External Trade Policy prepared a counter-draft with an escape clause to enable Canada to take protective measures for its own industries.[4] It provided that a product imported in such increased quantities and under such conditions as to cause or threaten serious injury to domestic producers could have values for ordinary and special duties established by the Canadian government. That is, the Canadian government could set a value on a Japanese import and levy duties based upon this value to remove the advantage in price which it had over a competing Canadian product, when its producer was injured or threatened with injury by the Japanese product.

The advantage of this rather roundabout approach was that it conformed with the escape clause, GATT Article XIX, which permitted a member who had made tariff concessions to another member to suspend them in case of unforeseen developments when increased quantities or other conditions caused or threatened serious injury to the domestic producers.[5]

The essential problem of foreign competition is precisely that the foreign product may undersell the domestic product which has higher costs and cannot easily meet the lower price. Usually the objection is that the foreign product is being "dumped," that is, sold at an unfairly lower price abroad than at home where the larger receipts may even permit the product sold abroad to be priced below its actual cost. As the committee and cabinet both noted, it was quite possible for a Japanese import to harm Canadian producers without any increased quantity. In other words, consumers might refuse to buy the Canadian product if they could buy the Japanese one cheaper. Even where the item was not dumped, but merely sold at the equivalent price in both countries plus the duty and transport and freight, it might still undersell the local product. To meet this competition, American legislation had recently defined "dumping" as selling a foreign product in the domestic market at less than the cost, plus a ten per cent margin for overhead, plus eight per cent for profit.[6] This pushed the price of the foreign product considerably above that of competing domestic ones, to provide super-protection.

Canadian officials in 1953 reasoned that the current Japanese imports were so few that they would all increase anyway, permitting them to become subject to arbitrary valuation in case of injury or even the threat of such injury.[7] Since so much Canadian trade was with the United States, Canada had a great interest in keeping the escape clause as narrow as possible, to avoid American use of it against Canadian products. They also wished to obtain Japanese concessions to limit the application of restrictions on Canadian trade for balance of payments reasons.

The Canadian representative on the GATT Intersessional Committee meeting in February 1953 supported the admission of Japan with the minimum amendment to existing provisions of GATT, assuming that Canada could negotiate as indicated above while conforming with Article XIX procedure. That is, Canada joined the American effort to gain relatively liberal admission for Japan because of its own interest in liberal trade, especially with the United States. It proposed that Japan's accession be merged with the general negotiations made necessary by the expiration of the tariff schedules later that year, and thus ensure that adequate effort was made to accommodate Japan within GATT as it was bound to be a major component of that world trading community. Britain and Australia, fearful of Japanese competition, pressed for amendments of a more far-reaching character because of their alleged fear of Japanese dumping and unfair trade practices.[8] The committee decision favored Japanese entry as soon as possible, with the necessary preliminary tariff negotiations for joining merged with the general multilateral negotiations as Canada had envisaged.

Although the Reciprocal Trade Act was extended by Congress, President Eisenhower decided not to use his power to negotiate tariff decreases at the scheduled multilateral GATT conference planned for that autumn. Without the United States, however, no conference was practical because the American market was so large and important to all trading countries. This put off the opportunity to negotiate simultaneously with Japan, which was frustrated by this obstacle to its ambition to enter on favorable terms with the major trading countries.

In August 1953 Japan proposed a new procedure which had not been used before: to enter GATT as an associate member.[9] It wanted to be admitted even without the negotiation of most-favored-nation status for the time being. The eighth general meeting in September turned the matter over to a ten-nation committee. Despite the strong support of the United States and all the Japanese powers of persuasion, the opposition of Britain, Australia, and France prevented Japan's entry as an associate member. The committee then proposed a compromise solution, whereby a larger part of the customs schedule (about 860 items) would be postponed and current rates of duty be used, but, for those countries willing to sign the declaration of Japan's accession as an associate, the other aspects of GATT would apply. Japan was to have the right to speak, make proposals, and vote.

The general meeting accepted Japan's associate status under this compromise by twenty-five out of thirty-three countries on 23 September 1953. By the end of the year, the time limit for signing the declaration, twenty-one countries had signed and three more joined them soon afterward. Also, by October there was acceptance of the general lines which Canada wanted in the bilateral commercial agreement with Japan; so the Canadian delegation to the United Nations in Geneva which handled GATT matters was instructed to support Japan's temporary accession.[10] Canada intended to apply GATT schedules to Japan "in due course"; that is, when the commercial agreement was ratified by the Japanese Diet the following February or March.

The reaction in Japan was favorable, even though most of the most-favored-nation low tariffs had still not been attained. The opportunity to participate in GATT was welcomed, and not only supporters of Japan's accession, such as Canada, Indonesia, the Dominican Republic, Nicaragua, and

Brazil, but abstainers such as the United Kingdom, thought it would at least inhibit any further attempts to discriminate against Japan.[11]

Canada was anxious to guarantee an entry to the Japanese market for Canadian exports and hoped to limit Japan's ability to reduce or block these exports for balance of payments reasons. The United States was a chief competitor of Canada in its supply of food grains, minerals, and wood products. Canada hoped that here, too, Japan could be dissuaded from taking measures discriminating in favor of the Americans. A serious problem which still distresses farmers is that special low-cost sales or gifts of grain seriously reduce the market for commercial sales and influence the world price which is very sensitive in raw materials. Canada wished to prevent or at least limit such disposal of American grain on concessional terms.

Japan, of course, was short of foreign exchange and had to ration its dollars. Even GATT permitted certain discriminations and deviations from its rules for the sake of keeping a balance in the payments position. Japan ran a chronic deficit up to about 1965, which required some limitation of imports whenever the deficit threatened to become severe. From the beginning of the negotiations in 1953, Canada pressed for liberalization of quantitative import restrictions for exchange reasons. When the problems over its entry to GATT became acute in the summer of 1953, Japan became more amenable to Canadian wishes in order to win its support for accession.

The result was the liberalizing of nine items: wheat, barley, wood-pulp, flax seed, primary copper, pig lead, zinc spelter, synthetic resins, and milk powder. Japan undertook to grant unconditional non-discrimination in the import of these items from Canada and not to apply exchange restrictions. As they were the chief food, forestry, and mineral products exported by Canada and would not be subject to any restrictions for exchange reasons, this represented an important concession by Japan.[12]

The importance of the Japan trade to the British Columbia forest industry was indicated by the brief sent to the federal government by the B.C. Lumber Manufacturers' Association, which was anxious to expand markets for fir, spruce, hemlock, and veneer logs. The managing director of Alaska Pine and Cellulose, Ltd. of Vancouver, Walter Koerner, went to Japan to urge an increase in dollar allocation for dissolving pulp, required by Japanese concerns in the summer of 1953. The allocation was not forthcoming for the third quarter, so Canadian ability to compete in the market along with American and Swedish firms was threatened. Koerner's appeals from Tokyo to the Japanese embassy and Department of Industry, Trade, and Commerce in Ottawa linked the allocation with "fair and equitable treatment" and application of only regular commercial considerations, which was being discussed in connection with Article IV of the commercial agreement.[13] The final note to the liberalization agreement mentioned above made it no longer possible to hold up exchange allocation when a Japanese customer wished to buy woodpulp from Canada and ensured that the Canadian producer could compete on equal terms with American suppliers.

The commercial agreement was signed by Lester Pearson, the trade minister C. D. Howe, and Koto Matsudaira, the Japanese ambassador, in Ottawa on 31 March 1954 and was ratified and came into force on 7 June. Both countries accorded most-favored-nation treatment to each other's trade. For Japan this meant a substantial reduction in duties on its main exports, including textiles. Since Japan had only one tariff schedule, it meant no immediate reduction in duties on Canadian goods, although those on raw materials were very small. With Article I, Canada granted use of its lower most-favored-nation tariff schedule, the only exception being the continued even lower tariff on some items with Commonwealth partners.[14]

Article III prohibited restrictions on imports except for essential security or balance of payments reasons. Where it was necessary to restrict them because of balance of payments, there could be no discrimination as between dollar or convertible currency countries. This prevented special discrimination in favor of American competition.

Article V provided for fair practices to be followed, especially with respect to patents, marks of origin, and trade marks. The agreement was initially valid for one year, to be extended thereafter unless three months' notice were given by either party. The agreement is still in force thirty years later.

In the exchange of notes, the Canadian government reserved the right to establish values for ordinary or special duty purposes as a result of unforeseen circumstances if any product was being imported into its territory in such increased quantities and under such conditions as to cause or threaten serious injury to the domestic producers of like or directly competitive products.[15] As the opposition was to point out in Parliament, there was nothing unforeseen about the increased quantities to be imported. Donald Fleming, whose riding included mill towns suffering acute unemployment, was worried that this might vitiate the government's ability to take effective protective action even under the escape clause.[16]

In Canada, the reaction to the new agreement was positive regarding the need to extend most-favored-nation treatment if Canadian exports were to be sustained and the market for such items as wheat ensured. The safeguards received close scrutiny.[17] The Canadian Manufacturers' Association was somewhat apprehensive. The Japanese press reported that the president of the Canadian Export Association thought the safeguards would protect the businessmen who felt threatened; the president of the Canadian Textile Association, however, frankly felt that the effect of the new agreement was unfair in the blow expected to his industry, and he also commented on cases of copying of Canadian patents and exporting at lower prices than those charged in the home market.[18]

Trade Minister Howe introduced the resolution in the Commons to approve ratification of the agreement on 12 May 1954.[19] He emphasized the advantages to Canada of: (1) the guarantee of most-favored-nation treatment for Canadian goods, (2) the promise not to discriminate in favor of other dollar countries, and (3) the promise not to discriminate even for exchange control reasons against the nine important Canadian exports enumerated in the exchange of notes. The minister pointed out that although imports from Japan would increase, there was no need to fear them. He underlined that the Japanese would be on the same footing as the American or German producers in the Canadian market and that Japanese imports would remain a comparatively small part of the total, even with increases. The safeguards would take care of the emergency conditions of sudden increases injurious to Canadian producers.

The strategic aspect was mentioned as tying in closely with the economic and commercial aspects of the relationship with Japan. Keeping Japan out of the Communist orbit and a member of the democratic group of countries was given strong support by all the speakers, government and opposition benchers alike. This reflected Canada's own involvement in the Cold War and the Korean War and its deep interest in maintaining the balance of power, such as it was, in East Asia. It was acknowledged that Japan had to be encouraged to trade with the NATO countries if it was to achieve a viable economy. The American assistant secretary of state for Far Eastern affairs, Walter Robertson, was quoted concerning the need to provide outlets for Japanese trade to keep Japan from being drawn in with the Communist countries. The United States had already granted most-favored-nation treatment to Japan. Japan negotiated an agreement on more favorable payments with the United Kingdom on 29 January to reduce the protection of its textile and pottery industries from Japanese competition. The United States signed a friendship, commerce, and navigation treaty with Japan in April 1953 for precisely the same reasons in the face of industrial opposition.

Both the opposition speakers, Fleming for the Tories and M. J. Coldwell for the CCF, supported the agreement on the basis of the necessity to guarantee the Japanese market for Canadian producers and the strategic need to keep Japan on the Western side, although naturally the speakers with textile mills in their constituencies were anxious about the safeguards. Fleming recalled the difficulty in applying protective steps against American textile dumping in the previous year. The Trades and Labor Congress was also cited for its concern over unemployment in textiles.

Thus Canada obtained some assurance of entry into the Japanese market, chiefly for its raw materials exports, and some protection from flooding of the Canadian market by highly competitive products from Japan, particularly textiles. It also obtained some guarantee of non-discrimination in competing with the United States and Australia for a share of the Japanese market for raw materials. The Japanese obtained more favorable entry into the Canadian market for its manufactured products such as textiles by a lowering of the Canadian tariff wall and thus a better chance to reduce the unfavorable trade balance and reduce the drain on its precious dollar reserves. Perhaps equally important at this point was Canadian cooperation and support in Japan's struggle for full acceptance in the world trading community. Probably there has been no time when Canada was so important to Japan, despite the comparatively small size of their trade with each other. The problem that followed was how to implement those assurances and provide the desired support.

Unlike the other Commonwealth countries, Canada conducted tariff negotiations with Japan, made a commercial agreement with it in conformity with GATT, supported Japan's full membership of the latter, and applied GATT regulations to commercial relations between Canada and Japan. Thus Canada, together with the United States, was a major force behind Japan's struggle for acceptance.

Canada sponsored Japan's entry to the Colombo Plan at the meeting in Ottawa on 5 October 1954. This plan for economic cooperation and development in South and Southeast Asia was largely a Commonwealth effort. Japan's entry as a donor country had been opposed by Indonesia since 1952. Thanks to Canadian persuasion, an invitation to Japan to participate was now at last unanimous; Koto Matsudaira, the ambassador to Canada who signed the commercial agreement, represented Japan in the fifteen-nation organization. Because his country was itself still in the throes of recovery from the war, it was only able to offer technical assistance. Still, the symbolic significance was considerable in view of Japan's ambition for commercial acceptance. Canada seized the opportunity to be Japan's Commonwealth sponsor.

At the Intersessional Committee of GATT, meeting on 26 July 1954, a vote agreed to Japan's participation in multilateral tariff negotiations by the following February. Twenty-seven countries favored it at the Geneva general meeting on 29 October 1954, the five abstainers being Britain, Australia, South Africa, Southern Rhodesia, and France, chiefly Canada's other Commonwealth partners outside Asia. Japan thus finally obtained the necessary two-thirds majority of twenty-three countries to gain formal acceptance in GATT. However, fourteen members invoked Article XXXV against Japan. The article provided that the agreement did not apply if two contracting parties had not entered into tariff negotiations with each other or if either of them did not consent to apply it when the other joined.[20] Those refusing to apply the GATT regulations to Japan were the United Kingdom, Australia, New Zealand, Rhodesia, South Africa, India, Austria, Belgium, Luxembourg, the Netherlands, France, Haiti, Cuba, and Brazil. Ireland did not give up its application of Article XXXV against Japan until the mid-1970s.

Canada spoke in Japan's favor at the tenth session of GATT in 1955 when Japan joined. It accepted Japan's full participation and had put the regulations into force between it and Japan. Japan was a major trading country which, as most GATT members fully recognized, had to be accepted. But only Canada, the United States, Germany, Norway, Denmark, and a few smaller countries were willing to go all the way. The fact that so many members refused application of GATT rules made it hard to carry out the intention of GATT with respect to Japan.[21]

The Japanese were deeply distressed at this treatment. Their representative said, "Some contracting parties referred in the previous sessions to the flooding of Japanese products in world markets before the war. To this I wish to say that the structure of the economy has changed, and that the Japanese Government will be vigilant lest Japanese products should cause violent disruption of trade.... We are ready to participate in a constructive manner in the joint attempt to work out a satisfactory formula."[22]

At the eleventh session of GATT in 1956, the fourteen still held out against Japan. Australia had concluded a commercial agreement and indicated it was considering dropping its opposition to applying GATT rules to Japan. Canada's support was always appreciated by Japanese officials, even though it for long failed to persuade the other Commonwealth partners to abandon their opposition to Japan and to accept greater competition in their markets. Even in 1960, Canada and the United States were the only major markets giving Japan most-favored-nation treatment under GATT rules. Although these countries eventually applied GATT rules to Japan, and thus accepted it, they were to undergo severe competition from Japan's manufactured products on a massive scale twenty years later. But if they had been more cooperative in their approach to Japan when it was weak, would it have stemmed the impact later when Japan was very strong?

It is significant that Canada, like the United States, showed its appreciation of the need to welcome Japan into the circle of the advanced democratic countries and to accept a reasonable degree of Japanese competition in order to win its cooperation. It was also easier for them as their economies were comparatively strong then. It was a favorable time when Japan most needed acceptance and was willing to take constructive steps in international trade and finance.

Both Canada and the United States, as Pacific littoral nations with an active interest in the strategic situation in East Asia, had an incentive to create relationships with Japan for geopolitical as well as economic reasons. The more protectionist and competitive economic relations of the European and African states foreshadowed the attitude of the future EEC, which was to become a major economic rival of Canada, the United States, and Japan, notwithstanding their military cooperation through NATO and the Japan–United States security treaties.

IMPLEMENTING THE AGREEMENT

Despite the difficulties in reaching a commercial accord, it was perhaps simple compared to the implementation of the new agreement. As Canada was anxious to secure a good market in Japan for its raw materials, it wanted to be sure the provisions for non-discrimination were carried out on the nine items which Japan had promised not to restrict. The Japanese supplied figures on their imports showing how they stood on the nine items listed in the exchange of notes. They also supplied supplementary data when requested by Canada. It was thus possible to learn what Canadian competitors were doing in the Japanese market.

Wheat and barley were especially important to Canada and were subject to strong competition from the United States, Australia, and Argentina, the other big world grain exporters. Fortunately for Canada, even when transportation inadequacies—some of which still remain to be remedied—held up shipments or strikes slowed down supply, Japanese sales continued to be strong.

In the case of Public Law 480 of 1956, the United States arranged to dispose of surplus grain abroad which had been bought up under price support programs for farmers. It could be paid for with local currency, which in turn was made available for use in educational exchanges and various sorts of aid in the days when Japan was short of foreign exchange and had to maintain strict exchange controls. This naturally gave an advantage to the disposal of American grain and reduced the market for Canadian grain being offered on commercial terms. Australia also established good commercial relations and a favorable reception as a reliable supplier to Japan. From the Canadian point of view this appeared somewhat discriminatory, but Japan promised not to cut back its purchases from Canada. Indeed, its need for grain continued to expand as dietary habits changed, so that it was able to take large and increasing quantities from all three of its major suppliers; this is still a major export for Canada to Japan. In other agricultural products not on the list, such as beef and pork, Canada has run into considerable barriers or variable quotas that sharply limit the market. It enjoys only a nibble of this trade compared to the Australians and Americans.

In fixing customs charges on Japanese imports to Canada, it was necessary to establish a fair market value for duty purposes. Thus it was necessary to find out what an item cost to produce in Japan or what it sold for there if it was intended for the domestic market. But on this point Japanese producers were reluctant to cooperate with the Canadian customs attaché in Tokyo. In 1957 cotton textile exporters became antagonized by the Canadian attaché's attempts to investigate Japanese costs, threatening to abandon voluntary export restraints and even the Canadian market.[23] The Japanese Ministry of Trade and Industry and Ministry of Foreign Affairs eventually offered to transmit the information in order to mollify their exporters in what has continued to be a sensitive industry.

The agreement on commerce has continued to apply, although Japan has from time to time proposed a commerce, trade, and navigation treaty conferring broader or more favorable reciprocal treatment. Although Canada only resorted to global quotas in 1976 when the Québec textile and clothing industries were threatened with extinction, the threat then came from the newly industrializing low-wage countries and Japan itself was besieged by cheap manufactured imports.

3

Restraining Competition from Japanese Manufacturers

VOLUNTARY QUOTAS

The pattern of trade relations between Japan and the other developed countries has tended to persist from the prewar period and postwar settlement right up to the present. That is, Canada and the United States have applied more liberal trade policies to Japan than has Western Europe, which clung to more restrictive policies and quotas to protect such industries as textiles. Canada did induce Japan to restrict specified manufactured exports in the late fifties and early sixties, but avoided contravening the letter of the liberal GATT rules. The Europeans, and later the EEC, frankly maintained quotas specifically against Japan. The United States eventually persuaded Japan to agree to institute "voluntary" quotas for lengthy periods, thus protecting and reserving eighty per cent of its textile market for domestic producers. Canada never went quite so far and until 1976 negotiated only very short-term restraint agreements for clearly defined and limited items and opened its market much wider to foreign exports.

Although GATT Article XIX authorized the use of unilateral quantitative restrictions in an emergency to prevent serious injury or the threat of it to domestic producers, this has its drawbacks. Any unilateral quota, surtax, or prohibitive tariff must be non-discriminatory, applying to all countries. Thus injury by one or two countries cannot justify sanctions levied equally against all the others, some of whom may retaliate. Unless the injured party can prove the damage or threat, he may even be subject to retaliation by the party causing the trouble, and all may ask for compensation. Canada has used Article XIX several times on a short-term basis to institute a surtax on

some agricultural imports. The first time it used it against injury from manufactured goods was in November 1971, on men's and boys' shirts with
tailored collars.[1]

When the United States first pressed Japan to institute limitations on its
exports of cotton textiles and apparel in the second half of the 1950s, it was
not because the American market was flooded or because there was market
disruption; in fact, Japanese cotton textiles never amounted to more than
two per cent of the United States market.[2] The forceful entry of American
textile producers into politics threatened to defeat the Reciprocal Trade Act,
which the Eisenhower administration was trying to renew, and thus to sabo-
tage Japan's trade with the United States.

To avoid import controls, Japan fixed export quotas on fabrics, made-up
goods, and clothing destined for the United States. As a rule, when goods
destined for the United States are blocked or restricted, it is convenient to
divert them to the Canadian market, which can easily be flooded because of
its much smaller size. Countries such as Japan, the United States, and Britain
have large markets, and their mills have long production runs up to millions
of yards which can readily be dumped in Canada at low prices. For this
reason, Canada immediately requested Japan to take steps similar to those
being used for the United States to restrain excessive concentration on Canada. Initially, the restraint was exercised by Japan, according to its own judg-
ment, in what were truly voluntary restraints as far as Canada was concerned.

On several previous occasions the United States had asked Canada to
adopt voluntary export controls, which it refused to do. The Canadians were
loath, therefore, to ask Japan to do so in too direct a manner on this occa-
sion, as it could undercut its relation with the United States. The latter was in
as strong a position to retaliate against Canada as against Japan, since the
United States was and still is the major market for both. Canadian officials
suggested it would be nice if the Japanese could make some announcement
of voluntary restrictions on cotton piece-goods and made-up goods. The
Japanese, in their turn, were reluctant to weaken their own hand in their
uphill battle to get rid of the discriminatory restraints under which they had
labored since the earliest days of their industrialization. However, they did
indicate informally to the Canadian textile industry what they expected to
export. Since the Canadian industry is easily overwhelmed, knowledge of its
competitors' export plans is very valuable in planning its own production or
new investment.

The low-cost producers in 1957 were Japan with twenty-five per cent of
Canadian clothing imports and Hong Kong with four per cent. By the end of
1959, Japan's share had risen to forty-four per cent and Hong Kong's to ten
per cent.[3] During 1956 and 1957 Japan had set limits to its exports of cotton
textiles, fabrics, blouses, coats, knitwear, tablecloths, and pillowcases, after

discussions with Canadian officials which were called "negotiated arrangements." These items were allowed to increase at a relatively moderate rate compatible with the wish of the Canadian industry for "orderly marketing." However, overall exports to Canada increased quite substantially from 1957 to 1958 at a rate of twenty-five per cent, but from 1958 to 1959 at a rate of forty-two per cent. As a result of complaints from Canadian producers, additional restrictions were placed on table cutlery and plywood in the summer of 1959.

In 1959, when imports of spun rayon garments increased nearly eight times in a two-year period, the Canadian side proposed that some limits lower than the 1959 exports be set for 1960. Japan balked at this attack on the orderly marketing principle associated with gradual moderate increases, although it was lack of moderation to which the Canadians objected. Japan finally bowed to Canada's wishes and suspended the export of rayon garments in June.[4]

Canada was in a favorable position at that time, when it was a comparatively more important market for Japan; even today it is one of the world's biggest markets for textiles and clothing, taking more imports than Japan and one-third as much as the United States.[5] Japan's economy was then not much larger than Canada's, but Canada was one of the few relatively affluent postwar nations. Japan was still seeking entry into United Kingdom and German markets on a most-favored-nation basis and had not yet established the global trading scope it now enjoys. It was sensitive to any charges of flooding North American markets. At a GATT conference in Tokyo in November, Léon Balcer, the solicitor-general, said, "Canada and Japan have found that when problems arise in our trade, it is possible in a friendly and constructive way to find workable solutions acceptable to both countries."[6] Canadian satisfaction at Japan's cooperation was expressed by the Canadian ambassador to Japan despite the acute competition felt in various sectors, especially textiles. Canada also experienced the pressure of large volume low-cost imports from Hong Kong and Taiwan, as unilateral and discriminatory quotas were applied to these countries as well as to Japan by Britain and other European countries, still invoking GATT Article XXXV to deny Japan most-favored-nation tariff treatment.[7]

The voluntary quotas were at least subject to frequent renegotiation, which was probably preferable to the more arbitrary unilateral trade barriers.[8] Ambassador Hagiwara made clear that Japan was dedicated to a better trade balance through increasing exports to Canada, not by restricting them, nor by restricting Japanese imports of Canadian raw materials which, then as now, were far greater in value than Japan's exports to Canada. When Prime Minister Ikeda visited Canada, he inserted this policy in the communiqué issued jointly with Prime Minister Diefenbaker.[9]

The year 1961 was somewhat critical: a new Long Term Arrangement Regarding Trade in Cotton Textiles (LTA) was negotiated among major trading countries in an attempt to check the strong protectionist trend in textiles and to bring current practice under the auspices of GATT, whose rules were being increasingly violated by refusal to follow the safeguard measures laid down in Article XIX. The LTA permitted discriminatory restrictions against cotton textile imports when there was "market disruption"; it also permitted unilateral quotas if no agreement was reached on "voluntary" restraints, while countries with unilateral quotas were pledged to increase the latter annually and eventually eliminate them.

A relatively concise policy was developed under Donald Fleming, then minister of finance, whose constituency's textile mills were suffering from foreign competition. He said that the flooding of the Canadian market by Japanese products could not continue.[10] Canadian policy prescribed that Japanese imports could grow only five to ten per cent a year when demand was increasing, in order to ensure orderly growth of the imports. Japan was expected to take steps to curb items when they exceeded this limit. When business was poor, as was not the case then, Japan might need to forego increases or even to take cutbacks. The "voluntary" quotas were applied to rubber footwear, transistor radios, television and radio tubes, and buttons. The results of the yearly negotiations on what were really involuntary quotas were tabled in the House of Commons, in the form of a letter from the Japanese ambassador detailing the items agreed to in what was almost tantamount to a formal agreement.[11]

Thus by 1962 the quota system was at its height, at least in the sense that it covered the most extensive array of items. Thirty classes of textile products were included, as well as footwear, electronics, plywood, vinyl raincoats, and polyester buttons. Sixty-five per cent of Japanese exports to Canada, ninety per cent of which were textile items, were now restricted. The protective intent of the commercial agreement of 1954 was attained in practice, although the annual bilateral restraint negotiations were not provided for in the agreement or in the exchange of letters—nor would the Japanese have wished them to be spelled out. Moreover, Canada did not have to use the special duties provided for in the agreement, which would have tended to clash with its obligations under GATT. The tabling of the yearly agreements had sufficient publicity and authority to impress employers and employees alike in hard-pressed Canadian industries that their interests were protected. The government could garner credit in the textile-manufacturing areas where it relied on political support in the two most populous provinces: Ontario and Québec.

These measures were liberal compared with the restrictions imposed by the Europeans, and in some respects the Canadian market was more open than that of the United States to Japanese imports. Nevertheless, the annual negotiations with Japan were rather long and even acrimonious; the Japanese were extremely reluctant to see the voluntary quota system outside the GATT arrangements or the commercial agreement with Canada reimpose restrictions which they felt to be unfair and contrary to the spirit of liberal trade enshrined in GATT. Business expanded only moderately in Canada in 1962, but all but six of the quotas allowed some increase, averaging three to four per cent and some were as high as eight per cent.[12] Canadian practice was also compatible with the new LTA for cotton textiles under GATT. Importing countries had agreed not to reduce purchases below a twelve-month total out of fifteen previous months and to permit increases of at least five per cent after two years.[13]

Canada claimed it was more generous than Japan's other advanced trading partners because it permitted a bigger growth rate of Japanese exports than any other except the United States and took more Japanese goods per capita than any other except Australia, as well as giving the more generous GATT tariff rates. Canada did apply an emergency surcharge on imports briefly in 1962 for balance of payments reasons, which was allowed by GATT Article XIX, and had to ask for emergency credit from the International Monetary Fund, Britain, and the United States. This amounted to an added duty, but an editorial in the *Asahi Shimbun* urged the Japanese to cooperate with it.[14]

In 1963 the amount of imports covered by quotas dropped to around thirty per cent. For example, vinyl raincoats were removed from the list of restricted items. The letter from Ambassador Nobuhiko Ushiba to Finance Minister Walter Gordon provided for increases of three to five per cent except for a few running to thirteen per cent.[15] Dan Rosenbloom, former director of the Canadian Apparel and Textile Manufacturers' Association, said Japanese shipments of clothing and textiles were forty-five per cent higher during the first five months over the same period the year before and required drastic adjustment. He demanded that quotas be kept at the previous year's level without increases and feared that Japan would get up to twenty per cent of the Canadian worsted fabric market in 1965. However, the government did not go as far as he wished in its arrangements with Japan.

Regular increases were allowed in 1964, but Canada pressed for adding worsted fabrics to the restricted list. Japan had 1.5 per cent of the Canadian worsted fabric market in 1960 which grew to ten per cent by 1963, mostly at the expense of Britain. Japan was quite adamant that it did not want to restrict its exports to Canada just to benefit some third country—a principle that it was to incorporate in its annual ambassadorial letter tabled in the Commons.[16] Ambassador Ushiba complained rather bitterly at the British Columbia Trade Fair in May 1964 that Japanese goods were restricted for no other reason than high quality and low price;[17] he also protested the voluntary quota system. In that year, Japan was able to become a full member of the International Monetary Fund by abolishing its biggest currency controls, so that the ambassador was expressing the Japanese desire to reach a more equal footing with the leading advanced countries.

The ambassador's protest may not have been without some political calculation, as the West Coast was traditionally opposed to the protection of eastern industry at considerable economic disadvantage to itself. This theme was echoed in the speech of British Columbia's trade and commerce minister, Ralph Loffmark, who urged lowering barriers to encourage trade with Asian countries.[18] The provincial government was worried about a weakening of the international market for forest products and was aware of Japan's threats to cut back on its purchase of Canadian resources if it could not sell enough to Canada, which continued to have a large surplus in its trade with Japan.

Japan did finally receive some satisfaction in its continued drive to end voluntary quotas or set a time limit, as had been done with Britain and was being attempted in various GATT negotiations: Canada removed five more items from a list which was now about twenty-five.[19] Spun rayon blouses and shirts, canvas and waterproof footwear, and dish towels were removed, but textiles, transistors, radio and television tubes, polyester buttons, and stainless steel cutlery remained.

Many of these items belonged to the period before 1960 when Japan's industrial development relied upon the labor-intensive items which dominated Canada's imports, such as textiles, footwear, toys, paper goods, canned sea-foods, and mandarin oranges. It was from 1960 that Japan's concentration on heavy and chemical industries became intense, with development of steel, shipbuilding, petrochemical complexes, metal and oil refineries, and pulp and paper mills. Producer goods began to replace some of the earlier concentration on such things as textiles. The rapid rise of Japanese heavy industry required large volumes of ores and fuels from Canada, Australia, and the United States.[20] From 1965 Japan entered the period of mass consumption of consumer durables and motor vehicles, which began to filter into its foreign trade as well.

By the mid-sixties Japan was able to take the lead in moving into higher quality textiles such as synthetic and mixed fibre fabrics and garments, while suppliers like Hong Kong were entering the cheap textiles industry. This was also a period when production turned away from cotton textiles, so that the new fibres and fabrics now fell outside even the LTA for cotton and were subject to the quotas and unilateral restrictions which undermined GATT principles once more. In 1965 Japan was producing cotton fabrics at seventy per cent of capacity, and even though it was a year of recession, it still produced synthetic fibres up to eighty-five per cent of capacity. The Ministry of International Trade and Industry in Japan instituted a program to build one new spindle for each two old ones and to install continuous automated equipment which lowered costs and upgraded the industry. While the Japanese share of American imports of cotton fabrics declined from seventy-six per cent in 1956 to twenty-six per cent in 1964, Hong Kong gained twenty-six per cent of American imports from none earlier.[21] Japan made biggest gains in the Canadian market with synthetic fibres, worsted wool and broad woven fabrics, poplin broadcloth, and cotton. However, this constituted only ten per cent of Canada's total textile imports, at just over thirty million dollars in 1964. Shinichi Arai, former director of the Textile Bureau of the Ministry of Trade, said that Japan intended to produce higher quality goods and not to compete with the developing countries. The Japanese Spinners' Association did not expect any dramatic expansion in the Canadian market beyond orderly growth with rising Canadian incomes.

By mid-1966 the Canadian textile industry was suffering from sharp setbacks in sales, and demand for curbs on Japan again arose from the industry. Canadian producers had also begun to make the new polyester fabrics, and they claimed that disruptively low prices were set by Japanese makers. The Japanese were slow in responding to the new Canadian pressure, so that the annual negotiations dragged on much later than usual. Finance Minister Mitchell Sharp, in a speech in British Columbia, defended the Canadian policy by attacking Japan's own protectionism: "The market in Japan for manufactured products is very large, and it is doubtful whether Japanese producers any longer need to shelter behind protective barriers to trade."[22] He insisted that Canada was comparatively liberal, as only a few areas of textiles and clothing were now restricted and Canada had permitted yearly increases, unlike some other advanced countries.

In 1967 a slowdown in Canadian textiles resulted in a drop from ninety per cent of capacity to seventy-five, while inventories doubled. Plants began to shut down in the Eastern Townships of Québec and eastern Ontario, and there were heavy layoffs.[23] Under-Secretary of State for External Affairs Marcel Cadieux summoned the Japanese ambassador on 25 July to suggest that Japan hold exports at 1966 levels by monthly averages for the time being. The government was prepared to invoke GATT Article XIX and resort to special duties under the commercial treaty.

The Japanese minister of trade, Wataro Kanno, stopped in Ottawa with a team of senior officials on his way to Washington. He requested a meeting with the Department of Finance to discuss what was viewed as a dangerous precedent proposed by Canada. It would amount to the first new quota in five years, on precisely those burgeoning synthetic fibres in which Japan was a leader and was under attack internationally. Canadian officials were concerned about the competition in mixed polyester and cotton fabric, polyester rayon, spun rayon, nylon, and acrylic yarns.

Negotiations on the existing quotas were finally completed, although later than in any previous year. Finance Minister Sharp tabled the letter from the Japanese chargé d'affaires on 17 October in the Commons. The restraint agreement permitted the usual orderly increases in 1967; however the minister was able to state that the manmade fibres not covered in the agreement were unlikely, as a result of the recent talks, to reach 1966 levels. Thus a new quota was avoided, and the Japanese were able to give assurances of orderly marketing. Canada continued its normal policy of increases and took no sanctions against Japan.[24]

Although the surveillance program of Revenue Canada estimated later that thirty per cent of Japanese textile exports were subsidized by such non-tariff measures as tax rebates, concessional export financing, and so forth, Canada did not attempt to use countervailing legislation under Section 7(1) of the Customs Tariff.[25] Instead, the restraint agreements were depended upon to remove any disruption occurring in Canada. However, in 1968 Section 40A(7)(c) of the Customs Act, which established fixed values for ordinary and special duty purposes against injurious imports, was replaced by Section 8(2) of the Customs Tariff Act whereby the governor-in-council, on the recommendation of the minister of finance, may apply a surtax on imports of any kind from any country which cause or threaten serious injury to Canadian producers. This was to be incorporated in agreements with Japan by Canada. Prior to the quota legislation of 1971, surtax action was the only unilateral measure available to deal with disruptive textile imports, and it was used almost entirely to deal with disruptive agricultural products from the United States. Once, when it was used against Mexico for imports of cotton yarn in 1969, that country retaliated against Canadian newsprint and automotive exports.

The year 1969 also saw the enactment of a new Anti-Dumping Act, which provided for an Anti-Dumping Tribunal. If this body does not find injury to Canadian producers, the Department of National Revenue must return the special duty it has collected for selling goods here for less than in the foreign producer's home market. When the tribunal did find that Algoma Steel Co. was injured by European steel beams dumped in eastern Canadian markets, British Columbia companies which bought their steel from Japan were seriously harmed by this move; they could not afford to transport the steel from central Canada, and Algoma was not willing to supply them. Eventually, pressure from the British Columbia members of Parliament resulted in a remission of the duties for the province.[26]

The Canadian anti-dumping system was the outcome of the 1966–1967 Kennedy Round of multilateral trade negotiations which produced a new international Anti-Dumping Code to implement Article VI of GATT.[27] This brought Canadian practice into line with that of the United States and Britain which had complained mightily about Canadian practice. It also provided protection for new producers, which had not been possible before.

In the late sixties, the technological change, by which synthetic and mixed fibres replaced cotton, produced a trend toward unilateral protective measures outside both GATT and the LTA for cotton. The situation was further aggravated by the explosive crisis between the United States and Japan over the textile issue from 1969 to 1971,[28] in which Canada managed to obtain some satisfaction by voluntary restraint negotiations, however.

The letter from the Japanese ambassador to the finance minister was tabled in the Commons on 21 November 1968. It concerned restraints to be applied in 1969. Japan acknowledged that the Canadian textile and garment industry was in difficulties and agreed to accept smaller increases for the year. It also promised to monitor the polyester-cotton mix fabrics.[29] However, in 1968 there was a distinct swing in imports from Hong Kong from fabric piece goods to finished garments, which increased by three times in 1967, as did those from Taiwan and the United States. Canadian textiles continued to be under pressure from the increase in manmade fibre fabrics from abroad. Apart from textiles and garments, the only items put on voluntary quotas in this period were receiving tubes for radio and television sets, and stainless steel tableware.[30]

THE NEW CANADIAN TEXTILE POLICY OF 1970

In 1970, a new Canadian textile policy was initiated on liberal principles, through the Textile and Clothing Board which was set up to investigate injury to Canadian firms and workers and recommend protective measures to the minister of industry, trade, and commerce.[31] The Textile and Clothing Board Act contains the radical idea that protection should only be contemplated if the industry is viable and, if applied, it should be temporary as well as conditional on carrying out a plan of rationalization to make the industry competitive. Apparently, this denies protection beyond the ordinary tariff to industries that do not appear to be viable in the face of foreign competition. However, the tariff is ineffectual against low-cost yarns, fabrics, textile products, and clothing from Japan and developing countries. Treating such competition as not "normal" or "fair," the Textile and Clothing Board grants protection, and thus treats Canadian production as viable, in all cases where it has found injury. Nor has the board been able to police the confidential plans for rationalization filed with it. Although the industry has tended to rationalize and modernize itself on a par with other advanced countries, it cannot compete with the low wages of South Korea or India or the artificial prices of Communist state trading countries in Eastern Europe.

Despite the seeming denial of protection in the Act, the board has usually granted it where injury threatens or occurs.[32]

The Textile and Clothing Board Act also includes amendments to the Export and Import Permits Act and to the Customs Act. Section 26 enables the government to put any goods on the Import Control List if the board finds they are likely to cause serious injury or over which it wishes to institute surveillance. At the same time, an import permit is granted, while importers must inform the Office of Special Import Policy of the quantities and prices of the goods they order. Section 27 amends the Customs Act to permit an embargo on goods circumventing a restraint agreement. The Office of Special Import Policy thus has a strong hand in negotiating restraint agreements, and the government also has the power to stop imports being controlled. Nevertheless, the board has tried to limit the scope of these actions in being precise about types and weights of products protected and has tended toward reducing the number of items protected. It has generally recommended protection against Asian and Eastern European low-cost producers, but not those of developed countries. As a result of the moderation of this protectionism, in 1976 the board was to come under attack by the industry for its laxness.

The restraints on textiles and clothing changed very little in 1969 and 1970, as the Japanese continued to avoid a formal agreement on the newer fibres, such as polyester-cotton mix, and contended that Canadian production of the latter had been stable for three or four years.[33] Canadian producers wanted to be assured of a ceiling on Japanese imports, so that they could plan on investment for a bigger share of their own market. The Japanese, however, did not want to take any step that would undermine their resistance to American pressure for restraints on the new textiles. In the meantime, the shift from plain cotton to mixes rendered the old agreements of lesser importance. Two of the earliest investigations of the Textile and Clothing Board were of acrylic fibres and knitted fabrics, of which Japan was a principle exporter.[34] Canadian officials were particularly concerned that without a board report they might not be in a position to check an onslaught of imports diverted from the United States, once it carried out its threats of stringent quotas on textiles such as those contained in the Mills Bill which was before Congress in 1970. That measure envisioned a limit on all imports, to a fixed fifteen-per-cent share of the American market, without proof of injury or market disruption.

Canada brought the new items under voluntary restraint in September 1971, just weeks after the Nixon import surcharge was imposed, aimed at forcing Japan, Europe, and Canada to a realignment of currencies and a more favorable trade balance. As part of the fallout, the Japanese industry gave up its resistance and capitulated to American pressure by agreeing to restraints on the new textiles. Both Japan and Canada were so shaken by the surcharge that they attempted to reorient their foreign policies in a more independent direction.

At the Pacific Basin Economic Cooperation Council meeting in Vancouver in May 1971, Industry, Trade, and Commerce Minister Jean-Luc Pépin reminded the Japanese that Canada was the most open of any industrial country to textile imports and bought ten times the amount per capita that the EEC did. He also contended that Japanese import licensing kept many Canadian manufactured items out of Japan.[35] After inconclusive negotiations in April, renewed negotiations in the summer finally reached agreement on all types of woven shirts, including manmade fibres, with specific amounts on quota; polyester pillowcases and sheets were added, together with fabrics of polyester filament and polyester-cotton mixtures, for the first time. Permitted increases were limited to five per cent instead of ten as before. These quotas still only amounted to five per cent of Japan's sales to Canada, and included radio and television tubes as well as textiles and clothing.[36]

Thus Canada resolved the outstanding difficulty with respect to fabrics and clothing items of the new manmade fibres, wool, and mixed fibres, which were deemed threats to Canadian production. The United States also brought its struggle over Japanese textile imports to a conclusion on 15 October 1971, with a memorandum of understanding followed by a new and more comprehensive restraint agreement in January 1972. Outright unilateral quotas by Canada on imports of low-cost textiles were avoided, except for the single global quota on men's and boys' shirts with tailored collars under GATT Article XIX, as already noted above. Canada and the United States continued their voluntary restraint agreements with Japan and other Asian suppliers. Nevertheless, the whole multilateral trading system established under GATT was shaken by the struggle between Japan and the United States. It was part of a broader international battle over unilateral quantitative restrictions, carried on by major importing countries against Japan and other suppliers of massive low-cost imports.[37] So in June 1972 the director-general of GATT, Olivier Long, who had attempted to help the Japanese in their struggle with the United States over textiles, got fresh negotiations going to cover the newer materials which had not been dealt with in the LTA on cotton.[38]

THE INTERNATIONAL MULTI-FIBRE ARRANGEMENT OF 1974

The result was the Arrangement Regarding International Trade in Textiles (ITA), also called the Multi-Fibre Arrangement (MFA), which became effective on 1 January 1974 for four years and was renewed in 1978 and 1981. It was an advance over the LTA for cotton, permitting expansion and liberalization of the textile trade while providing protection against disruption of the production in the importing countries. Existing bilateral restraint agreements and unilateral quantitative restrictions were to be phased out over three years unless they already conformed to these new requirements of GATT. Canada had already included manmade fibres and mixed fabrics in its restraint agreements. Full application of the ITA was acknowledged in the agreement between Canada and Japan in 1976, in the note from the secretary of state for external affairs, Allan MacEachen, to Ambassador Yasuhiko Nara.[39] The annex to the note included only three textile items, which were all that remained under restraint.

The ITA specifically permitted unilateral restraint agreements on certain products, based on proof of market disruption or, failing agreement, by unilateral action. There were liberal provisions for the growth of textile imports, base periods for calculating quotas, carryovers, and interproduct transfers. For example, an annual minimum growth of six per cent in imports was to be allowed unless exceptional circumstances warranted a smaller rate of growth. A new Textiles Surveillance Body was to receive notification of all restraint arrangements which were to be reviewed by it, and it could recommend as to the admissibility of the imposed restrictions. Canada was successful in getting the inclusion of an expanded definition of the concept of market disruption, basing it on the International Anti-Dumping Code, Article 3. The new arrangement permitted Canada to carry out its already comparatively liberal policy within a vastly improved GATT framework.[40] In liberalizing the major textile importers' markets, it provided some relief for Canada, where huge amounts were frequently dumped below cost of production when they were shut out of the bigger markets by unilateral restraints.

The anticlimax of the epochal struggle with Japan was that by this time Japan itself was invaded by low-cost textile imports from developing Asian countries such as South Korea and Taiwan, often using Japanese technology and investment. By 1973 Japan imported more made-up goods than it exported, whereas exports had been five times the quantity of imports only three years before. The polyester-filament fabrics restraint, incorporated in the annual agreements by Canada after long consideration, was only partially used by Japan.[41] Japan has since phased out many of the cheaper textiles and less efficient operations, but it remains an important exporter of higher quality fabrics and clothing. Like Canada, it has made considerable room in its home market for the developing countries' textile and clothing exports— although unlike Canada it reserves over eighty per cent of its home market for its own producers.[42]

Initially, the new textile policy under Jean-Luc Pépin as minister of trade was a success. There were efforts to modernize and upgrade the industry in Canada to make it more competitive.[43] The rise in Japanese prices with the revaluation of the yen made restraints less necessary. By 1973 there was a world shortage of textiles, when big exporters turned to traditional markets and did not dump excess production in Canada. In 1972 and 1973 the Canadian government permitted some restraints to lapse, when the protection seemed no longer necessary. However, in Québec unemployment still was considerable and Pépin's loss of his parliamentary seat in 1972 was attributed by some to his over-liberal textiles policy.

The years 1975 and 1976 proved to be very bad. In some of the Eastern Townships of Québec and small communities of Ontario where the textile or clothing industry was the chief or sole employer, plant shutdowns were disastrous, unemployment reaching as high as twenty-seven per cent in some parts of Québec. In that province one in four of those in the manufacturing sector was employed in textiles, while in the rest of Canada the proportion was twelve per cent, or two hundred thousand. Women and immigrants who spoke neither English nor French made up a large part of this work force, which was not easily absorbed elsewhere. The burden of social welfare payments was heavy and it was difficult for the workers to move.[44]

The renewed onslaught of foreign exporters in 1976 resulted in an increase in clothing imports of forty-six per cent over the year before. In fibres and fabrics the Canadian industry had gone from nearly ninety per cent of the home market in 1949 to only forty per cent by this time, in contrast to the United States which reserved nearly ninety per cent of its home market for domestic producers, or to Europe which reserved seventy-five per cent of its market. In Canada the share of the clothing market held by domestic producers fell from over sixty-four per cent to below fifty-six per cent between 1975 and 1976.[45] Bruck Mills in Québec, which looked like a desirable investment in the better days of 1973, had sold a controlling interest to Marubeni Trading Company and Toyobo (Oriental Spinning) Co. They introduced new technology and improved the plant, spending six million dollars on new buildings; but it too had sustained heavy losses by 1976.[46] The Japanese owners reported that their home industry was under even more severe competition from low-cost imports.

The Canadian industry was now thoroughly disillusioned by the slowness of the new government arrangements, as well as by their inadequacy compared to the much more comprehensive protection provided by the United States and the EEC to their own producers. Its anxiety was balanced to some extent by the concern of the importers' and consumers' organizations, as well as by the efforts of some of the western Canadian representatives in cabinet to make the inexpensive imports available. The latter opposed what they viewed as excessive protection for the central provinces' textile and clothing industries. This balance was to be rudely upset by the political developments of 1976.

The Canadian producers had been on intimate terms with the officials negotiating with Japan in 1970, whom they accompanied to Tokyo in that year. But under Pépin's successors in the Department of Industry, Trade, and Commerce and under the new Textile and Clothing Board, they were kept at arm's length by the newer and more neutral process of handling the industry. When Senate hearings were held in February, March, and April 1976, they had their first opportunity to air their resentments and frustrations over the unfavorable situation they found themselves in.

The Senate hearings resulted in considerable criticism of the government and the minister of trade, Don Jamieson, struck an ad hoc committee, which included textile and clothing manufacturers, labor unions, and provincial representatives, to study the situation; the importers and consumers were not invited to participate.[47] The opposition introduced a motion in the House of Commons condemning the government on its textile policy, to which the Ontario minister of industry added his own condemnation. Most important was the Cabinet reshuffle of 14 September that brought Jean Chrétien to the post of minister of industry, trade, and commerce in place of Jamieson. He was a Québécois, and may well have heeded the fate of his provincial colleague, Pépin, because of these important issues.

THE GLOBAL QUOTAS OF 1976

The new minister, Chrétien, immediately called for an interim report from the Textile and Clothing Board and was said to have remarked in connection with foreign textile imports that Canada was the Boy Scout of the world.[48] To this was added a joint Emergency Interim Submission of the clothing associations of Ontario, Manitoba, and Québec, demanding immediate action to curtail imports, which was supported by the unions and the primary textile industry. The interim report of the Textile and Clothing Board of 8 November 1976 called for a rollback to 1975 levels of fourteen items of clothing from all sources, covering virtually all types.

Despite considerable objections from other departments represented on the Interdepartmental Committee on Low Cost Imports, and doubts in the Cabinet Committee on Economic Policy, Chrétien succeeded in getting support for drastic action along the lines recommended by the board's report. Crucial for his cabinet colleagues was the November victory of the

Parti Québécois, dedicated to separation of the province from the rest of Canada.[49] The need to woo Québec by support for its principal industry, and to woo its vote for the sake of Canadian unity, is made explicit, for example, in the pamphlet on the industry in 1978, mindful of the coming referendum on sovereignty association.[50]

The decision of 29 November 1976 followed the recommendations of the board without compromise. Global quotas were applied, based on the worst year of the recession in 1975. Article XIX was invoked in the GATT safeguard procedure concerning a threat to domestic industry. The restrictions applied to all foreign trade partners for a period of at least thirteen months to the end of 1977, and included all fourteen clothing items singled out by the board. The penetration of the Canadian market in 1976 varied from nine per cent to 370 per cent. Some critics said certain items did not need to be included, while several of the partners could hardly be held responsible for the threat, opening the possibility of retaliation. American retaliation could be very damaging, but Canadian national unity was more important.

Bilateral agreements with Hong Kong and South Korea and another being drawn up under the MFA were abrogated without the advance consultation or evidence of disruption promised in the agreements, and the MFA itself, which had been so assiduously sponsored by the Canadian government, was breached. In Washington an international trade group spokesman said, "The question raised by the Canadian action is whether there should be any rules at all in world trade, or should we all tear up agreements and live by the law of the jungle."[51] Canadian officials argued that the GATT Article XIX procedure superseded bilateral agreements; however, the Canadian action also violated the MFA.

The Textile and Clothing Board's final report in May 1977 recommended that five-year bilateral agreements be negotiated with twenty-one countries covering fifteen items of clothing.[52] The drastic policy, closely adhering to the interim report, was not fully maintained: after consideration within the government, and a return to more normal input of departmental and consumer interest, the final government decision was to negotiate three-year agreements with the seven largest exporters, instead of five-year agreements as proposed by the board in its final report. The unilateral global quotas were extended to 31 December 1978, and the new restraint agreements were to begin on 1 January 1979.[53]

Japan was not named by the board as a country to be restrained and no longer constituted a large exporter of garments, although there was to be continued restraint of its synthetic fibres, the category in which producers in the developed countries still outstripped those in the developing. Between 1970 and 1977 Japan shifted from exporting low-cost apparel to importing it. By 1978 close to half of all shirts sold in Japan were imported at about half the cost of those made locally.[54] Japan's producers were not only hampered by the competition from low-wage countries, but its own prices had risen with yen revaluation and the escalating cost of energy in Japan. In Korea and Taiwan, wages were only a third of those in Japan. Toyobo had invested in Taiwan, Indonesia, Brazil, Costa Rica, and El Salvador to surmount import barriers. Its plants were doing well there, unlike its Bruck Mills investment in Montréal. Teijin, which had invested in Korea, was being squeezed out by the Korean government just as its joint project was beginning to flourish.

The Japanese industry, therefore, moved out of apparel production and low-cost textiles within its own country, to concentrate on synthetic fibres and sophisticated products based on them. Higher technology and value-added were intended to compensate for higher Japanese wages and other costs. Unfortunately, the same strategy was being followed by the EEC and the United States. Thus even the synthetic fibre producers in Japan had been in the red for three years, and some American fibres were competing successfully in Japan as well. With the world recession and overcapacity, the Japanese producers formed temporary cartels in both 1977 and 1978 in order to cut output by fifteen to twenty per cent. Special loans from the government to industry enabled it to scrap or mothball facilities which were deemed to have about twenty-five per cent excess capacity. Older employees were helped to retire and young ones to retrain for other employment.[55] The Japanese producers could not be protected by bans and quotas as in Canada, because they depended on many of the low-cost exporting countries for essential imports, and had favorable trade balances from their own sales there which they did not wish to jeopardize.

The report of the C. D. Howe Research Institute of Montréal by Caroline Pestieau brought out a sober assessment of the Canadian industry; it raised the possibility of phasing out the industry in order to improve international competitiveness and lessen its long-standing divisive influence in Canada, since the other provinces would have to pay more for protected goods manufactured in Québec and Ontario.[56]

The Canadian industry was significantly helped by the new clothing quotas. In 1977 it regained what it had lost in the incoming flood the year before, and managed to get back its 64.6 per cent share of the Canadian market.[57] Employment was considerably up, as well.[58]

Only a few leading synthetic fabrics imported from Japan were still restrained in 1976. These were polyester-filament and nylon fabrics, and elastic braid,[59] and in 1977 even elastic braid was omitted.[60] The next agreement covered the two-year period from 1 January 1978 to 31 December 1979. It added acrylic spun yarn for hand knitting to the polyester-filament and nylon fabrics in Annex A. Worsted fabrics, elastic braid, and elastic webbing were to be closely monitored. When they were thought likely to exceed limits set down in Annex B, Japan agreed to consult quickly at Canadian request and to apply a year's restraint above the indicated level if no other solution was reached.[61] The agreement for the 1980 calendar year repeated the arrangements for 1978 to 1979, but on an annual basis once more.[62]

Thus as Japan itself joined the ranks of the advanced developed countries, it had to cope with the same problems as Canada with respect to the influx of low-cost imports—especially in the volatile textile and clothing sector. After 1973 it ceased to be much of a threat to the Canadian industry. Only in the category of synthetic fibres was an element of the voluntary restraint system retained to ensure orderly marketing. Canada does remain comparatively liberal in its textile policy by allotting a much bigger share of its market to imports, even though its market is smaller and its protection less comprehensive than Japan, the United States, or the EEC.

The textile policy of 1970 has never been implemented in its aim of granting only temporary protection in addition to the regular tariff to make the Canadian industry fully competitive. Probably none of the advanced countries could remain in the industry if they did not maintain some sort of special protection against the low-cost developing countries or state trading countries. The defeat of the Parti Québécois in the 1980 referendum made it even less likely that the federal Liberal government would leave the industry exposed to the tender mercies of full international competition, even if the agreements stemming from the latest round of GATT multilateral trade negotiations were implemented.

The divisive issue of protection of the manufacturing industries of Québec and Ontario, at the cost of higher prices to Canadian consumers and the inability of Canada to compete internationally, has probably been decided in favor of the protection of the two central provinces' industries by the federal election of 1980, which brought the Liberals back to power. They were sustained principally by the voters in Québec and Ontario, though repudiated by Conservative or New Democratic majorities everywhere else in Canada. The Liberals promised lower gasoline prices to consumers, but permitted them to rise as soon as they concluded the oil price war with Alberta in 1981. Japan, with almost no oil of its own, absorbed the full increases in oil prices from the beginning and began to phase out much uneconomic domestic production, becoming even more competitive than before.

Nearly seventy per cent of Canada's exports to Japan originate in the two western provinces, where they consist largely of processed or relatively unprocessed raw materials.[63] This trade has a generally beneficial effect on the development of those provinces and is sought by large Japanese companies. In the case of British Columbia, about a quarter of its foreign trade is with Japan. Canada's imports from Japan consist largely of manufactured goods, many of which compete with those made chiefly in Québec and

Ontario and have been able to leap the tariff barriers by virtue of low price and good quality. While all the consumers or recipients of those goods benefit, especially in central Canada where the population is concentrated, the central Canadian producers and workers have succeeded in slowing or blocking Japanese competition, as we have seen in the case of textiles and clothing.

The restructuring of Japanese exports in clothing and textiles, either scrapping or upgrading them, has gradually relieved the Québec industry of competition from Japan, but it is now undergoing even more severe competition from low-cost production in Taiwan, Hong Kong, and the Republic of Korea. The brunt of Japanese competition now falls on Ontario producers of durable goods. Canadian manufacturers in these newer sectors of competition have not attracted the same sympathy and protection, primarily because of the smaller number of their workers and votes.

TELEVISION PENETRATION

Television sets, which are one of the most outstanding cases of Japanese market penetration, have not received the kind of massive protection vouchsafed to clothing manufacturers in Québec, nor do they involve such a huge work force.[64] Canadian producers have chosen to make large-size sets that do not compete with Japanese sets, or have diversified into new lines, providing a more stable profit.[65] Both Canada and Japan abandoned the manufacture of small black-and-white sets to low-cost Asian producers, while the United States has insisted on quantitative restrictions to reserve a substantial market for their own television industry.

Japanese-made television sets first reached Canada in the early 1960s, and had captured a substantial share of the Canadian market by 1967.[66] R. G. Simpson, chairman of the consumer products division of the Electronics Industry Association and general manager of the RCA Victor Home Instrument division, said that Japanese black-and-white sets increased a hundred per cent in each of the years 1965, 1966, and 1967. Color television was introduced in Canada in 1966. In 1967, sixty-eight per cent of the color sets with nineteen-inch screens or smaller came from Japan, a huge increase in only eighteen months.[67] By the autumn of 1968, Japanese imports held about a quarter of the Canadian market.[68]

The Canadian customs ruling handed down 27 June 1968 raised the valuation for duty, as it found that the sets were being imported at fifteen to twenty per cent below the Japanese domestic price. Sets imported below the new value had to pay the difference in an anti-dumping duty, and the flood of sets immediately slowed. The Japanese Trade Ministry urged the five major Japanese companies to cut their domestic prices by ten per cent to bring them into line with the export prices, in order to get the dumping duty removed. Roy A. Phillips, president of the Electronics Industry Association, still feared that, under the pending new Anti-Dumping Code, it might take too long to investigate the damage which was required to be shown. In these circumstances the domestic industry faced a grim prospect.

Japan did go on to capture nearly thirty per cent of the Canadian market in the early 1970s, but that market was far from uniform. Japan concentrated on the smaller sizes, nineteen-inch and under, but was pushed out of the market for small black-and-white sets by Hong Kong, Taiwan, and the Republic of Korea after 1972. Canadian producers concentrated on the larger size sets in which the other chief source of imports, the United States, was also active. However, the Canadians were gradually edged out of both small and large size sets, going from over eighty-eight per cent of the market in 1965, to about forty-seven per cent by 1975; this resembles the pattern with textiles.

There was a recession related to the oil crisis from 1973 to 1975 when demand dropped nearly thirty per cent, but in 1976 it recovered. Imports from Japan doubled, as did overall imports, but at the same time, domestic sales declined to sixteen per cent lower than 1966 and forty-six per cent lower than 1973![69] Consumer preference shifted to color sets as the prices fell, chiefly due to pressure of the lower-priced imports. The nine active domestic producers in the early 1960s produced tubes, cabinets, and chassis, but with more efficient assembly-line operation there was a closing down of component plants between 1967 and 1974 and an increase in the assembly of imported components, as the switch from tubes to transistors in the chassis turned most Canadian producers into assemblers. Japanese producers not only enjoyed lower wages but also economies of size and flexibility of a variety of models for quick shifts of taste. A minimum plant capacity is estimated at three hundred thousand to be competitive, whereas the average Canadian production run in 1976 was only fifty thousand sets; some Japanese plants even had capacities of one million sets. In Canada, there were too many firms producing too many lines for too small a home market, although some sets are now exported. Consumers probably gained, in that they would have had to pay more than double the price for sets if there had been no imports and the same volume of sales had been reached.[70] Workers in the consumer electronics sector declined from 1971 to 1975, going from eight to seven thousand and then in 1978 to six thousand.[71] Thus the number of workers involved appears to be far smaller than the vast numbers involved in the case of textiles and clothing.

The Canadian federal government introduced a duty remission scheme in 1977 which enabled Canadian production to hold at the levels of shipments of 1974 and 1975. This enabled components to be imported with a waiving of the duty to reduce the cost to assemblers.[72] At first the program only permitted the import of TV sets to qualify for remission of duty and sales tax, but chassis were later added; the scheme required plans for restructuring to make the participating companies more competitive, as well as for the usual Canadian content and benefit. Initially it applied to RCA Limited, Canadian Admiral Corporation Limited, Electrohome Limited, Hitachi Sales Corp. Canada Limited, Sanyo Canada Limited, and Panasonic Industries Canada Limited. The program permitted dramatic increases in Canadian exports which reached 192,000 units in 1978, nearly all to the United States. In 1977 the federal government also withdrew the General Preferential Tariff and the British Preferential Tariff on all color TV sets until 31 December 1981, to favor domestic producers.

AUTOMOBILE PENETRATION

Japanese passenger automobiles have enjoyed an unusual success in Canada, which at times has ranked only behind the United States, the United Kingdom, and Germany as an automobile export market for Japan. Australia is more highly saturated, but the vehicles are assembled with a high Australian-made content as required by the government there. In Canada in 1981 Honda came second only to Chevrolet as the most popular new car model. Three Japanese models were among the top imports, although they paid a higher duty than either American-made or British-made cars. Even with rising prices, the popular models continue to be cheaper than the equivalent makes of other nations.

From 1965 to 1969 Japanese cars went from 0.4 per cent to 5.2 per cent of Canadian sales. In 1970 they reached 10.2 per cent and in 1971 11.8 per cent. There was a decline in 1974 and 1975 during the oil recession, back to 9 per cent, but by 1977 they were 13.3 per cent, with a dip again in 1979 when oil prices suddenly doubled.[73] In 1980 and 1981 sales soared.

In numbers of Japanese vehicles imported to Canada, they reached over 100,000 in 1971 and rose to 116,860 in 1972, but declined to 72,226 in 1975. By 1977 they reached 127,058 and declined again; in 1979 they were just above 60,000, less than half the 1978 total.[74] In 1980, however, Japanese auto exports more than doubled, to 158,375 units,[75] although that was only a 24 per cent increase over the previous peak in 1977.

Japanese cars have enjoyed a relatively ready reception in Canada, where small cars have long been a steady proportion of the market. The car-makers and government officials of the United States and Europe have frequently noted the vast difference between export and import of vehicles by Japan: in

1982 it exported about five-and-a-half million and imported under forty thousand. Foreign car prices have greatly increased in Japan due to the expensive inspection required there: a Buick Century cost about twenty-nine thousand dollars in 1981 after inspection.

However, in 1980 and 1981 the climate altered drastically in Canada, the United States, and Europe when there was an enormous drop in the purchase of new cars other than those of Japan. In North America, demand for the large models declined markedly as the smaller, fuel-efficient cars became more popular, but demand for even these was sluggish. But for Japanese automobiles, this was not so: demand for them held up or even increased while North American and European makers experienced big decreases with consequent unemployment in this leading heavy industry. The historically unprecedented high interest rates also greatly discouraged would-be car buyers, except for those turning to the Japanese models. Thus enormous pressure arose for governments in the United States and EEC to restrict the entry of Japanese cars. In Italy, France, and Britain a low ceiling was already set, with only Germany, the Benelux countries, and Denmark fully open to Japanese car exports.

Bill Pickett, president of American Motors (Canada), which had a drop in sales of nearly thirty-five per cent in the twelve months to June 1980, accused the Japanese of selling cars in the United States below cost and below the Japanese selling price.[76] He called for government action to get the Japanese to adopt voluntary restraints on car exports to Canada.

In the United States, Ford Motor Company and the United Auto Workers' Union appealed to the International Trade Commission to rule that Japanese auto exports were causing injury to their industry, a decision which would permit the president to curtail the exports. However, the Commission found by one vote that Japanese exports were not the chief cause of the unprecedented downturn in the American auto industry; it was the change in consumer taste favoring the smaller, more fuel-efficient models. This made presidential action difficult, and fueled the moves in Congress to curtail the Japanese penetration by legislation. The Danforth Bill became the chief threat to the Japanese industry.

The Canadian minister of industry, trade, and commerce, Herb Gray (a native of Windsor, where automobiles are the major industry), visited Japan in August 1980 to try to persuade the Japanese makers to invest in new production in Canada and use more Canadian-made parts.[77] He warned that measures to protect the industry might be forced on the government if no positive steps were taken by Japan. In October a high-powered mission of Canadian auto parts makers also toured Japan urging greater purchase of Canadian-made parts.[78] But it was not until May of the following year that Premier Bill Bennett of British Columbia revealed that Toyota Motor Company, Toyota Canada Incorporated, and Toyota Motor Sales Company were conducting a feasibility study of an auto parts plant in his province.[79]

Herb Gray went to Washington in April 1981 in an effort to concert policy with the United States, where the White House wanted to curtail Japanese exports to 1.7 million units a year from the 1.9 million units exported to the United States in 1980. There was strong lobbying in Ottawa by the Canadian auto industry to restrict Japanese exports, which had risen by sixty-two per cent during the first three months of 1981.[80] The minister said, "We will take whatever action is necessary to prevent a disruptive diversion of Japanese cars to Canada." He hoped that any restrictions on the Japanese in the American market could be extended to Canada, for the sharp increases of Japanese car exports to Canada and Europe in February and March suggested that a diversion was already under way by the Japanese industry in anticipation of American restraints. Coincidental with Gray's visit to Washington was the Canadian government mission to Tokyo under Campbell Stuart, chairman of the automotive task force of the Department of Industry, Trade, and Commerce; they told the Japanese that if Japan curbed its auto exports to the United States, it should similarly reduce its shipments to Canada.[81]

The dénouement came on 1 May 1981 when Japanese International Trade and Industry Minister Rokusuke Tanaka offered to limit auto exports to the United States to 1.68 million units in the fiscal year 1981, a decrease from 1980 of 7.7 per cent. William Brock, the American special trade representative, expressed satisfaction in Tokyo, promising that the Reagan administration would persuade Congress to withdraw protectionist bills such as that of Senator Danforth.[82] Some degree of restraint was to be continued in the following two years, the amount depending on improvement in the American car market. The voluntary restraint was intended to roll back the Japanese share of the American market from 21.3 per cent in 1980 to 17 per cent or 18 per cent in 1981, from the start of the fiscal year on 1 April. The Japanese share of the American market contrasts with the minuscule limit of twenty-two hundred cars permitted by Italy, fixed in 1956 before Japan won full acceptance in GATT, the three per cent limit set by France's administrative officials, or the approximately ten per cent limit agreed to by the automakers of Britain and Japan.[83]

The announcement in Tokyo, however, was greeted with dismay in Canada and Europe, where fears of diversion were already high as officials and industry leaders nervously watched the Japanese-American negotiations. The Japanese industry itself was angry at its own government for giving in to the Americans; they were even less disposed to listen to concession demands by the Canadians and Europeans. Campbell Stuart was dispatched to Tokyo again to appeal on behalf of Canada for similar treatment to that vouchsafed to the Americans. Prime Minister Trudeau also appealed to Prime Minister Suzuki, who happened to visit Ottawa about this time. The commission of the EEC demanded reciprocity as Viscount Davignon, the industry commissioner, strongly criticized Japan's trade offensive in Europe at the European Parliament in Strasbourg.

When Stuart met with the Japanese trade officials, they said they had already cautioned their manufacturers to show restraint and were considering requiring them to file their export plans with them to forecast shipments.[84] The issue was resolved when Herb Gray was informed by letter from Trade Minister Tanaka that Japan would reduce auto exports to Canada by six per cent in the current fiscal year. Canadian officials were quite pleased that a limit was placed on the Japanese share of the Canadian market, as had been done in the United States.[85] Although the fiscal year 1981 would show a decline compared with 1980, the calendar year 1981 would show an increase of about ten per cent over 1980 because of the flood of cars in the first three months of 1981. The United Auto Workers' Union and the industry criticized this arrangement because it permitted an increase in 1981 and did not reduce car exports as in the United States, which obtained promises of greater restraint for a three-year period. Ian Deans of the New Democratic Party told the House of Commons that he believed Japan had flooded the market during the first three months to boost its bargaining position.[86] The minister, Gray, said that the Japanese promise ended fear of diversion from the American market to Canada, and that he continued to feel satisfied with the outcome. A similar arrangement was made between Japan and Germany which still welcomed Japanese exports. In Belgium, the other Benelux countries, and Denmark actual cutbacks were undertaken; in Belgium the Japanese had captured a quarter of the car market in 1980, while the domestic foreign-owned producers were cutting back or closing down.

At his meeting with Suzuki, Trudeau had requested the long-term goal of Japanese production in Canada and the purchase of Canadian parts. At the Fourth Canada-Japan Businessmen's Conference in Vancouver, Herb Gray revealed on 18 June that Toyota intended to dispatch a team within two weeks to conduct a feasibility study for a parts plant in Canada.[87] Premier Bill Bennett said that there was the future possibility of a complete assembly plant in British Columbia, a project which would be supported by both federal and provincial governments.[88] The project was held up by the abrasive negotiations over extension of the Japanese "voluntary" restrictions on auto exports for 1982. It was only after several months' slowdown of customs clearance of Japanese cars at Vancouver that the Japanese government agreed to a reduction in the level of car exports, but only for a six-month period. Toyota then announced its plans to go ahead with a plant to produce twenty thousand aluminum wheels a month, starting in mid-1985 with eighty per cent going to Japan. The plant would cost twenty-three million dollars; this was later lowered to nineteen million with federal and provincial government loans of five-and-a-half million. A new company called Canadian Autoparts Toyota Inc., capitalized at seven million dollars, would be headed by Yukiyasu Togo, president of Toyota Canada Inc. One hundred workers would be hired locally.[89]

In the first quarter of 1981 fiscal year, the export of cars did not abate; indeed, they continued at a rate of seventy per cent over the year before;[90] in September, when new domestic-made cars were selling at fourteen per cent below the year before, the rate was seventy-three per cent greater than September of 1980.[91] However, the quantity did eventually subside as had been agreed, although Japan felt special compulsion to make more concessions to the United States. As the chairman of Nissan told European auto-makers, "The Japanese government agreed to these quotas [with the U.S.] because of the special trade and defence relationship Japan has with the U.S."[92] The kind of special relations with Canada, envisaged when the prime minister signed the Framework for Economic Cooperation, have not materialized.

Although Japan has continued the restraints on a six-month basis with some reduction on passenger cars—trucks have not been restricted as Canada has asked—pressure has not abated for some significant assembly and purchase of auto parts in Canada, on the part of the United Autoworkers or the Automotive Parts Manufacturers' Association. A federal task-force report on the auto trade in May 1983 recommended that Japanese cars sold in Canada should have at least sixty per cent Canadian content. The members of the task force represented the auto union and auto-parts makers; the Japanese car importers' and consumers' organizations were excluded from it. Both British Columbia Industry Minister Don Phillips and the Japanese ambassador have condemned the report. Phillips called it, "A self-serving document produced by those who have a vested interest in promoting protectionism."[93] Ambassador Mikanagi warned, "It might totally destroy all good intentions for expansion of trade."

Thus pressure to protect vulnerable but even more important industry in Ontario and Québec, especially during the severe recession of 1980 to 1983, has arisen and may continue. It is also a time when equally important resource industries which are not obsolescent or uncompetitive in the Western provinces are suffering from cutbacks in Japanese offshore purchases, especially in the energy sector. Should Canada shed its role as a leader in liberal trade policies, Japan would be fully entitled to retaliate under GATT rules. Japan can also obtain the resource imports elsewhere with ease, and the step would delight Canada's competitors.

we come to Canada...Based on our knowledge, factors related to labor are not really favorable...To be more specific, we understand labor costs are very high and that days lost through work stoppages are extremely high." He also felt that import duties on imported components were unduly large. As a result, the Japanese did not see any great advantage in investing much beyond the current interest in raw materials, and the processing of these in some cases. Even in the case of refining metals like nickel, Japan had its own nickel refineries to utilize and would be willing to look for ore elsewhere, if necessary, to keep its own refineries going. Other factors that concerned the visitors were increased government regulation or control of profits, as occurred under Anti-Inflation Board regulations, and greater regulation of business by the provinces, such as those under the New Democratic Party. Labor costs, strikes, and taxes were all higher in Canada than in the United States, for example; and Canada as a single market was too small.

This visit was unusual in the frankness with which the Japanese businessmen expressed their views of Canada. Although polite and considerate as always, they did drop their usual reluctance to say anything critical, stating clearly what they thought. The assessments contained in the lengthier Japanese report of the mission were even more critical. However, federal and provincial governments have subsequently followed more moderate policies in regard to the control of resources, royalties, and environmental considerations, and soon after the mission's visit the trend toward resource nationalism abated somewhat; thus, with some improvement in demand and the fall of the Canadian dollar, the business climate in Canada improved. Still, there was toward Canada nothing like the interest displayed by Japan toward newly industrializing countries such as Mexico, Brazil, or even Australia, during most of the economic troubles of the late 1970s.

In short, the outcome of Japanese business missions following the Trudeau initiative in Japan did not augur at all well for success in carrying out any new economic ventures—particularly at that time. It also made Trudeau's approach to Japan seem rather unreal, symbolic of a policy that never seemed to have its feet on the ground. Even the prime minister did not seem to expect any immediate economic benefit from his "third option" policy. His cabinet's subsequent economic sanctions against Japan in banning uranium shipments, although aimed more specifically at the Europeans who were also the target of that policy, ignored any intent to improve relations with Japan.

The Joint Economic Committee, provided for by the Trudeau-Miki Framework Agreement, met in Vancouver in June 1977. Foreign Minister Iichiro Hatoyama participated, as well as External Affairs Minister Don Jamieson, who emphasized the aim of closer relations with Japan to build a sounder economy and reduce its economic vulnerability (the "third option"). More frequent meetings of political leaders as well as academic and cultural exchanges were proposed as one means developing the relationship. The large number of Canadian purchases per capita of Japanese consumer electronic goods and automobiles was linked to the desire to sell high technology and manufactured goods from Canada. Some members of the Makita mission the previous year had feared that the desire to upgrade the percentage of manufactured goods sold to Japan would be linked to the availability of raw materials; this condition was specifically disavowed. However, further Japanese capital investment in joint projects of benefit to both countries (that is, they would have to meet the criteria of the Foreign Investment Review Agency) would be welcomed.[55]

In September that year, Premier William Davis of Ontario visited Japan, and a strong pitch was made for the advantages of Japanese investment in his province. He was met by Eichi Hashimoto of Mitsui, who had been with the Makita mission; Hashimoto again cited labor disputes, high taxes, and low productivity among other deficiencies of the investment climate in Canada.[56] Back in Ottawa, federal cabinet ministers Chrétien and Munro both criticized Hashimoto, accusing him of exaggerating the situation in Canada.[57]

However, they in turn were countered by Canadians who supported Hashimoto's statements. J. Laurent Thibault, director of economics of the Canadian Manufacturers' Association, said, "We have been trying to tell Canadians the same things for several years but very few would listen." Robert Scrivener, chairman of Northern Telecom Ltd., agreed with Hashimoto that high taxes in Canada made the United States a much more attractive area for investment and establishment of branch plants. He said it cost forty per cent more to build a plant in Canada than an identical one in the United States.

Perhaps more in concert with Japanese thinking was the symposium on "Resource Development and Economic Cooperation between Canada and Japan," held in Toronto on 7 November 1977, and sponsored by the Toronto *Globe and Mail* and *Nihon Keizai Shimbun* (Japan Economic Journal). Canadian officials and businessmen taking part in it emphasized not only present and future resource trade and investment, but the desirability of further processing. Gardiner of the Royal Bank noted that the raw materials passed through processing and finished stages had declined from thirty-five to twenty-two per cent of Canada's exports to Japan in the previous nine years. He urged further processing for the new joint investment projects in uranium mining, synthetic crude oil, and coal mining.[58]

When External Affairs Minister Jamieson visited Japan in January 1978 during an Asian tour, it gave him the opportunity to be present when the Japan-Canada Atomic Energy Cooperation Agreement was initialled—an agreement that would soon bring an end to the uranium ban by Canada.

Japanese Foreign Minister Sonoda and Jamieson agreed that the economic and trade ties between the two countries had improved as a result of the 1976 Framework on Economic Cooperation Between Canada and Japan.[59] It is difficult to understand this statement. The long-drawn-out nuclear safeguard negotiations were anything but favorable, and the new fisheries agreements that restricted Japanese fishing both inside and outside the new two-hundred-mile economic zones were no better. Jamieson stated that the Japanese had promised to expand their imports of Canadian semi-finished and finished goods.

At the persuasion of federal officials, Canadian businessmen joined with their Japanese counterparts to create a Canadian-Japan Business Cooperation Committee, that would meet annually in the two countries alternately. David Culver, president of Alcan Aluminum Ltd., headed the first Canadian delegation which met in Tokyo at the Keidanren Kaikan, headquarters of the Federation of Economic Organizations, the main big business association of Japan. The Japanese were once again headed by Hisao Makita, who took the lead in business relations with Canada. The first meeting dealt with the needs of Japan for stable sources of raw materials, and of Canada for increased manufactured exports.[60]

The Japan-Canada Joint Economic Committee held its second meeting in Tokyo, and took on the job of urging Canada's interest in exporting its manufactured and processed goods. Thus there was now a channel, on both a regular annual official level and a business level, to handle the chief economic objectives of the two countries and take over the part so long played by the more casual visits of top government and business leaders to each other's countries. These were backed up by working-level committees for specific fields of interest. In addition to this economically oriented series of exchanges, there were technological and cultural meetings sponsored by the Canadian federal government that were intended to give more spread and depth to the relationship.

Although exports classed as "end products" in Canada were only two per cent in 1980, fabricated goods came to twenty-nine per cent and included many manufactured items. Canadian embassy officials felt considerable satisfaction with the two hundred million dollars' worth of manufactured exports to Japan,[61] although James Taylor, the commercial minister at the embassy in Tokyo, thought the chief reason for this degree of progress was the fifty per cent rise in the value of the yen relative to the Canadian dollar in the previous two years, as well as the Japanese liberalization and lowering of trade barriers. In view of the general growth in overall trade, the export figures represented a considerable increase in such things as jewelry, furs, electronics, fish products, and auto parts. The decade-long effort by federal officials, together with that of the central provinces, seemed to have only a moderate effect on raising the manufactured content of Canadian exports to Japan and failed to eliminate the fear of some federal officials that, in the eyes of the Japanese, Canada remained a primitive country in the wood-hewer image.

The decade of the 1970s was a period of great economic difficulties compared to the sixties, and one in which the relatively rapid advance of the economic relationship could not be expected to continue unabated. Canadian government policies never really achieved an industrial strategy to restructure the economy, improve Canadian productivity, or evolve trade initiatives that could have given more substance to a "third option" policy. Those officials who had the necessary vision and expertise had little impact on policy, nor could they keep the attention of the prime minister and cabinet which was constantly pre-occupied with the non-economic side of domestic politics or the more glamorous aspects of international politics. The connection with Japan thus altered little during the decade. Canadian business, too, apart from a few medium and large companies which were quite successful in the Japan trade or joint ventures, was preoccupied with its traditional ties to the United States or Western Europe, or perhaps with other global trade which could more easily be carried on in English with more familiar business practices. The Japan market demanded willingness to enter a unique arena and a great deal of effort by any Canadian medium or small entrepreneur; few felt impelled to lavish the time and expense required, nor did they have anything like the big Japanese trading companies to act as their attack force upon the world economy.

6

Safeguarding Nuclear Materials and
Selling CANDU Reactors

EARLY URANIUM SUPPLY AND SAFEGUARDS AGREEMENT

Unlike most mineral sales to Japan which resulted from Japanese business initiative, the supply of uranium to Japan resulted from a Canadian government initiative. The Canadian embassy in Tokyo approached the Japanese Foreign Ministry in 1958 to propose discussions on cooperation in the peaceful uses of atomic energy.[1] Japan did not respond immediately, and only in March 1959 did it accept the invitation to send a delegation to Ottawa to negotiate the agreement, which was tabled in the Commons on 2 July.

To augment Japanese interest, the Canadian government offered three metric tons of natural uranium for research purposes, which was eventually accepted by Japan on 12 December 1958. This was arranged through the auspices of the International Atomic Energy Agency (IAEA) in Vienna, and included early safeguard provisions on nuclear facilities, such as international inspection to prevent diversion to military use. Canada was early committed to a policy of no transfers of this material beyond its two great power allies, the United States and Britain, except for peaceful purposes. To ensure peaceful use, Canada required a bilateral agreement with another country before that country could receive Canadian uranium or nuclear equipment or know-how. The agreement necessitated safeguards of nuclear material with verification by the IAEA.

The safeguards policy on peaceful uses originated in the agreement between Canada, the United States, and the United Kingdom—the last two engaging in their own weapons programs. Closely involved on the Canadian side were the former trade and commerce minister, C. D. Howe, and his deputy, Robert Winters. Before adequate uranium was discovered in the United States, the American and Canadian governments were anxious to expand production in Canada, one of the few places where uranium had been found, and therefore essential for the American and British weapons programs. The largest mine was at Elliot Lake in Ontario in the riding of Lester Pearson, leader of the opposition in the House of Commons in 1959.

Virtually all of the Canadian supply was shipped to the United States under short-term contracts. By the end of the fifties, however, adequate supplies of uranium had been discovered and developed in the United States. The need for weapons stockpiling declined and, hence, the need for Canadian production. Eisenhower's "Atoms for Peace" Policy was to eventuate in the widespread use of light-water reactors for electric power, which would create a demand for Canadian uranium later on. These light-water reactors were manufactured by General Electric and Westinghouse, using enriched uranium. Canada developed the Canadian Deuterium Uranium (CANDU) reactor for power generation using heavy water as the moderator, one of which was about to be built in Ontario for power production that would provide a demonstration of Canadian technology for would-be buyers. It was due to be in operation by 1964. In the meantime, the United States was widely believed to be several years in advance of Canada in its production of enriched uranium light-water reactors.

The implications for Canada were serious in respect to export of both uranium and the CANDU. The Canadian uranium mining industry was geared up for the foreign market, which in 1959 amounted to about three hundred million dollars in export sales. It was threatened with collapse during this period when little uranium was needed for military purposes and before the civilian power reactors came into operation in the second half of the sixties. Communities such as Elliot Lake were threatened with closure as uranium production dwindled. Pearson, as leader of the opposition, pressed the Conservative government on its plans to promote the sale of uranium to other countries such as Japan, and also urged it to convince the United States it should renew or extend its contracts with the mines in Canada.[2]

Another Ontario M.P., Arnold Peters, launched quite a sharp criticism of government nuclear policy on behalf of both the citizens of Elliot Lake and the uranium mining industry. He argued that the restrictions on Canadian sales of uranium should be scrapped, alleging, on the basis of an article in *Saturday Night*, that the United States was engaged in an attempt to corner the market on the civilian uranium industry. He also suggested that both Howe and Winters had been duped into safeguarding arrangements in order to inhibit Canadian sales.[3] He urged the development of uranium enrichment facilities in Canada to compete with the United States in this promising market, and criticized the government for failing to foresee the recent uranium discoveries and the need to adopt an independent policy in promotion of the industry. With respect to Japan, he thought the South Africans had already sold uranium to it without any safeguards at all and were capturing further promising sales there.

Minister of Trade and Commerce Gordon Churchill was taken aback by the onslaught from Peters. He pointed out that the new discoveries could not have been predicted at the time the current contracts were negotiated, and that the government was promoting the industry including the development of the CANDU as rapidly as possible, for Peters had also spoken of the need for urgency in CANDU construction. Pearson then agreed that the recent discoveries in the United States could not have been foreseen, but nevertheless he urged greater initiative by the government. He proposed that the American government should be persuaded to continue to take Elliot Lake uranium to enable the Canadian industry to survive during the adjustment period, waxing indignant over American disregard for the Canadian contribution to the common defence in the provision of uranium during the period that Canada had been the only secure source. The Americans owed greater consideration to Canada than merely to walk away from the Canadian connection when they were no longer in need of it. He said the Conservatives must press the matter, at the level of the President himself if necessary, to keep Elliot Lake operating.

Pearson noted that the United States had made a safeguards agreement with Japan over a year and a half earlier and had agreements with seventeen other countries. The agreement with EURATOM, the European Atomic Energy Commission, included a loan of $135 million and a ten-year guarantee of uranium supply. The American agreements also included easy terms on the sale of American reactors using enriched uranium. He was afraid that the Canadian reactor, as good as the American or British models, would be left behind in the international competition.[4]

Unfortunately, the fears of the leader of the opposition proved to be correct. The United States, with its light-water reactors and its facilities for producing the enriched uranium fuel they required, went on to acquire most of the world market. Even Japan later came to depend almost wholly on the American reactors and enriched fuel, and only acquired one British-type reactor. Without its model ready and functioning on a commercial scale, it was probably already too late at that stage for Canada to have won a big part of the world civilian reactor market; the Americans managed to sell their model to Europe before it was even proven at home—although the Europeans were not to know that.

The secretary of state for external affairs, Howard Green, tabled the agreement with Japan on the peaceful uses of atomic energy on 2 July 1959.[5] It covered the exchange of technical information, provision of equipment and materials including uranium, and applied to any source material supplied to Japan from Canada.[6] It was welcomed by Pearson as protecting and advancing the export interests of the Canadian uranium industry, particularly when the United States was supplying reactors of a type that required enrichment. Pearson was also concerned about the minister of finance's recent announcement that Japan had agreed to limit some of its exports which were too competitive with Canadian manufacturers. As Japan was buying much more from Canada than it sold, it was dangerous to begin to shut Japan out of the North Atlantic markets; from both an economic and a strategic point of view, it would be very unfavorable if Japan were eventually driven to depend upon China and the Soviet bloc countries for its economic needs.[7] Pearson's perception of the potential economic importance of Japan to Canada was thus keen, at least in the period before he became prime minister. Despite this, however, he never rated Japan's importance great enough to go there himself, and is the only postwar prime minister who never visited Japan while in office.

A drastic reduction in demand for uranium and consequent difficult period for the industry ensued, as foreseen, during the sixties. Mining activity managed to continue by dint of Canadian government stockpiling arrangements, which permitted some production to go on. It was only later in the decade that Japan came to Canada for uranium which, nevertheless, had first to be sent to the United States for enrichment in order to use it in Japanese power reactors, which were almost all of the American type. Thus the American suppliers were successful in the Japanese reactor market. The United States forbade the import of any foreign uranium for their own domestic reactors, which had to use uranium mined in the United States to support their mining industry. They also monopolized the enrichment business for most of the foreign as well as domestic power reactors, as Pearson had anticipated in the fifties. Canada did manage to sell a million dollars' worth of technical data and know-how on atomic matters from research done at Chalk River in Ontario during the 1960s, but it was a drop in the bucket.

Although uranium was sought in Japan, only about twenty-five hundred tons were found economically minable, scattered in about a hundred deposits throughout the country. So in 1967 when a power utilities survey returned from Canada, it recommended that Japan buy as much as possible there. Canadian uranium oxide was deemed plentiful, of good quality, and reasonable in price. It was also conveniently close to the United States for the enrichment process.[8]

As a result of this recommendation, Tokyo and Kansai Electric Power Companies negotiated on behalf of the Japanese electric utility companies with Denison Mines Limited for 10,500 tons of uranium concentrate, and with Rio Algom Mines Limited for an additional 5,000 tons. Deliveries were to start in 1969 for a ten-year period.[9] Thus sales to Japan began to materialize as Pearson had earlier hoped. The first commercial operation in Japan began in 1969 at Tokai Mura by the Japan Atomic Power Company with a capacity of 160 megawatts. Tokyo Electric Power Company also signed a contract with Consolidated Denison in 1970 for another 16,750 tons, for delivery in 1974–1983 to the Japanese utilities.[10] In 1974 Tokyo Electric Power Company signed a further contract with Denison Mines for 20,000 tons of uranium concentrate, or "yellow cake," to be delivered between 1984 and 1993, subject to Canadian export policy. These contracts, together with open market purchases, resulted in Japanese reliance on Canada for about forty per cent of its fuel requirements for nuclear reactors. If the Canadian government had been willing to issue permits for export of a greater volume, Japan might have bought even more.

By the mid-seventies the supply position was reversed from ten years earlier, as a large number of civilian reactors had come into operation. It was now a seller's market for uranium, with the price four times higher than in the early sixties, and soon to double again, as did the other major power source: oil. Both Canada's own domestic needs and those of its overseas customers, as projected into the future, called for increased exploration and development of mines to augment the amount of fuel. Canada welcomed Japanese efforts which became involved in prospecting by 1969, when Kerr Magee Corporation and Denison Mines worked together with fifteen Japanese companies, including nine power and six non-ferrous metal mining companies, in the Elliot Lake area. Denison Mines also had a six-year contract with nine Japanese utilities to explore in the North Thompson River and Highland Valley in British Columbia, as well as around Port Radium and Marian River in the Northwest Territories. They also drilled in Colorado. Rio Algom Mines had a joint venture drilling program in Wyoming with Mitsubishi Metal Mining Company, which first started in 1967.[11] The partly government-owned Japan Power Reactor and Nuclear Fuel Development Corporation prospected in British Columbia and had plans to search in Alberta, Saskatchewan, Manitoba, Ontario and Québec.

Japan was anxious to reduce its excessive dependence upon Canada and the United States for fuel, and sought to diversify its supply by broadening the search to Africa, South America, and Southeast Asia. Almost the only joint project to reach the production stage was in Niger, where the Overseas Uranium Resources Development Company of Japan had a twenty-five per cent interest in a joint venture with the Commissariat à l'Énergie Atomique of France, which had forty-four per cent, and the Niger government which had thirty-one per cent. Production at an annual rate of two thousand tons was scheduled by 1979, with Japan taking forty-three per cent of production. In Japan itself in 1975, only nine thousand tons of "yellow cake" appeared to be available, at the going rate of fifteen dollars per pound, so that Japan still had to keep up its search abroad for uranium to supply its growing needs. In most countries, available supplies were earmarked for domestic consumption with little available to foreign consumers. Only South Africa and Australia appeared likely to be Canada's major competitors for surplus uranium. But in Australia under the Labor Party a moratorium was placed on production and export for several years.

INDIAN NUCLEAR EXPLOSION AND NEW CANADIAN POLICIES

In 1965 Canada adopted the policy that Canadian uranium could only be used for non-military purposes. It terminated its involvement in the nuclear weapons programs of the United States and Britain. This may have confirmed the wisdom of the United States in making itself independent of foreign supplies for military purposes, but it also boomeranged for commercial users when world prices for uranium rose along with oil, and Westinghouse was no longer able to honor its contracts with foreign customers in supplying fuel. This caused lawsuits to be brought against the uranium cartel in which Canada was an active participant.[12] Canada's policy was to increase the availability of nuclear power as a reliable source of energy for peaceful purposes, and to ensure that civilian nuclear power programs do not produce material for explosive or military uses.[13]

The IAEA had been created in 1957 to administer nuclear safeguards as well as to promote access to nuclear technology for peaceful uses. The administration of safeguards under Canada's 1959 agreement with Japan was transferred to the IAEA by a tripartite agreement of 1966 between Canada, Japan, and the agency. Japan also signed the Treaty on Non-Proliferation of Nuclear Weapons in 1970, although it failed to ratify it for a number of years, due to the reluctance of some conservative politicians to forego the nuclear option in Japan. The treaty puts signatories under the IAEA safeguards for all their installations; they are pledged to refrain from making nuclear weapons. They may, however, allow the "weapons states," like the United States, to bring nuclear arms onto their territories, as does the German Federal Republic. The nuclear weapons powers are also pledged to assist other states in gaining access to nuclear tests for possible peaceful uses, and have agreed to carry out these explosions on behalf of the non-nuclear-weapons states. Thus, nuclear explosions, even for peaceful purposes such as creating reservoirs or exploiting underground resources, are classed the same as military explosions. As yet, none of the IAEA signatories have availed themselves of the weapons states' facilities for nuclear explosions.

Canada's supply of nuclear materials and technology to the developing countries is intended to give them the benefits of peaceful uses which Canada is well placed to provide. Two Commonwealth members, for whom Canada has provided economic and technical aid since the inauguration of the Colombo Plan, are India and Pakistan; part of this aid has been nuclear. Canada, in collaboration with the United States which provided the heavy water, supplied an experimental reactor and two commercial power reactors to India, as well as a commercial reactor to Pakistan. With the huge increase in oil prices after 1973, the value of nuclear power as a cheaper or more secure source of energy was enhanced, and would lessen some of the growing debts and financial weakness of the developing countries that do not have oil. This increased the value of the Trudeau government's nuclear aid and should have increased the opportunities to sell uranium reactors.

Canada has sought to enhance its global stature with two foreign policies: efforts for peace and aid to developing countries. Moreover, Canada is the only one of the early nuclear leaders, such as the United States, Britain, and France, that does not make nuclear weapons and devotes all its nuclear effort to peaceful uses.

It was, therefore, a profound shock when India exploded a nuclear device in May 1974, even though insisting it was for peaceful purposes. The plutonium used for the Indian explosion was produced in the American experimental reactor, the CIRUS, using heavy water provided by the United States, while Canada had been providing technical information and fuel. India, like France, refuses to sign the Non-Proliferation Treaty or accept IAEA inspection, and is intent on a completely independent fuel cycle.

India is keeping its options open and, apparently, has all but acquired the technology and capacity to produce weapons. Because of its frequent wars with Pakistan, that country too wishes to keep its options open and to acquire a complete fuel cycle—judging from the contract with France for a reprocessing plant. Pakistan also refuses to sign the Non-Proliferation Treaty or to accept IAEA inspection for all its nuclear facilities.

After the Indian explosion, the Canadian government put a ban on all nuclear aid to India and on export of all nuclear material. Although India maintained its explosion was peaceful, the Canadian government had told India, even before the explosion, that it considered any development of explosive capacity to be contrary to the spirit of nuclear cooperation between them, since an explosive device is the same as a weapon, if it is so used. Consequently, a new Canadian safeguards policy was announced by the minister of energy, mines, and resources on 20 December 1974.

The new Canadian comprehensive safeguards went considerably beyond those of the IAEA. They applied to all materials, facilities, and technology, and to any items or material produced in them, which had to be used exclusively for peaceful, non-explosive purposes. Binding assurances of full IAEA safeguards or bilateral ones with Canada must be accepted. Canadian consent was required prior to the transfer of any items, material, or technology of

Canadian origin to another country. Irradiated fuel could be reprocessed for plutonium extraction, uranium could be enriched up to twenty per cent, but plutonium and uranium enriched beyond this point could be stored only if Canada agreed that they would constitute no proliferation risk. To ensure that economic aid did not support proliferation, even indirectly, Canadian International Development Agency (CIDA) funds could henceforth only be applied to countries that had ratified the Non-Proliferation Treaty.[14]

It had been expected that the Canadian government would actually disallow sales to countries thought likely to use them to produce nuclear explosive devices.[15] The opposition Conservatives and New Democrats were critical of the government's policy, and the leader of the New Democrats later demanded a moratorium on domestic nuclear expansion as well as foreign sales of reactors and technology.[16] Nevertheless, when the new comprehensive safeguards rules were announced in December 1974, the temporary ban on export of some nuclear materials was lifted. Atomic Energy Canada Limited was permitted by the government to conclude a CANDU reactor sale to the South Korean Power Company because the Korean government was willing to subscribe to the new Canadian rules.[17]

The prime minister, when questioned by the Progressive Conservatives and the New Democrats, said that the Koreans had abandoned their plans for a reprocessing plant before Canada agreed to sell them a reactor. In the case of Pakistan, however, Canadian officials believed that the reprocessing plant it had decided to buy would have no other use than to make explosive materials. Moreover, the Pakistanis had already decided to buy the plant before purchasing five or six reactors from countries other than Canada. As Pakistan had already built up a supply of spent fuel from the Canadian reactor it had purchased in 1971, it could use the plutonium from the reprocessed fuel to make explosives. When Prime Minister Zulfikar Ali Bhutto of Pakistan visited Ottawa in early 1976, he said his country had no desire to use the spent fuel to make a bomb, a statement suspiciously like Mrs. Gandhi's in Ottawa just before she exploded her "peaceful" nuclear device. Canadian officials were demanding a Canadian veto on Pakistan's use of spent fuel. Without it, they were prepared to stop sending the fuel needed for the Canadian reactor already functioning near Karachi. Perhaps some of the enthusiasm for Canadian reactors was that they produce twice as much plutonium as do the more widely used American light-water reactors. It can also be harvested daily, while in light-water reactors plutonium can only be gathered at the shut-downs, at intervals of twelve or eighteen months.

South Korea may have signed the Non-Proliferation Treaty, persuaded by Canadian pressure, but Argentina did not. The Argentine military junta wanted heavy-water reactors in order to be free of American control over the enriched fuel used in the light-water reactors, and in order to get the increased amounts of plutonium.[18] Siemens of West Germany built Argentina's first reactor at Atucha, and Canada a second six-hundred-megawatt plant at Rio Tercero. Argentina agreed to accept IAEA inspections of the Canadian-built facility, and thus ensure no nuclear weapons are built with materials supplied by Canada. However, within ten days of the Indian explosion in May 1974, the Indian foreign minister visited Buenos Aires. A few days later the director of Argentina's Information Agency announced that an agreement had been signed with India to allow it "to enter the limited circle of nations endowed with nuclear arsenals."[19] Argentina began building its own heavy-water plant in Patagonia so as to be independent of Canadian as well as any other foreign supplies, and bought a heavy-water reactor from the Federal German Republic and the necessary technology from Switzerland.

Although the IAEA had only about 186 inspectors in 1976, it was thought that it could be at least ninety-five per cent effective in guarding the approximately 640 nuclear installations in thirty-eight countries.[20] That left some margin for unobserved operations. However, even those who have signed the Non-Proliferation Treaty can withdraw with only six months' notice. In addition, if a country breached its safeguards agreement with Canada, it would be difficult for Canada to resort to force to recover Canadian materials if the buyer refused to return them voluntarily. Canada's most effective sanction was to discontinue nuclear cooperation and stop the export of nuclear fuel, but this would not prevent the misuse of facilities or fuel already supplied.

The oil crisis and price hikes of OPEC not only affected the developing countries, making them seek other energy sources, but also Japan and the EEC became anxious to rely more upon nuclear power for energy. Reprocessing used fuel, and using plutonium as fuel, would vastly increase their potential output. It is possible for the new breeder reactor using plutonium to produce more plutonium than it consumes. Both Japan and the EEC were short of oil and uranium, so that they were eager to see the development of reprocessing and the new generation of reactors using the plutonium which promised to economize greatly on the basic nuclear fuels. The increasing amounts of plutonium produced in irradiated fuel as well as in breeder reactors can easily be processed to make atomic bombs. Thus, the economic needs of those developed and developing countries alike run counter to the risk of the spread and use of plutonium for weapons.

Countries like Canada, Australia, and the United States, which have large supplies of all types of energy including uranium, are not under the same economic restraints as the other developed countries. As nuclear suppliers of fuel, equipment, and technology they are more mindful of the dangers of weapons proliferation for which they might be responsible. It is natural for them to be more concerned about safeguards, and to be willing to use embargoes to impose their policies. Because both Canada and the United States have been long involved with nuclear weapons programs, they are more conscious of the military implications of nuclear power development. They are also less conscious of the economic necessities that influence countries that are short of energy, such as Japan, Germany, or France which also suffered immense destruction and privation in the last great war.[21]

In dealing with the advanced countries that used Canadian uranium, the Canadian government found Japan, the EEC, and Switzerland all unwilling to accept its policy of 1974. The government then indicated it would be willing to wait a year to conclude new safeguards agreements. But by the end of 1975 it had not obtained agreement, and extended a six months' "grace period," and then another six months to the end of 1976, still without obtaining any new agreement.

Meanwhile, Canada was negotiating with Pakistan for a ban on any reprocessing of nuclear fuel. The United States was also threatening to stop arms aid to Pakistan if it went ahead in acquiring the reprocessing plant from France. At first Canada warned that it would cut off all nuclear supplies if the Pakistanis "staged any nuclear explosion whatever materials were used," according to an American report.[22] Pakistan apparently agreed to acknowledge Canada's right to stop supplies if Canadian materials were used to build a bomb, but it hoped to circumvent international controls by making it difficult to identify any Canadian material being used for this purpose.

It was too risky for Canada to be found instrumental in the making of any more bombs or "explosive devices," in view of the opposition party's anger at the priority given to commercial motives over the requirements of safety in the cause of non-proliferation, and the desire for Canada to be accepted as a leader in the cause of world peace.[23] After its flirtation with Pakistan, Canada announced a new and even more stringent policy of comprehensive safeguards. It would supply nuclear materials or cooperation only to countries that would accept its comprehensive safeguards on all their nuclear facilities without exception; they must be "full-scope."

On 1 January 1977, shipments of uranium for Japan, the EEC, and Switzerland were suspended until these safeguards were accepted. In the absence of an upgraded safeguards agreement with the United States, shipments for use in American reactors were also subject to restraint.[24]

Thus, the Canadian government ignored the views of those officials who argued that Canada would lose its influence in the nuclear field if, in the end, it drove its customers away. The latter would then be encouraged to obtain materials under even less rigorous safeguards than those they would have been willing to negotiate with Canada. The opposite view, which won out in Canada, argued that a moratorium on nuclear sales abroad, until more effective international supervision was achieved, would enhance and not diminish Canadian moral authority and challenge other supplier countries to join.[25] However, unlike Pakistan, India, and Argentina which, frankly, had bomb-making intentions, Japan and West Germany had no such ambitions. They were much more concerned with the urgent need for a reliable energy supply in an increasingly unstable international environment.

Other suppliers did follow Canada's example to some extent; the United States and Australia, for instance, modeled new regulations on Canadian lines. However, up to that point most of the user countries, such as Germany and Japan, were not very sensitive to the military and safety aspects of nuclear power—nor was the Atomic Energy Commission in the United States itself—and were scarcely conscious of the threat to the nuclear balance from states like India, Pakistan, and Argentina, not to mention countries such as Libya receiving Soviet nuclear aid, or Taiwan which had an unguarded Canadian experimental reactor supplied with fuel from South Africa. They all looked forward to the plutonium economy where the deadly substance would become a convenient and commonly used fuel for breeder reactors.

As the United States was the principal large-scale supplier of both types of light-water reactors as well as of the enriched fuel they required, its role was the most important on an international level, especially if it were to restrict supply. It had briefly banned exports of enriched uranium to the EEC on 28 March 1975 to put pressure on the Europeans to adopt more secure measures against the theft of uranium by terrorists.[26] As the Anglo-German-Dutch gas diffusion plant for enriching uranium was not completed, Germany feared it might be left with only the Soviet Union to turn to, for supplies of fuel for its fourteen power reactors.

Critical reaction to the threat to international controls represented by the Indian explosion of 1974 was not confined to Canada and its Parliament. In the United States, Congress expressed considerable concern at earlier Nixon administration plans to provide reactors to Egypt and Israel, and at later French and German plans to supply reprocessing plants that could produce weapons-grade plutonium in Korea, Pakistan, and Brazil. The American Atomic Energy Commission, with largely technical aspects in mind, had been fostering the development of reprocessing and breeder reactors abroad. For example, Japan was encouraged to go ahead in its plans for a reprocessing plant at Tokai Mura, the site of its first large power reactor.

With the advent of the Carter administration in 1977 under a man who, as a naval officer, had been a nuclear engineer, a new policy was inaugurated. It aimed at slowing down nuclear development, which was threatening to undermine the existing safeguards system and to lead to greater ease in evading it for the sake of diversion to weapons purposes. The president's decision, backed by the Nonproliferation Act of 1978, was to defer reprocessing and the use of plutonium in existing reactors, and to restructure its breeder reactor research and development program to stress safer fuel cycles, rather than early commercialization, both at home and abroad.

The policy was received with consternation in Japan, which had up to then received American support in completing its reprocessing plant at Tokai Mura. Japan was one of the least likely countries to embark on a nuclear weapons program, in view of both its experience of the atomic bomb and its vulnerable population crowded into one corner of its tiny islands.

The United States began to bring pressure on Europe to forego plans to supply reprocessing or enrichment plants to other countries, and on Japan to delay its reprocessing plant. They urged more stringent safety measures and postponing the use of reprocessed or plutonium fuels. The Europeans suspected that the new policy was a way of maintaining an American nuclear monopoly. Both they and the Japanese were particularly resentful that the United States, which has large uranium resources, could cheerfully contemplate continued wasteful consumption by deferring indefinitely breeder reactors or reprocessing of fuel. They, on the other hand, had virtually no fuel of their own and a global shortage loomed ahead.[27]

During 1976, Canada terminated its arrangements with India, who agreed to apply Canadian safeguards policy to its two Canadian reactors, RAPP I and RAPP II, for the lifetime of the two.[28] Cooperation was suspended with Pakistan, and neither it nor India would agree to sign the Nonproliferation Treaty or apply "full-scope" safeguards as demanded by Canadian policy. Canada completed its work on the RAPP II reactor and also went ahead on the contracted Argentine reactor. Although Argentina was willing to purchase further reactors, it would not accept "full-scope" safeguards either, or sign the Nonproliferation Treaty, thus precluding further cooperation with Canada. Fortunately for the Korean sale, the United States brought pressure to bear on South Korea to sign the treaty.

Negotiations between Canada and Japan began in Tokyo in January 1977. Verbal accord was reached on most points by March, but Canada was reluctant to lift the embargo until it had some formal agreement in writing. The Canadian negotiating team for the EEC in Brussels had hoped to have the Japanese agreement at a sufficiently advanced stage to encourage similar action from Europe.[29] Initially, Japan had objected, particularly to the Canadian veto on enrichment beyond twenty per cent. Enrichment to three or four per cent is sufficient for light-water reactors, and above this level it raises concern about use for explosive purposes. Also contentious was Canada's insistence that received technology should be transferred to a third party only with permission. Naturally, Canada preferred to sell its technology directly to other countries, while Japan wanted to be sure it would not be required to agree to stiffer requirements than the EEC. Canada was willing to resume shipments as soon as a formal agreement was put into effect, even if ratification were to take some time.[30] Substantial agreement was finally reached at the working level in Ottawa in May.

Meanwhile, Japan had already negotiated an agreement with Britain to reprocess almost three thousand tons of Japanese irradiated fuel, according to Japan's plan of relying on Britain and France for reprocessing services. In March the United States, which enriched Japan's fuel, demanded that the plutonium from Japanese fuel in Europe not be returned to Japan.[31] The United States was also delaying fuel shipments to Europe, to back up its attempts to forbid transfers between European countries. American policy differed from that of Canada, which was not opposed to reprocessing per se but only wanted the right to veto in case it mistrusted the use to which the material might be put in a particular case.

In the negotiations with the EEC, the Europeans had difficulty in accepting Canada's right of prior consent to reprocessing of material of Canadian origin. They feared that it would give Canada a veto over the right of member states to determine their own energy policies, and prevent the fullest possible degree of energy self-sufficiency from being attained. Japan was also concerned that it would be subject to a double set of safeguards on the same material going from Canada to the United States for enrichment before reaching Japan.[32]

Both Prime Minister Trudeau and External Affairs Minister Jamieson discussed the problems with their foreign colleagues at the London economic summit meeting in May 1977. At President Carter's suggestion, an International Nuclear Fuel Cycle Evaluation was instituted, and it was decided to examine the problems of reprocessing and the safeguards implications of the plutonium economy. In June, Jamieson also talked to the Japanese foreign minister at the Canada-Japan Economic Cooperation Committee meeting in Vancouver, where the Japanese minister tried to facilitate the resumption of uranium shipments. At a meeting between Prime Minister Trudeau and Chancellor Helmut Schmidt in July, it was further agreed that, since the summit meeting had decided to take up the issue of reprocessing in the Nuclear Fuel Cycle Evaluation, and the EEC was willing to consult with Canada before reprocessing Canadian material, deliveries of current needs of uranium could be resumed if other outstanding issues were resolved; the latter included the transfer of Canadian nuclear technology and deliveries to France for civilian reactors not covered by the Nonproliferation Treaty. However, France shortly afterwards agreed to IAEA safeguards on the civilian nuclear cycle, which removed this barrier to Canadian cooperation.

The timing of the embargo was particularly inconvenient for Canada itself, which had just managed to negotiate special agreements with both the EEC and Japan for closer economic cooperation. They were the culmination of several years of effort to reduce dependence on the United States by enhancing ties with Canada's other two principal trading partners. The prime minister had gone to Japan in October of 1976 to sign the Framework for Economic Cooperation only a few months before the uranium embargo was imposed, and apparently the incompatibility of the two policies did not occur to him. Despite the elaborate negotiations, the special ties sought by the Trudeau government with the Europeans and Japanese had little of a substantive nature, which mystified the leaders of those countries. Perhaps suspecting that they were being subjected to some elaborate publicity stunt, Japanese officials refused to call the new arrangement an "agreement." Needless to say, the embargo was hardly a good way to inaugurate a new era of economic cooperation, and although the governments of Europe and Japan avoided voicing their anger publicly, a lasting impression among Japanese officials was that they could not rely upon Canadian economic cooperation.

Despite the embargo decreed by Ottawa, the supply of enriched fuel to Japan was in fact never halted completely as it progressed through the United States. The attention of Japan and Europe was attracted away from the Canadian safeguarding strictures by the even more serious American anti-plutonium policy, since the Carter policy threatened their access to cheaper and more plentiful nuclear fuel supply. The Trudeau policy, on the other hand, did not aim at stopping reprocessing or breeder development, but at an elaborately idealistic system of safeguards which could shut down the recipient country's nuclear industry and control its foreign nuclear policy if Canada insisted and the other country complied. In mid-November 1977 Canada reached an interim agreement with the United States. Final arrangements were to wait upon the passage of the American Nonproliferation Act of 1978, and meanwhile Canadian restraints on shipment of uranium to the United States were removed.

In late November and early December, External Affairs Minister Jamieson, together with Energy, Mines, and Resources Minister Gillespie and their negotiating team met with the EEC Energy Commissioner Brunner, with whom they finally reached agreement.[33] Canada received binding assurances on the peaceful non-explosive use of Canadian-supplied material, equipment, and technology and of material of any origin produced in equipment designed or supplied by Canada. They even affirmed Canada's right to demand prior consent to transfer of supplies of Canadian origin outside the EEC countries. All Canadian material, whether supplied directly or through a third country, was subject to the agreement. This allowed France—who had held up earlier agreements—to enrich uranium for other countries, but excluded Canadian uranium from use in French reactors until France accepted safeguards, as it subsequently did.[34]

An interim arrangement was also agreed on, whereby reprocessing was covered in accordance with the Trudeau-Schmidt formula worked out in the Nuclear Fuel Cycle Evaluation. Canada was given the right to in-depth consultation prior to reprocessing; continuation of the supply of uranium hinged on the outcome of the evaluation and was to be further negotiated by the end of 1980;[35] and transfer of nuclear technology was left up to bilateral agreements of member states with Canada. Uranium shipments to Europe were resumed in December 1977.

Japan was naturally reluctant to move ahead of the EEC or the United States, which it viewed as the most important participants in the handling of safeguards. The interim agreement with the United States reduced many of the inconveniences stemming from the two sets of safeguards inflicted on Japan for the same materials; thus it was persuaded to accept these double controls at the end of 1977 after agreement had been reached with the EEC, and a settlement was agreed to when Secretary Jamieson visited Tokyo on 26 January 1978.[36] Uranium oxide and hexafluoride being accumulated in Canada for Japan resumed its way to Japan via enrichment in the United States.

Although Canada was willing to make its requirements of Japan no more stringent than those it set for Europe, the 1959 agreement already provided for prior Canadian consent to reprocessing; whereas the agreement with the EEC did not, nor did it limit shipments for current need. Japan decided to continue to accept prior Canadian consent on reprocessing, as well as on storage of plutonium and enrichment of uranium above twenty per cent. Unlike the agreement that was to be renegotiated with the EEC, the one with Japan was a permanent model settlement with Canada's most important uranium customer. Canadian officials regarded this agreement as satisfying Canadian safeguards fully, and a demonstration that the latter did not constitute impediments to a national energy program where there was no likelihood of proliferation.[37]

Despite the success of the diplomats in negotiating a settlement, the Liberal Democratic members of Japan's Diet were still suspicious of Canada's intentions and of the way the protocol would be implemented. They feared that, if Canada was determined rigidly to enforce its rights under the settlement, this could seriously interfere in the operation of Japanese nuclear facilities, and they consequently delayed ratification by the Diet. The possibility of interference in reprocessing was a major Japanese worry. In addition, the impact of the new Canadian policy and the negotiation of the protocol had an unfavorable influence on Canada's attempts to sell a CANDU reactor to the Japanese, who were also anxious that their own heavy-water reactor program might be blocked if the Canadian technology transferred with the CANDU was deemed to pre-empt the sphere of development on Japan's own new reactor program. Their experience of the uranium export ban just after

Trudeau had signed the Framework for Economic Cooperation left an uneasy feeling that it could happen again. Canadian officials admitted that they knew Japan had no intention or likelihood of engaging in a weapons program, but the sanction was levied anyway. The independent provincial governments were another source of disquiet. Saskatchewan declared a moratorium on uranium development about that time, and in 1980 British Columbia, where Japanese companies were involved in prospecting for uranium, suddenly also declared a freeze on exploration or development for seven years, even before the premier's inquiry had made a report on whether to restrict development or not.

The Japanese Foreign Ministry assigned its director-general for scientific and technological affairs, who had considerable experience as their representative with the IAEA in Vienna, to lobby the Liberal Democrats concerning the protocol with Canada. He succeeded in getting it ratified by the Diet just before Prime Minister Ohira's visit to Canada in May 1980, even though it was only one of fifty treaties awaiting Diet action.

THE ATTEMPT TO SELL A CANDU REACTOR TO JAPAN

The semi-governmental company, Electric Power Development, began serious consideration of the CANDU reactor in late 1975. It had played an important role in the development of new electric power generation technology in an earlier period, but now looked to Canadian technology as a way to continue its role, which the nine electric utility companies would have preferred to see ended. Those companies had built their own light-water reactors, and had already contracted with Canadian mining companies for a large share of their uranium. They favored the advanced thermal reactor being developed by the other semi-governmental corporation, Japan Power Reactor and Nuclear Fuel Development, as the new medium-term more advanced reactor.

The Electric Power Development Company had by 1979 already spent close to seven-and-a-half million dollars on preliminary research and testing of the CANDU technology, looking into its suitability to earthquake-prone Japan, while Atomic Energy of Canada Limited, the Canadian crown corporation which sells the CANDU, spent a similar amount. This effort was backed by the Japanese Ministry of International Trade and Industry, which preferred to diversify from over-reliance on American light-water reactors, to the Canadian heavy-water reactor using natural uranium which did not require enrichment in the United States. The ministry hoped that this arrangement would not only bring with it Canadian long-term guarantees of a thirty-year uranium supply, but also open up access to future supplies of oil from the tar sands and natural gas.[38] The Electric Power Development Company was closely tied to the ministry, and its president, Yoshihiko Morozumi, was a former vice-minister of the Trade Ministry: a career civil servant retired to a subsidiary agency of the ministry.

The Power Reactor Corporation's advanced thermal or converter reactor was a competitor to CANDU. It was also a heavy-water moderated reactor which used slightly enriched uranium, natural uranium, and a tiny amount of plutonium for fuel. It was considered a step in the direction of a breeder reactor, which was Japan's long-term hope for a more independent nuclear future. The prototype reactor, FUGEN, was already operating in Tsuruga City, Fukui Prefecture, with an output of 165 megawatts.[39] The Science and Technology Agency, which was responsible for the development of experimental reactors, backed the advanced thermal reactor.

The Trade Ministry and Electric Power Development Company contemplated buying from Canada four reactors, each one of which could cost up to one billion dollars and would constitute a more independent second-generation reactor. However, the government departments, the development companies, and private industry were divided between those favoring a heavy-water reactor developed in Japan, which had always depended on foreign nuclear technology before, and those who preferred a heavy-water reactor developed in Canada, which promised diversification from reliance on any one foreign country, as well as more secure access to a future energy supply. The so-called "second oil crisis" of 1979 brought almost as dramatic an increase in prices as that of 1973, which, according to the minister, Masumi Esaki, emphasized the need for access to other fuel.

Until October 1978, this conflict of views within Japan was kept under control and moved toward a compromise which might have permitted both programs to go ahead, if it had not been for a struggle for funds under the budget control of the Finance Ministry. Unfortunately, at this point the newspapers entered the fray to catapult CANDU onto the front pages of the Japanese newspapers for almost the first time.

The agency charged with the decision for the Japanese government was the Japanese Atomic Energy Commission. That group was nominally an advisory body to the prime minister, but its advice in this case was required by law to be binding. The commission had previously had its credibility badly damaged by lengthy disputes over the nuclear-powered merchant ship, *Mutsu*, whose reactor had developed a minor leak during its first sea test. The ship literally drifted for months before a way could be found to get it into port in the face of anti-nuclear fishermen and local inhabitants who did not want any radioactive ships in their vicinity, although the leakage of radioactivity was small and temporary. As a result of the poor performance of the commission, some of its members resigned and a largely new commission was headed by Susumu Kiyonari as acting chairman. He was a former head of the Power Reactor Corporation, which was building Japan's own advanced thermal reactor, and he was still an adviser to his old company, Hitachi Manufacturing Company, a leading electrical machinery manufacturer in Japan. The formal chairman of the commission was Iwazo Kaneko, director general of the Science and Technology Agency, cabinet minister and senior Liberal Democratic member of the Diet.

Both Kiyonari and Kaneko were beholden to their respective constituencies of the Power Reactor Corporation and the Science and Technology Agency. The corporation was naturally anxious to promote its own reactor, as were the younger officials of the agency. They constituted some of the important groups favoring the Japanese technology which thus far had always taken a back seat to foreign technology in reactor development. The new commission found itself in a situation where it could no longer meekly submit to pressure from the usually powerful Ministry of International Trade and Industry and opt once more for reliance on a foreign country. The ministry itself was in the unusual position of backing a foreign industry, instead of its more accustomed role as a defender of Japanese industry.

When the ministry put forward its proposals for the next budget year in August 1978, it asked for 1,800 million yen, about $7.5 million, for the planned introduction of the CANDU. The opposition of the Atomic Energy Commission and the Science and Technology Agency was so strong that the ministry drew back. Its two opponents had only received funds to complete the FUGEN reactor and were awaiting further funding to go ahead with the advanced thermal demonstration reactor. In October the ministry publicly demanded that the decision to accept the CANDU be made in November. This was eventually to prove a fatal step, opening up the low-key kid-glove struggle to an outright rough-and-tumble contest.[40]

The responsibility for a decision was structured so that the experimental reactors were under the Science and Technology Agency but commercial reactors were under the ministry. On that basis, the ministry tried to push through a decision. But because of the continued opposition of the Atomic Energy Commission and the agency, the ministry had to give up, as far as the 1979 budget was concerned. Open confrontation was put off for a while.

In the meantime, the Atomic Energy Commission had charged its new reactor panel with looking at the economic and technical aspects of the CANDU. In March 1979 its report was conciliatory. It recommended that planning for the CANDU be permitted to go ahead without foreclosing the question of whether it would be accepted or not.[41]

The Three Mile Island nuclear accident in the United States in March 1979 brought home the disadvantages of depending upon a foreign country for nuclear technology. Japan sent engineers to America to get information on what happened to a reactor the same as theirs. In view of the fears aroused over that accident, most of Japan's reactors were temporarily shut down for inspection, and it strengthened the case of those advocating support for Japan's own experimental reactor.

Proponents of the latter also raised the question whether the introduction of CANDU technology would pre-empt Japan's own efforts at heavy-water reactor development, in view of the new nuclear safeguards agreement. This was strongly denied by Canadian officials, and when Prime Minister Clark came to Tokyo for the summit meeting, he personally tried to reassure the Japanese prime minister on that point.

Japanese private business increasingly came out in favor of Japan's independent effort. Appearing before the new reactor panel of the Atomic Energy Commission, Toshio Doko, president of Keidanren, came out against CANDU. He was the former head of Toshiba, another important electrical manufacturer and long-term partner with Westinghouse, the leading maker of the American reactors purchased by Japan. Referring to his age and long-range national viewpoint, he said, "My life is drawing to a close. There will be a time when the oil is gone and we must use sea water to get our own uranium. I fear for the future of Japan if we do not take steps for energy independence for our light-water reactors and fast breeder reactors."[42] Hiromi Arisawa, chairman of the business group Japan Atomic Industrial Forum, also took a negative attitude toward CANDU at the panel hearings in April 1979, and in a speech to Keidanren in June he repeated this view.[43]

In June the panel decided that there was no reason to import the CANDU. The ministry argued that Japan's economic foreign policy and relations with Canada would be adversely affected by such opposition, and tried several times to get the commission to put off its formal decision. Because of the July summit meeting in Tokyo of the seven industrialized countries, the decision was in fact postponed. At the summit, Prime Minister Clark lobbied Ohira to accept the CANDU, explaining how greatly it would improve relations with Canada, which, as a technically advanced country, would consider it a vote of confidence for Japan to buy its high technology. Public interest was aroused as Doko of Keidanren objected to the intense lobbying for the CANDU and was himself criticized.

On the morning of 10 August, just before the departure of Minister of Trade Esaki for overseas, he tried to get a postponement of the formal decision until September. However, both the chairman of the commission, Iwazo Kaneko, and the acting chairman, Kiyonari, apparently fearful that they could not much longer resist the pressures on them, decided to hold the formal meeting of the commission for a final decision on that very day, despite the entreaties of the trade minister. The decision went against the purchase of the CANDU, on the grounds that no valid arguments for introducing it had been adduced. The decision was softened for the sake of good Canadian relations by stating that if conditions changed significantly in the future, the question could be taken up once again. The formal report was sent to the prime minister who had no option but to accept it.

Masumi Esaki held a press conference on the evening of 10 August, deploring the commission's decision;[44] however, that decision was generally welcomed by the press on the grounds of greater self-reliance.[45] The Trade Ministry reluctantly bowed to defeat at the unaccustomed hands of the normally unassertive advisory body, but continued to campaign for CANDU. By October the ministry at length also acknowledged that it could do nothing but accept the decision of the commission.[46] Apparently the tactful Japanese efforts to soften the blow succeeded in keeping Canadian hopes alive that the question might be reconsidered.[47]

The Japanese Atomic Energy Commission had recognized the advantages of the CANDU as a viable alternative. It was a proven system that could be put in place quickly, whereas the demonstration commercial heavy-water plant envisaged by Japan had yet to be built, which would need five to ten years. The CANDU use of natural uranium offered diversification of technology and fuel, away from dependence on the United States. But the commission argued that it would take too much money and skilled personnel away from Japan's own effort in what would be a fourth nuclear power system. For its part, the Finance Ministry was reluctant to see both systems go ahead at once, even though the CANDU would have brought low-interest Canadian loans which would have freed Japanese general revenues more than the independent program. Thus, hope lingered on in Canada.[48]

In Japan the 1980 budget provided 15,575 million yen for the Power Reactor Corporation and the electric power industry to construct a full-scale fast breeder reactor, MONJU.[49] The corporation's experimental 50,000 kilowatt breeder reactor, JOYO, had already started up in 1977. Thus, Japan was going ahead with two advanced types of reactor to enable it to keep up with developments in Europe.

Despite the close cooperation of the Japanese Trade Ministry with Atomic Energy of Canada, and the advanced stage it had reached, Japan finally came down against CANDU. The failure was not due to any lack of support from the Canadian government or lack of interest or favorable assessment by Japanese agencies. Even the Japanese Atomic Energy Commission had good things to say about CANDU. But the question of introducing the Canadian reactor brought to a head the long-standing debate within Japan itself, whether to put more effort into its own development or not, and how important greater independence in nuclear matters would be; the internal interagency struggle was also unfavorable to CANDU. The matter reached a critical point at an unpropitious moment, and in addition the Three Mile Island accident had just occurred.

Once again, as in other cases such as the attempted sale of a water bomber, Canada failed to sell its high technology and break out of its role as a purveyor of raw materials with Japan. Even when Canada had a powerful ally in the Ministry of Trade, it failed to deflect the Japanese drive to achieve technological independence.

7

Encouraging Participation by
Japanese Investors in Canada

STEPPED UP RESOURCE INVESTMENT

The 1960s was a period when Japan began to produce on a large scale its popular advanced consumer durables like color television sets, motorcycles, and automobiles, as well as machinery and other sophisticated products of both heavy and light industry. It was also the chief period of investment in Canada by Japanese companies to develop and ensure a stable supply of raw materials to feed their new industries. These were concentrated in forest products, copper, and coal, and were mainly from British Columbia which was the principal exporter to Japan. Investment took the form of participation in joint enterprises in some forest industries, the provision of loans and long-term supply contracts, and the acquisition of usually only minor equity in Canadian companies whose output was desired by Japan.[1]

That decade was a time of economic cooperation between Canada and Japan, as the two countries' leaders constantly mentioned in the 1970s. The maturing of the Canada-Japan relationship was probably the outcome of the relatively strong Canadian support to Japan in the forum of the advanced countries, second only to the sponsorship of Japan by the United States. This was examined in the discussion of the GATT negotiations and the Colombo Plan in Chapters Two and Three.

The decade was led off, appropriately enough, by the visit of Prime Minister Ikeda to Ottawa in June 1961 for two days, and the return visit of Prime Minister Diefenbaker to Tokyo and Osaka for five days in October the same year.[2] Ikeda was on his way to Washington, the main objective of his trip overseas. It was appropriate, too, that the second Canadian prime minister to be born in a western province should express the western Canadian interest in Asia with an official visit devoted exclusively to Japan.

Ikeda was attempting a "third option" policy to diversify from Japan's excessive dependence on the United States by building stronger ties with other industrialized countries like Canada, Britain, and France. During the previous three years, Japan had been rocked by massive protests, principally by adherents of the Socialist parties, against the defence arrangements with the United States and against nuclear arms and tests in general. Although he followed the old policy of close defence reliance on the Americans, Ikeda wished to show greater independence from them in the economic sphere by a more conciliatory policy toward China, as well as by extending trade and investment to other countries, chiefly Canada and Western Europe.[3] This policy resembled that of Pierre Trudeau ten years later, when he also tried to break ranks with the United States by recognizing China.

During Ikeda's visit to Ottawa, the Canadian prime minister announced new liberal arrangements for Japanese executives and experts to come to Canada in connection with their investment and business activities here.[4] The two leaders also agreed upon a Canadian-Japanese Ministerial Committee of cabinet ministers to meet alternately in Japan and Canada for informal discussions on problems and policies. Seven of these meetings were held during the next fourteen years, mainly during the 1960s, which enabled Liberal Party leaders to become personally acquainted with subsequent Japanese prime ministers and many of the top politicians in the ruling Japanese Liberal Democratic Party.

This interchange at cabinet rank undoubtedly enabled cordiality and understanding to develop at a level of government where otherwise there would have been almost none, as both countries' leaders were normally absorbed in other relations. Ikeda and Diefenbaker professed a high regard for each other in a period when it was not very common for prime ministers to spend so much time abroad. As this was a time when Japanese leaders were just beginning to establish new contacts and Japan was breaking out of the Pacific regional sphere, cabinet interchanges were welcomed and tended toward considerable warmth—more so than in the harsher environment of the 1970s. It is perhaps a measure of the great change of circumstances that Trudeau's initiative to create special contractual links with the EEC and Japan fell on such barren ground later on. Of course, by that time the relative global roles of the two countries had shifted, from one of near equality to great asymmetry where Japan was a major world power.

Diefenbaker's Osaka speech spelled out Canadian policy toward Japan with unusual clarity. Canadian devotion to the North Pacific Fisheries Treaty was expressed, concerning its protection of eastern Pacific salmon, herring, and halibut. Japan was anxious to get rid of the abstention principle under the treaty which excluded it from fishing on the high seas in much of the eastern Pacific. On the other hand, as the time for renewal of the treaty approached, Canada was equally anxious to keep the abstention in place.

With respect to the development of Japanese investment in Canada, managerial, supervisory, and technical personnel for Japanese-owned enterprises were to be admitted for three years, subject to automatic renewal. Permanent admission was to be granted to some similar key personnel in mining and manufacturing, in which a majority of Canadian citizens or residents were employed.

Regarding the Canada-Japan commercial agreement, the prime minister mentioned the granting of most-favored-nation treatment and the support of Japanese entrée to the world trading community on an equal footing. He defended the trade gap in Canada's favor as providing a larger trade volume that was brought into balance on a multilateral basis, and pointed out that virtually all Japanese exports competed with similar products made in Canada. He noted the contribution of Canadian food and raw materials to Japanese industrial expansion, declaring that the Japanese had freer access to the Canadian market than to "any other industrialized country in the world." The restriction imposed by Japan on textile exports to prevent Canadian "market disruption" still permitted relatively large sales to Canada, and the special duty procedure had not been used at all in the first seven years of the agreement to safeguard Canadian industry.

Diefenbaker also defended the necessity for the items covered in 1960 and 1961—and even their increase—under the quotas on Japanese exports to Canada. The Canadian "orderly growth" policy was applied to Japanese products that were competitive with Canadian industry, and could increase about five to ten per cent in years when the Canadian economy was buoyant, unemployment was not above normal levels, and demand was rising. Where flooding of the Canadian market was threatened, slowdown or even cutbacks might be necessary.

Thus the protective devices developed in the 1950s, such as fisheries abstention and quotas on competitive Japanese exports, were strongly supported in the 1960s, as spelled out by the Tory government under Diefenbaker, and were subsequently continued under Pearson's Liberal government. The more independent initiatives of the Ikeda government were soon blunted, and the subsequent Sato cabinets in Japan followed a complaisant pro-American policy. The result was that Japan remained firmly in the Western bloc; furthermore, Canada was not involved in Pacific or Asian hostilities as it had been in the 1950s in the Korean War. Canadian security in the Pacific was maintained by the Japanese-American defence arrangement and American hegemony.

Sparked by the prolonged rapid growth of world trade and the even faster growth of the Japanese economy, Canadian exports of raw materials, particularly minerals, increased. They were eagerly sought by Japan and no serious obstacles to this trade arose on either side; concomitant with this, Japanese funds and participation in Canadian resource industries became significant. Japan's improving economic strength, liberalization of trade and currency, and subsequent surpluses with other countries like the United States also allayed Japanese concern over the trade gap with Canada. However, Japan remained dissatisfied at the basically unequal nature of many of the restrictions placed on it by the other advanced countries, among whom Canada was a lesser offender. Canada's friendly and supportive actions should not be minimized, and for Japan they probably did outweigh the negative aspects of their relationship. With respect to investment, Canada in the 1960s maintained few restrictions except for the uranium industry and the banking system.

BRITISH COLUMBIA FOREST PRODUCTS

The more active years of Japanese investment in Canada were from 1964 to 1973, years in which the largest Japanese firms were taking the initiative. Thereafter, currency changes, oil crisis, inflation, and escalating wages and taxes in Canada all conspired to make the subsequent period comparatively unfavorable to investment. In the case of forest products, medium- or small-sized companies had been prominent before the war in exporting lumber and logs. Some of these were run by Japanese immigrants settled in Canada, and a medium-sized firm based in Japan, Tamura and Company, exported quite a few logs. By the 1960s the trading companies Mitsubishi, Chu Itoh, Marubeni, and Sumitomo became participants in joint forest enterprises along with Canadians, and in some Japanese paper companies.

The largest company was—and is—Crestbrook Forest Industries of Cranbrook, British Columbia, with about a thousand employees engaged in a pulp-mill, three sawmills, and a veneer plant; there is also a plywood plant at Fort MacLeod in Alberta. The pulp-mill at Skookumchuck required $42 million when it began in the West Kootenays in 1968, and it undertook a $16.8 million modernization program in 1976.[5] The company is jointly owned by the trading company, Mitsubishi Corporation, and Honshu Paper Company, who hold all the preferred stock on a fifty-fifty basis and half of the common stock. The Skookumchuk pulp-mill produces 450 tons of bleached kraft pulp daily, and the entire output up to 1987 is committed to the two parent companies.[6]

Finlay Forest Industries started in 1969 with 350 employees in its ground-wood pulp-mill, producing 160 tonnes daily; Jujo Paper Manufacturing Company and Sumitomo Forestry Company each has 37.5 per cent of the ownership, with Cattermole Timber Ltd. of Chilliwack holding twenty-five per cent. From 1972, Cariboo Pulp and Paper Company has had 300 employees in its Quesnel pulp-mill and produces 750 tonnes of bleached kraft pulp daily; it is jointly owned by Daishowa-Marubeni International Ltd. of Vancouver and Weldwood of Canada Ltd. of Vancouver, on a fifty-fifty basis. Daishowa-Marubeni International is in turn a joint venture of the trading company, Marubeni Corporation, and Daishowa Pulp Manufacturing Company who each hold half. The usual pattern is for both the general trading company and a Japanese manufacturer to go into a project together with a Canadian company.

Sawmill operations have been much smaller: CIPA Lumber Company with a sawmill in Nanaimo, British Columbia, produces sixty million board feet annually, and is owned eighty per cent by the trading company, Chu Itoh and Company (Canada), and twenty per cent by Pacific Logging Company, which in turn is owned wholly by Canadian Pacific Investments. The company began in 1964 with a five-million-dollar mill employing eighty men. In 1972 other sawmills included Q.C. Timber Company, wholly owned by Chu Itoh; its mill at Pitt Meadows, British Columbia, produces another sixty million board feet per annum, cut to Japanese sizes. Mayo Lumber Company is sixty per cent owned by Mitsubishi Canada Ltd. and a local Nanaimo family with a sawmill. Prince Rupert Forest Products Ltd. is seventy-five per cent owned by the trading company, Nissho-Iwai Canada Ltd., and produces forty million board feet per annum at the mill in Prince Rupert. Cindarella Daiei is a lumber concern one-third owned by Daiei Housing Co. Ltd. since 1973; its Canadian partners include Cindarella Cedar Project Co. Ltd.

DEVELOPMENT OF BRITISH COLUMBIA COPPER

In the mining industry, the production of copper concentrates went from nearly zero to second place in Canadian exports to Japan, and the British Columbia industry was almost rebuilt to meet the needs of the expanding Japanese industry. Although five of the ten principal copper-mines in British Columbia were foreign owned, in no case did Japanese companies acquire majority ownership or control.[7] However, the Bell Copper division of Noranda Mines Ltd. was the only case where the Japanese received none of the output and were without a connection.

One of the first mines to be opened was the Phoenix Mine of the Granby Mining Company, where there had been an underground operation which was closed down in 1919. Small-scale production began in 1959, and was increased considerably in 1963 by the loan and equity investment of the Ataka and Sumitomo trading companies.[8] Two-thirds of the equity was held by the Zapata Corporation of Houston, and the Sumitomo companies took the output which grew from seven hundred tonnes per day in 1959, to two thousand tonnes by 1963. Most of these new copper operations were open-pit large-scale mines, with copper at less than one per cent of the ore. The concentrates were smelted and refined in Japan, with smelting, refining, and transportation charges to the mines.

The Granisle Copper Ltd. property was initially under development in 1928–1929 by the Consolidated Mining and Smelting Company (now Cominco), but it recommenced production under Granby Mining Company in 1966. Sumitomo Metal Mining Company, Sumitomo Corporation, Mitsubishi Metal Corporation, and Mitsubishi Corporation (Mitsubishi Shoji, the trading company) loaned part of the capital costs, as did Granby Mining Company and a Canadian bank. The four Japanese companies purchased the entire output for ten years. Granby Mining Company owned nearly all the shares of Granisle, while the Sumitomo companies had one per cent of the equity. In 1972 a new long-term contract was arranged.

The Craigmont Mines Ltd. mine was brought into production without Japanese participation in financing, although Nippon Mining Company contracted for all the production. During 1971 and 1973 the Japanese company was forced to cut back twenty per cent on contract deliveries during a copper glut in Japan. The principal owners are the Canadian companies, Placer Development Ltd. and Noranda Mines Ltd; it closed down in December 1982, due to exhaustion of copper reserves.

The Bethlehem Copper Corporation developed both the Jersey Mine and the Huestis Mine in the Highland Valley south of Kamloops. They came into production in 1962 with a loan and purchase of shares by Sumitomo Corporation and Sumitomo Metal Mining Company, which agreed to take all the production for over ten years; the current contract goes to 1983. The Sumitomo Corporation sold its 20.8 per cent of equity to Newmont Mining Corporation of New York, keeping only about three per cent of the mining company's shares. Gränges Exploration Aktiebolag of Sweden, the original partner with Sumitomo, had 24.5 per cent of the shares in 1970; slightly over half remain with British Columbia investors. By 1980 Cominco had acquired a large share of Bethlehem which is adjacent to the huge Valley Copper Mines in the Highland Valley. Further development of this body of ore will make it the largest copper-mine in Canada.[9]

The molybdenum-copper property of Brenda Mines Ltd. went into production in 1970, financed by Nippon Mining Company and the Mitsui Trading Company as well as the Bank of Nova Scotia and Noranda Mines—

Noranda holding fifty per cent of the equity in addition to being the manager. The copper concentrate is sold to Nippon Mining Company under an exclusive five-year contract, renewable by the company up to 1986, and Noranda sells the molybdenum elsewhere. Nippon Mining holds 9.2 per cent of the equity and is on the board. In 1971 the Japanese cut back by twenty per cent on deliveries under a *force majeure* clause, as had Sumitomo Metal Mining Company in the case of Bethlehem Copper.

Utah Mines Ltd. in the north of Vancouver Island commenced operations in 1971. Mitsui Mining and Smelting Company contracted for 63.6 per cent of the production for ten years, and Mitsubishi Corporation together with Dowa Mining Company contracted for 36.4 per cent for five years. The company is wholly owned by Utah International Incorporated of San Francisco.

Gibraltar Mines Ltd. in the McLeese Lake area commenced production in 1972. As early as 1967, Mitsubishi Metal Corporation participated in exploration with Cominco Ltd. and Duval Corporation, a subsidiary of Placer Development. The mine capital was provided by loans from the Bank of Nova Scotia and the Canadian Imperial Bank of Commerce. Nippon Mining Company contracted to take all the output until the end of 1981, but like the others was obliged to cut back in 1971. The Canadian company, Placer Development Ltd., owns seventy-one per cent of the shares.

Similkameen Mining Company near Princeton is wholly owned by Newmont Mining Corporation and has never had Japanese financing. Its output was contracted for by Mitsubishi Metal Corporation for nine years.

The Lornex Mining Corporation mine is in the Highland Valley area and commenced production in 1972. Rio Algom Mines Ltd., which is fifty-five per cent owned by Rio Tinto Zinc Corporation of London, did the principal exploration work and financed a considerable part of it, together with shareholders such as Yukon Consolidated Gold Corporation. Six Japanese smelting companies and three Japanese trading companies provided $26.5 million in loan funds and received 150,000 common shares. The Japanese companies were Dowa Mining Company, Furukawa Mining Company, Mitsubishi Metal Mining Company, Mitsui Mining and Smelting Company, Nippon Mining Company, Sumitomo Metal Mining Company, Mitsubishi Corporation, Mitsui and Company, and Sumitomo Corporation.[10] Three Canadian banks provided a sixty-million-dollar loan, and an additional forty million dollars was provided between 1970 and 1973 by Rio Algom and Yukon Consolidated through shares and debentures. The Japanese companies agreed to take the entire output for twelve years.

Some additional copper involvement was in Valley Copper Mines, where Marubeni Corporation took two per cent of capital shares with six million dollars in 1964; Cominco and other Canadian investors held 69.7 per cent. Sherritt Gordon's mine borrowed fifteen million dollars from the Mitsubishi group,[11] and its output went to Mitsubishi Metal Corporation for smelting. Southeast Asia Bauxites Ltd., Montréal, received investment from Japan Light Metal Company in August 1960.[12]

Despite the rather wide scope of Japanese investment in mining, especially of copper, in the form of loans and share holding, it has been only a small fraction of the total investment in the mining industry in Canada, or even in British Columbia where much of the industry is concentrated. The most important aspect has been the willingness of the Japanese mining and smelting companies to take almost all of the copper output on long-term contracts. Even in the investment in the mines, the largest share of the financing has come from Canadian banks, and from Canadian and American mining companies. The Japanese financing has only been water to prime the pump, but with firm agreement to take the output. Here Japan was carrying out its primary foreign economic policy objective: to obtain a stable source of essential raw materials through its private enterprise sector. The Japanese mining and smelting companies evidenced the usual policy of collaboration with a big trading company, which itself invested to a minor extent but brought to bear its worldwide information network. The Japanese firms in the mining sector were not interested in majority ownership or control, even to the partial extent that it prevailed for pulp, lumber, or paper in the forest products industry.

The oversupply of concentrates in Japan in 1971 was due to a recession which was reducing effective demand. The Japanese producers needed to cut back on their supply contracts for the first time in over a decade of almost continuous and rapid large-scale expansion. This caused quite a shock to the Canadian companies, which had come to rely on the growth of the Japanese economy and the dependability of the supply contracts which were very valuable in obtaining financing for the industry. Nearly all of the 250,000 tonnes of copper concentrate produced in British Columbia went to Japan at that time; new mines were coming on stream and were due to increase production to 400,000 tonnes per annum by 1975, just when the Japanese demand was slacking off. New mines were also coming into production in Australia, New Guinea, the Philippines, and West Irian.

The Social Credit government in British Columbia had passed a Mineral Processing Act in 1970, requiring half of the concentrate produced in the province to be smelted there. However, there were no longer any smelters in operation, so the law was of no effect for the time being. The provincial mines minister, Frank Richter, told Japanese companies that the government wanted copper ore to be processed locally, with proper pollution controls. Partly due to new pollution regulations in Japan also, smelters there were subject to rising costs, which their companies wanted to pass on to the Canadian mines.[13] The minister welcomed Japanese capital for a smelter in

British Columbia, a policy aim continued by the New Democratic government that came to power in 1972, which set up a special task force to foster it.

By 1972 the Japanese companies were pressing for fifteen to twenty per cent cutbacks in copper-ore shipments, as well as trying to get the Canadian mines to absorb some of the cost of the recent seventeen per cent revaluation of the yen that had resulted from the Nixon trade and currency sanctions. The pressure on Canadian firms by virtually all the Japanese customers to alter the hitherto sacrosanct contracts produced hard feelings on both sides. Federal Energy, Mines, and Resources Minister Donald Macdonald met the problem head-on, by telegraphing twenty-two copper producers asking them to not renegotiate their export contracts with the Japanese. As the minister wrote, "The Japanese previously have given every indication in the mineral field of a commercial policy of dependable markets in accordance with obligations entered into. We are particularly concerned with the signal that a major change in the reliability of Japanese commercial policy is indicated." The federal government feared that the Japanese were acting in concert to pick off one Canadian mine after the other, which, acting singly, could not defend themselves. The Canadian firms, however, were not uniformly pleased with this government intervention.[14]

The federal minister released the companies from this requested moratorium on negotiations at the end of April, when it appeared that the Japanese were prepared to compromise. The Canadian companies accepted some cutbacks and increased charges, while the federal budget provided some tax concessions for custom processing to encourage smelting in Canada. As there appeared to be a good demand in other markets for processed copper, companies such as Bethlehem Copper, Noranda, Placer Development, and Newmont Mining submitted proposals to the government for the construction of a copper smelter near Kamloops. Cominco also considered setting up a copper smelter near Kimberly for ore from its Valley Copper Mine property in the Highland Valley.[15] The new premier, Dave Barrett, had indicated before being returned to office that the New Democrats favored a publicly owned copper smelter to provide jobs and create more provincial revenue.[16] Accordingly his economic development minister, Gary Lauk, now sought Japanese capital for a smelter in British Columbia to handle ore destined for Japan.

However, the Mineral Royalty Act of the New Democratic government in February 1974 added to the woes of the industry, by greatly increasing mining royalties. At that time the province was providing nearly thirty-eight per cent of Japan's copper concentrate imports, even with the cutbacks of 1972 and 1973.[17] In addition to the new royalties and very low copper prices, the Canadian producers faced Japanese requests to accept higher smelting charges. These were now running from sixteen to twenty-three cents a pound for smelting, refining, and shipping to Japan, and in 1975 the increased charges threatened to push costs over the selling price of copper for the major British Columbia mines.[18]

Rising costs in Canada meant that to process the concentrates in the province would cost thirty-seven cents a pound, considerably higher than the current Japanese costs.[19] Consequently Placer Development, Noranda Mines, Cominco, Bethlehem Copper, and Granby Mining all rejected the idea of building a smelter, at least until the end of the decade. One company, Afton Mines Ltd., fifty-five per cent owned by Teck Corporation, decided nevertheless to go ahead with provincial government cooperation, although its output was intended for companies in Britain rather than Japan.[20] The provincial government was to grant a sum of five million dollars, based on a payment of two cents a pound for smelter production of 25,000 tonnes a year—about a tenth of what was going to Japan. Thus the proposals to Japan for a copper smelter fell through, as had that for a steel mill, due to adverse economic trends which dampened earlier Canadian hopes of large Japanese investment in processing and upgrading resources. Copper—mainly in unprocessed form—and coal continued to go to Japan which took most of British Columbia's production with only minor success in diversification away from dependence on Japan for a market.

DEVELOPMENT OF BRITISH COLUMBIA AND ALBERTA COAL

Japanese participation in the coal industry in British Columbia and Alberta has been especially important. Since the oil crises of 1973 and 1979, the enormous cost of what had been a cheap and abundant fuel during the expansive sixties has made coal more and more attractive. Even the Japanese steel industry, which depended on British Columbia for about nineteen per cent of its coking coal, has substituted thermal coal for oil to supply its auxiliary fuel needs. By 1981 Japan's steel industry relied on Australia for over half of its metallurgical coal, but as with the United States it was apt to be cut off by strikes for considerable periods from those two principal sources. It also obtained some from South Africa, Siberia, and China but these sources proved to be limited or unreliable. British Columbia offered a secure source of supply to help stabilize its import of this essential fuel.

When the Canadian Pacific Railway was converting its locomotives to diesel oil in the 1960s, it began closing down its mines in the Crowsnest Pass area of the Alberta-British Columbia border; the Japanese steel companies became interested in the coal as a new reliable supply for what was then a rapidly expanding industry. The Canadian coal was not of the best coking variety, but, blended with other coal, it proved to be satisfactory, and it was also cheaper than either Virginia or Australian coal. The South Africans at the same time began to press for reduced deliveries to Japan because of the needs of their own steel industry.

On behalf of nine Japanese steel companies, Mitsubishi Trading Company negotiated with Kaiser Steel Company of California for about two years before agreement was reached in January 1968, to take forty-five million tonnes over a fifteen-year period. Kaiser Resources Ltd. of Vancouver was formed to extract the coal at the Sparwood mine, and a new port was constructed south of Vancouver at Roberts Bank, which took delivery of the hundred-unit car trains from the mine six hundred miles distant. Passing through several mountain ranges, the route must be one of the toughest coal hauls to be found anywhere. The coal itself also proved difficult to mine; Mitsui Mining and Smelting Company provided the special hydraulic technique developed in the Soviet Union to win the coal from the open pit. The low prices and high startup costs resulted in losses of thirty-three million dollars during the first three years of operation from 1970; however, the 1973 oil crisis doubled coal prices and put the operation in the black.

The Japanese companies, led by Nippon Kokan (Japan Steel Tube Company) put up $27.5 million to bail out the company; Mitsubishi Corporation took ten per cent of Kaiser's shares and the other companies took another twenty per cent. They were Nippon Kokan, Japan Steel, Kawasaki Steel, Godo Steel, Mitsubishi Chemical Industries, Toho Gas, Sumitomo Metal Industries, Kobe Steel, and Nisshin Steel.[21] Edgar Kaiser, Junior, took the direction of the new company; his father's firm, Kaiser Steel Company of California, owned thirty-two per cent of the Canadian company after the Japanese companies came to its rescue in August 1973. The Japanese share became twenty-three per cent later, but with the buy-back of 1980 their share increased to 40.5 per cent.[22] In October 1980, Kaiser Resources was bought out by British Columbia Resources Investment Corporation, which became the principal shareholder; other shareholders are the ten Japanese companies. The company name changed to British Columbia Coal Ltd. in January 1981, while Edgar Kaiser Junior kept some of his senior management personnel and formed his own company, Kaiser Resources.[23] In 1983 B.C. Coal changed its name once more, becoming Westar Mining Ltd. Probably because Nippon Kokan became the principal negotiator for the Japanese companies involved in Kaiser Resources, its president, Hisao Makita, became a leading representative of the Japanese business community not only in connection with coal, but in relations generally with both the province and Canada during the 1970s.

The Japanese steel industry took only 860,000 tonnes of coal from Canada in 1969, but by 1973 it was receiving 9,300,000 tonnes. This amounted to about twenty-one per cent of Japan's coking coal imports, versus thirty-nine per cent from the eastern United States and thirty-two per cent from Australia. In 1974 the 10,100,000 tonnes exported broke down into 6,700,000 tonnes from British Columbia and 3,400,000 tonnes from Alberta. The slow-down in the Japanese domestic economy in the mid-1970s reduced steel industry operations to seventy per cent of capacity. Nevertheless, by 1978 Canadian exports were about 11,000,000 tonnes, half of which came from Kaiser, although 1981 and 1982 production fell to 9,500,000 tonnes, Westar Mining's new Greenhills mine starting up in southeastern B.C. will add another 1,800,000 tonnes in 1983.

The next most important coal exporter is Fording Coal Ltd. of Calgary, whose Fording River mine near Elkford, British Columbia, produces about three million tonnes a year. The company is sixty per cent owned by Canadian Pacific Investments of Montréal, and forty per cent by Cominco which operates the open-pit mine. Its coal is also exported from Roberts Bank to six Japanese steel firms on a fifteen-year contract. Three smaller mines on the Alberta side of the border are Luscar Sterco Ltd., McIntyre Coal Ltd., and Coleman Colleries Ltd., which also supply metallurgical coal to Japan; these do not have direct Japanese investment nor are they comparable with the Kaiser operation.[24]

Although it seems reasonable to assume that eventually steel production will expand again on a global basis, the continued weak demand in Japan has made steel producers there cautious about increasing coal supply contracts when business continues to be so sluggish. The South Korean and Taiwan mills can undersell the Japanese, but their production is still too small to cut deeply into Japanese output. Even though sales of Canadian coal to other parts of the Pacific and Europe would be possible, Japan remains by far the most important market for the time being. Coal has become the chief export earner for Canada, and promises further expansion because thermal coal is likely to be a major substitute for oil.

When the British Columbian Social Credit party came back to power in 1975, it was anxious to promote development of the northern part of the province, and for this purpose it looked to the coal deposits in the northeast; the existing coal mines were all in the southeast. The provincial government persisted in hoping that the Japanese could be persuaded to buy some of the northeast coal, and that development could be undertaken there. But it would cost a great deal to build all the facilities, as well as the mines themselves. On the visit of the Japanese business mission to Vancouver in October 1976, Hisao Makita of Nippon Kokan announced that it would be necessary for the provincial government to build the railway line, roads, town site, and harbor needed for the new coal fields in the northeast. Then the minister of economic development, Don Phillips, returned from a trip to

Tokyo in November, bringing the news that the steel-makers were reluctant to commit themselves to fresh contracts.[25] Clearly, the proponents of northeast coal needed more than the Japanese market, if they were to get sufficient supply contracts to make the new development feasible and able to pay for itself.

The British Columbian officials believed that at least ten million tonnes would have to be purchased per year to make the financing feasible. The coal task force issued a technical report recommending development, but it also outlined the difficulties.[26] Meanwhile Japanese steel-makers committed themselves to coal development in Australia on a bigger scale, and were unwilling to divert more business to Canada at that stage.

The Quintette property east of Anzac, which the British Columbia railway now reached, was the most fully explored in the northeast. Denison Mines Ltd. of Toronto initially held a 38.25 per cent interest, Mitsui Mining Overseas Company and Tokyo Trading Company Ltd. held 22.5 per cent each, and Imperial Oil Ltd. 16.75 per cent. Later, Imperial Oil surrendered its share to Denison and Esso Resources Canada Ltd., and Charbonnages de France joined them. Denison obtained a letter of intent from the Japanese steel companies to purchase five million tonnes of coal a year, but this was judged insufficient to go ahead with expensive infrastructure costs such as the railway line and the new port at Prince Rupert.

In the meantime Denison Mines said that Quintette Coal Ltd. had an agreement to supply the government of Romania with twenty-five to thirty million tonnes of high-quality metallurgical coal, over a twenty-year period to begin at the end of 1982 at an initial rate of 1.3 to 1.5 million tonnes per annum and four million tonnes by 1984. The property had an estimated 2.8 billion tonnes minable.[27]

In July 1979 it was the coal property of BP (British Petroleum) Canada Ltd. near Sekunka that was the object of a go-ahead in conjunction with the provincial and federal governments' plans for a rail line from Chetwynd to Sekunka, and town and road improvements for Chetwynd.[28]

Premier Bill Bennett and his economic development minister, Don Phillips, went to Japan and Korea in October 1979 to look for customers. But, like their predecessors Barrett and Lauk, they were unsuccessful in gaining any further commitments from the Japanese steel-men. Some limited success was achieved elsewhere, however: Norco Resources Ltd. (formerly Northern Coal Mines Ltd.) of Vancouver with coal licenses in the Bowron River area announced a billion-dollar twenty-five-year coal contract with Taiwan Power Company.[29] This was conditional on proving high-quality thermal coal up to sixty million tonnes. An eighty-million-dollar mine was planned, which would create six hundred jobs, seventy kilometers from Prince George; Taiwan Power would put thirty million dollars into it, for not more than thirty per cent of the equity. Both Norco and BP Canada hoped to use the planned Ridley Island coal port at Prince Rupert, but the federal government, temporarily in the hands of the Conservatives, was reluctant to start on the project of a new port before there was assurance of at least four million tonnes throughput a year.

The southeast of the province has also planned expansion. Federal approval has been given to triple the Westshore Terminals at Roberts Bank, which is currently overstretched to ship ten million tonnes a year for the two biggest coal producers, Westar Mining Ltd. and Fording Coal. Both of those companies are expanding their output. B.C. Coal, Westar's predecessor, was successful in exporting small amounts to Mexico, Brazil, Pakistan, and Korea, and the market for thermal coal is opening up, in addition to that for metallurgical coal. In the fall of 1979, B.C. Coal (then still Kaiser Resources) signed a five-year contract to supply 750,000 tonnes in 1982 and 800,000 a year thereafter to the Sam Chon Po power plant of Korea Electric Company.[30] Denison Mines also approached Korea Electric to supply thermal coal.

Crows Nest Resources Ltd., a wholly owned subsidiary of Shell Canada Resources Ltd., signed a contract to supply 350,000 tonnes of thermal coal a year to Korea Electric's power station in the fall of 1979. In the winter it signed a contract for another 400,000 tonnes for the Go Geong power station. It needed $180 million to start production on its property near Fernie in southeastern British Columbia.

The Electric Power Development Company was the first Japanese electricity company to participate in the development of thermal coal in Canada. It arranged with Manalta Coal Ltd. to strip-mine the McLeod River field to produce two million tonnes per annum by 1987. Costs would be shared, seventy per cent by Manalta and thirty per cent by Japan Electric Power Development Company. Mitsubishi Mining and Cement Company would provide some expert advice on the Japanese side;[31] no infrastructure investment was required.

Although demand for steel did not pick up, the prolonged strike in Australia in 1980 persuaded the Japanese companies to reconsider their reliance on the coal "down under." The long-held ambition of British Columbia leaders for further development in the north of the province seemed close to realization when a ceremonial signing on 10 February 1981 took place. Two coal companies, Quintette and Teck Corporation (with respect to its Bullmoose mine), succeeded in gaining Japanese acceptance of seven million tonnes per annum, starting in 1983 for fifteen years. Quintette would supply five million tonnes of metallurgical coal and one million of thermal coal, and Teck 1.7 million tonnes of thermal coal.[32] The province and federal government are financing the railway, roads, and harbor with revenues to be recouped from charges against the coal, and a new town is being built at Tumbler Ridge. Denison's current holdings in Quintette are 38.25 per cent, Mitsui Mining and Tokyo Trading have 17.5 per cent each, Esso Resources Canada has 16.75 per cent, and Charbonnages de France has 10 per cent. BP Canada is not scheduled to go ahead at the present time as it does not have any Japanese contract.

Meanwhile, Gregg River Resources Ltd. signed a thirty-million-tonne contract with the Japanese steel firms in January 1981, something the latter had wished to see proceed for more than a year.[33] This subsidiary of Manalta Coal Ltd. near Hinton in northwest Alberta is supplying 2.1 million tonnes a year beginning in 1983, and the contract price at $73.50 a tonne was a little less than that to be received by Denison and Teck. However, unlike Westar in the northeast, the Japanese companies took a forty per cent equity interest in Gregg River, and supplied forty per cent or $72 million of the $180 million development costs. The coal will be shipped from Neptune Terminals in North Vancouver.

The result of these new coal commitments becoming firm in early 1981 is to bring the Canadian share of Japanese coal imports up from nineteen to twenty-five per cent by the year 1985. This represents a greater effort at coal diversification and, hence, security of supply to the Japanese steel industry; it stems from Japan's concerted effort to ensure energy supplies for the new decade, and follows on the huge real oil price increases of 1979–1980 and reconsideration of the 1974 decision to rely mainly on Australia for coal. The Japanese industry now has two coal sources in Canada: southeast British Columbia and northeast British Columbia, for which a second shipping area at Prince Rupert is essential.

Considerable controversy arose in the province over the northeast development, in which it was feared that the charges on the Quintette and Teck coal would not be sufficient for the provincial and federal governments, and hence the taxpayers, to recoup the financing of the infrastructure. Low demand and low prices make it difficult to survive the start-up of so many new mines in 1983, but the Japanese companies will try to enable the new mines to cover their costs. Once some recovery occurs in the developed countries, steel demand should pick up enough to increase output. The Japanese industry is shifting a larger share of its imports to Canada at present.

PETROLEUM INVESTMENT

Japan was interested in Canadian petroleum resources even before the 1973 oil crisis or the discovery that Canada's conventional crude oil output was diminishing. The semi-governmental Japan Petroleum Exploration Company had discussions with the Alberta government in 1971, concerning extraction of oil from the tar sands for piping to the West Coast to be refined and shipped to Japan. With the realization of the decline in domestic crude oil, the Canadian government banned further exports and began to phase out current sales of oil to the United States from western Canada.

The provincial governments of Alberta and British Columbia strongly favored upgrading to the production of petrochemicals. The Japanese took the long-range point of view that, even if they could not obtain immediate supplies of oil, they would like to invest so they would have a foot in the door when it might be opened to them in the future. In the meantime, if they participated in domestic Canadian development, they would earn goodwill and perhaps at least make a profit in the process. In 1974 Hisashi Kurokawa, president of Mitsubishi Petrochemical Company, announced a joint project with Great Canadian Oil Sands (now Suncor), the first company to produce oil from the huge Canadian tar sands in Alberta. It was planned for Mitsubishi Metal Corporation to participate in the mining of the tar sands, and Mitsubishi Petrochemical Company to extract oil for the manufacture of the petrochemicals.[34]

At about the same time, Marubeni Trading Company and the Fuyo Petroleum Development Corporation joined Canadian Industrial Gas and Oil Ltd. to form the Fuyo-Marubeni Oil and Gas Company. They planned to build a test plant at a cost of twenty million dollars, with Japanese financing of half the cost and receiving half the concessions,[35] and would use the Exxon high pressure steam extraction process on the tar sands.[36] The Industrial Bank of Japan, Shin-Daikyowa Petrochemicals, Toyo Soda Manufacturing, Kuraray Industries, and Central Glass were also planning with Home Oil Company of Canada for a joint venture in the one-billion-dollar range, to extract feed stock and utilize spoil such as high grade silica to make sheet glass, caustic soda, vinyl acetate, ethelene, and polyethelene.

The Canada-Japan Joint Ministerial Committee had not held a meeting from 1971 until 1975, when the seventh and last get-together occurred in Tokyo in June.[37] The Canadian ministers argued in favor of more joint ventures in processing raw materials in Canada,[38] and the trade minister, Alastair Gillespie, strongly urged the Japanese to join in technological cooperation to develop Canadian energy resources. The Japanese ministers responded by promising to cooperate with Canada in the exploitation of the oil sand deposits.[39]

The governmental Japan Petroleum Development Corporation was selected to launch the oil sand development as a Japanese national project, something which had been recommended by Shinichi Kondo, former ambassador to Canada, in his energy report of 30 May 1973.[40] Japan Petroleum Development Corporation and Japan Petroleum Exploration

Company took over the venture which had been set up by Marubeni Corporation with Fuyo Petroleum in 1974. That project at Cold Lake, Alberta, had completed its first phase and had begun to inject steam in the nine wells drilled. They planned to drill up to forty wells for prototype oil production; if successful, they thought they might be able to move to modest commercial production of heavy crude by 1980.[41]

The two government oil companies took sixty-five per cent of the new Japan Oil Sands Co., with the trading companies and private oil companies as minor partners. Japan Oil Sands was in control of Japan Oil Sands-Primrose Ltd. of Calgary, which was a joint venture with the majority partner, Norcen Ltd. of Toronto, which had taken over from the Canadian Industrial Gas and Oil Ltd. The joint venture company doing the actual drilling was now Primrose-Norcen; Marubeni had ten per cent of Primrose and Fuyo had eleven per cent of Japan Oil Sands.

In 1978 the Canadian federal government oil company, Petrocan, and major American oil companies invited Japanese participation in twenty-five per cent of tar sand mining rights, with a Japanese contribution of $112 million over fifteen years;[42] it involved 1.2 million acres of oil sand permits southwest of Fort McMurray. The Japanese participant was Japan Oil Sands, Alberta (Josalta, formerly Japan Oil Sands-Primrose), which was backed by the Japan National Oil Corporation, Japan Petroleum Exploration Company, Indonesian Petroleum Ltd., and Nissan Motor Company. Non-Japanese participants were Petrocan, Esso Resources Canada, and Canada-Cities Service. In Japan, Josalta announced drilling to begin in October 1980.[43]

The success of Dome Petroleum in drilling the Kopanoar Well in the Beaufort Sea kindled Japan's desire to participate in Arctic oil exploration. Overseas Petroleum Corporation signed a contract with Columbia Gas Development Company for some of its oil exploration rights,[44] and planned to set up a new investment company with Indonesia Petroleum, Sumitomo Petroleum Development Company, Mitsubishi Petroleum Development Company, and the Japan National Oil Corporation. The actual exploration would be done by Dome.

Japan National Oil Corporation, in a cash-for-oil swap, arranged to finance three of the first four fields developed in the Beaufort Sea.[45] Under a letter of intent, the Japanese company was to provide four hundred million dollars in three instalments, covering most of Dome's summer exploration program up to 1982. Japan would receive ten to twenty-five per cent of the production from the designated fields, subject to approval by the Canadian government. If it received no production, the loan would be repayable by the year 2030. The Japanese company would have the right to provide development loans to bring on production, recoverable from the production. The added amount could go up to two billion dollars provided from the consortium led by Japan

National Oil. It was an unusual step for Japan to put up such large funds for almost the first time in hopes of getting some oil, perhaps in the second half of the 1980s.

In the drive for access to energy resources in 1980, the Japanese Ministry of International Trade and Industry set up an Alternative Energy Resources Corporation under the former vice-president of Hitachi Ltd. Its aim was to promote the liquefaction of natural gas, liquid natural gas tankers, and the transportation and distribution of gas currently coming from Alaska, Brunei, and Indonesia; its role was to help finance the arrangements being pursued on a more active scale by private companies and public utilities. Dome Petroleum and the trading company, Nissho-Iwai, on behalf of Chubu Electric Power, Kyushu Electric Power, Osaka Gas, and Toho Gas proposed supplying 2.3 trillion cubic feet of British Columbia and Alberta gas to Japan from 1986 to 2001.[46] The British Columbia government gave its approval in July of 1982 over competing proposals of Carter Oil and Gas Ltd. of Vancouver and a partnership of Westcoast Transmission Company and Petrocan. The base price of U.S. $6.86 was considerably above both the Canadian export price of U.S. $4.40 to the United States and the average price within the United States of $3.50. Dome and Nissho-Iwai obtained National Energy Board permission to export in January of 1983.

The proposal by Mitsubishi Corporation, Mitsubishi Chemical Industries, Mitsubishi Petrochemical, and Asahi Glass Company together with Dome Petroleum, Canadian Occidental Petroleum, and Westcoast Transmission was made to the British Columbia government in 1981 to set up a petrochemical manufacturing complex for ethelene, polyethelene, and vinyl chloride from natural gas.[47] Investment was expected to be U.S. $1.2 billion; production was to begin in 1986.

All these oil and gas plans have received a severe setback from the recession of 1981–1983, the fall in energy prices, and the vast oversupply of energy. With no certainty of an early return to shortages, all the new projects have been stopped or face doubts about going ahead. Most of the large projects in the Alberta tar sands were postponed as major participants withdrew. The Japanese also withdrew from their participation in Alberta oil sands development in 1982. The Dome Petroleum drilling in the Beaufort Sea in 1981 and 1982 was not encouraging. On top of that, the company underwent serious financial difficulties in 1982 due to high interest rates and reduced cash flow; it has yet to refinance its debt of over five billion dollars satisfactorily. In Japan, there are serious doubts about cooperating with Dome or raising additional large sums for the pending oil and gas projects, now that the immediate need for the energy resources is no longer evident. The British Columbia government turned down the Mitsubishi-Dome petrochemical proposal. Although the Mitsubishi group said they were only postponing the plans, they feared that there might be no need for new petro-chemical facilities for the balance of the decade and that transportation costs might make British Columbia unsuitable as a site for production.

The Canadian federal government has given strong support to Dome Petroleum in its financial difficulties and to the Dome-Nissho-Iwai natural gas export project, but the Japan National Oil Company has not been forth-coming in support of the electric utilities which must raise $2.4 billion for a liquefaction plant and special gas carriers. Perhaps to encourage Japanese support, the Canadian National Energy Board has permitted Dome to begin small shipments of shut-in Alberta oil to Japan from Vancouver in May of 1983.

JAPAN'S INVESTMENT BY INDUSTRY SECTOR

Most of Japan's investment in Canada is in resource-related industries. Of U.S. $585 million in March 1977, 51.5 per cent was related to resources, with 28.5 per cent in mining and 20.3 per cent in lumber and pulp. Investment related to commerce and services was 27.6 per cent, with 16.0 per cent in trading and warehousing, but only 0.8 per cent in construction and 0.5 per cent in banking and insurance. The remaining 20.9 per cent was in manufac-turing: iron and non-ferrous metals with 12.5 per cent, textiles 5.0 per cent, foodstuffs 1.4 per cent, and other manufacturing 2.0 per cent.[48] This invest-ment is heavily concentrated in British Columbia, particularly in copper, coal, and forest products, as noted above. The range, especially in other provinces, covers a wide variety of activities, from cattle raising and oil-seed crushing, to the Prince Hotel in Toronto, fish processing, television assem-bly, and the making of clothing, textiles, bearings, and steel wire. Most are medium-sized operations.

Some of these have not been successful, as in the case of a Japanese-owned textile plant, or the ill-fated Come-By-Chance oil refinery in New-foundland which undermined the large Ataka Trading Company; the latter has since been absorbed by Chu Itoh Trading Company. More hopeful are the processing and manufacturing projects connected with natural resources. The cheapness of electricity based on water power, compared with that pro-duced from oil, has conferred a big advantage on countries like Canada, Australia, Brazil, and Indonesia.

In 1979 the Japanese Ministry of Trade asked aluminum producers to shut down thirty per cent of their smelting capacity, and Japanese production began to move offshore to Indonesia, Australia, Venezuela, and Brazil where there was cheap power available. By 1980 the cost of producing aluminum in Japan had gone up to about five times that of steel. For electricity produced from oil, Japanese producers were paying up to fifty cents a pound, compared with the American price of only sixteen cents a pound. In Alcan Aluminum's Canadian production, the costs of producing aluminum were about nine cents cheaper than those of Alcoa in the United States.[49] Canada also benefited from an increase of sixty-three per cent in its 1980 exports to Japan, over 1979.[50]

Alpac Aluminum, owned half by Alcan and half by Nippon Light Metal, completed a 90,000-tonne plant in Canada in 1976. Nippon Light metal is itself half owned by Alcan. A new smelter has been built at Grande Baie, Québec; in addition, a huge smelter producing 500,000 tonnes a year is planned for Kitimat in British Columbia, which will have a million-kilowatt hydroelectric plant owned by the company.

The Sumitomo Trading Company and SKW Canada Ltd. of Montréal (owned by a German company) have proposed a ferro-silicon plant in British Columbia to supply silicon used to make steel, lured by the cheap power as well as high-grade silica deposits. Nippon Kokan has made similar proposals, as has the Mitsui Trading Company and Cominco. Nearly half the Japanese needs are met by imports which are up to forty per cent cheaper than their domestically produced silicon. Indeed, Japanese makers have accused Canadian producers of dumping, due to the low price of the imports. Production from these plants cannot commence until 1983 because of Japan's cartel agreement with the Canadian government.[51]

Thus the number of Japanese joint ventures in processing and manufacturing was increasing, because of the rising real cost of oil and the increased need of Japan for secure sources of energy. That seemed only prudent in view of the invasion of Afganistan, and the Iranian revolution and war with Iraq. Those threats to the supply of Middle East oil, as well as the 1979 exactions of the OPEC producers, gave impetus to Japan in that regard. The increasing strength of the Soviet Union's East Asian naval forces and its alliance with Vietnam constituted another threat, not only to Japanese commerce in Asia and the Pacific, but to that of the United States and Canada as well. Further development of Canadian resources and joint processing and manufacturing is bound to improve our own trade and domestic employment.

Japan's total investment in Canada reached $715 million by the end of 1979 (U.S. $1,087 million in March 1982), which was about 0.6 per cent of total direct foreign investment here; that compared with over $40 billion of American investment.[52] Not only is Japanese investment relatively small, but it tends to be of the type preferred by Canadian officials where the foreign investor is only a minor partner and not the controlling operator. The figures for direct investment do not include loans or even the contracts to take output which are often crucial to the success of an undertaking.

In 1979 and 1980 considerable criticism arose over the Japanese role in the herring-roe fishery in British Columbia as well as in fish processing in general, as was discussed in detail in Chapter Four. Control and undesirable influence was attributed to the Japanese companies involved in numerous fish processing operations where they often only had a minority ownership or agreements for first refusal on output, or had made loans. The criticism ignored the history of the industry in the province, where the biggest packing plants had usually been foreign owned for nearly a century. At present Canadian ownership is greater than at any other time.

In his book, *Men with the Yen*, Zavis Zeman elicited some lively press reaction to his suggestion that Japan might come to dominate Canada economically, although he denied that was the main point he intended to convey.[53] The record examined here seems to show that, if anything, the Japanese have been rather shy about investing in Canada; they have been much more active in Australia, Brazil, or the United States. They have invested mainly in the resource sector here to insure a reliable supply, especially of those minerals, energy supplies, and food needs in which they are so deficient. While they have made some modest investments in other sectors, these have not even been very conspicuous. The criticism often leveled at American investors, of owning and controlling whole sectors of the Canadian economy, can scarcely be made against the Japanese—nor does it seem likely in the near future. The ease with which suspicions can be aroused seems to be some irrational antagonism that stems back to wartime and beyond which may still linger in the Canadian community, for there appears to be little in the record that can justify these fears and suspicions. On the contrary, as foreign investors Japanese businessmen seem to have been, if anything, exemplars of what Canada would prefer.

8

Canadian Objectives Toward Japan

POLICIES OF CANADIAN GOVERNMENTS

It is useful at this point to summarize major Canadian policies toward Japan before considering the future. Turning to the federal government first, it was under Prime Minister Louis St. Laurent that Canada made peace with Japan and inaugurated postoccupation economic relations by negotiating the commercial treaty and the North Pacific Fisheries Convention. As described above, the commercial treaty emphasized entrée of the Canadian natural resource products which had historically been of chief importance in the trade between the two countries. It was based on the economic complementarity of Canada, well endowed with natural resources, and Japan which lacks them and must import. To pay for these, Japan must export manufactures made from the resource products.

At the same time, the commercial treaty sought to provide some measure of protection against flooding the comparatively small Canadian market with manufactured products and weakening the Canadian manufacturers who made similar items at higher cost. As it turned out, rather than relying on the imposition of special duties provided for in the agreement, which were not strictly in accord with the liberal principals of GATT, protection was obtained by inducing Japan to restrain its manufacturers voluntarily in some lines such as textiles before 1973, and, more recently, in automobiles.

In the case of fishing, through the device of a multilateral treaty, the North Pacific Fisheries Convention, Japanese fishermen were excluded from the best fishing off of the Canadian coast by a delimiting line of abstention. More recently, this has been superseded by the even more drastic system of a new convention, with a more inclusive abstention line and a bilateral agreement providing for a two-hundred-mile economic zone in 1977.

Canada was a strong supporter of Japan's re-entry into the postwar liberal trading regime under GATT, principally to induce it to cooperate closely with the NATO allies in their struggle to limit the expansion of the Communist states, to strengthen the liberal global trading system, and to defend their democratic governments. Thus in connection with the commercial treaty, Canada extended most-favored-nation treatment to Japan, including more lenient tariffs.

There have been important cooperative aspects entwined with the conflictive elements in our relations with Japan. With respect to trade, the complementary part has been the most important, where Canada has been happy to supply the raw (or preferably processed) resource products that Japan is most in need of. This has usually made up about two-thirds of our two-way trade. The most contentious aspect has been those Japanese manufactures that compete heavily with similar Canadian products, where a measure of restraint has been requested and extended. Even with Canada's restrictions, or the restrictions requested of Japan, they have not been as severe as those imposed by other developed countries. In the two important cases of textiles and motor cars, Canada has shared a larger part of its small market with Japan than have the much larger markets of the United States or the EEC.

To characterize briefly the policy of St. Laurent's Liberal government, it was to restore cooperation in trade matters with an independent Japan by the two major postwar treaties, and to attract it to the side of the Allies by extending the benefits of the new liberal trading system to Japan. It also opened, to a relatively generous degree, the market for manufactured products even where these competed strongly with our own manufacturing industry, which generally labored under the disadvantages of smaller runs, smaller investment capital, higher labor costs, and higher taxes.

Under the Conservative government of the flamboyant John Diefenbaker in the late fifties and early sixties, relations were informed by considerable cordiality, due to the high personal regard of the Canadian leader for Japanese Prime Minister Ikeda. Under them, an exchange of visits by cabinet ministers was inaugurated, which enabled the top leaders in both countries to come to know each other and each other's problems to an unusual extent during the sixties and the seventies.

The Diefenbaker government was, however, as devoted to protecting Canada's manufacturers as subsequent Liberal governments have been, mindful of the need to hold the loyalty of voters in the populous provinces of Ontario and Québec where most Canadian manufacturing is concentrated. Diefenbaker's finance minister, Donald Fleming, presided over the most extensive list of quotas or restricted manufactured products applied to Japan by Canada in the postwar period. Coming from an Ontario riding with textiles mills closed down by competition, he strongly opposed the "flooding" of the Canadian market by Japan.

Nevertheless, the government welcomed Japanese investment in both mining and manufacturing, and eased residence regulations for Japanese supervisory personnel. This was the period of rapid growth of world trade when Japan and Europe had recovered from wartime devastation. In Canada the waves of foreign competition were easier to bear. Japan's traditional light industrial exports were beginning to give way to the products of heavier and more sophisticated industry. This had the effect of a steadily increasing demand for the Canadian resource exports needed by Japanese industry— exports originating chiefly in the western provinces and especially in British Columbia. At this time Japanese industry was growing at nearly twice the rate of a very prosperous United States and Europe, traditionally Canada's most important markets.

Diefenbaker's policy, then, was one which took Japan into its scope much more closely than the policy of the following government of Lester Pearson, perhaps because the prime minister was himself from a western province. Also, the Conservatives relied much more on the western provinces for their voting strength. Historical trade patterns re-established themselves with strong government support for the prosperous western-based resource trade and equally strong protection for central Canadian manufacturers. In Japan, the Ikeda cabinet wanted to reduce its heavy dependence on the United States, and looked to Canada as part of its "third option" to diversify relations. Canada's market loomed much more important then, and was closer to Japan in the size of its economy. It was also a time when Japan did not have much trade or investment in Asia, Europe, or the Middle East and hence looked to North America more than it does now. Canada was one of the most prosperous developed countries and the rapidly expanding Japanese heavy industries sought not only markets there, but a stable supply of minerals and forest products to fuel those industries. One consequence was the re-establishment of the copper industry in British Columbia, a spin-off of Japan's world-record industrial growth. The Diefenbaker government strongly supported the western-based resource trade and encouraged the beginnings of Japanese investment, principally in the resource industries. It also aimed at protecting Canada's own light industry from Japanese competition, but still shared its market not ungenerously.

Under Pearson's Liberals from 1963 to 1968, the postwar prosperity and growth of world trade was at its height. Pearson himself never visited Japan during those years, but his cabinet ministers did so under the exchange arrangement worked out by Diefenbaker and Ikeda. This was the period of the Vietnam War, when Canada sought rather unsuccessfully to play a

mediator's role in Asia as a key member of the International Control Com-
missions in Indochina. Japan, therefore, receded in importance as a focus of
government attention. Canada tried to moderate American policy and to
help extract it from the quagmire of Vietnam—something it had accomplished more successfully in the Korean War of the early fifties, when the
NATO allies were more united in their Asian policies.

Nevertheless, Canadian–Japanese trade and investment both prospered
and in turn benefited from the economic activity due to the two Asian wars.
Japan's own economic activity increased not only in East and Southeast
Asia, but in the Middle East and Europe, too. In addition, the new consumer
durable goods industries arose in Japan that today characterize so much of its
exports in household appliances, electronic equipment, cameras, motorcycles, and motor vehicles. These were fostered in a strongly protected home
market, and then rapidly invaded overseas markets with the benefit of large-
scale domestic production, high productivity, and very high investment
using the latest technology from North America and Europe.

The sixties was the time of greatest Japanese interest in expanding and
stabilizing its sources of raw materials in western Canada in the forest and
mining industries. Through long-term contracts and minor ownership participation, it acquired the raw or partially processed materials it needed for
both its new and older industries, which were growing rapidly. Meanwhile
the Pearson government devoted itself to upholding its two historical purposes of support for the trade in resources and a moderate policy of protection for its industries in the relations with Japan. Neither side desired to take
any radical new initiatives toward each other.

If Pearson had his eyes fixed on the Vietnam problem in Asia, the contemporary Sato regime in Japan had its attention on the United States where
nothing was allowed to disturb their close cooperation. Sato's premiership
was the longest in Japanese history, in a steadily prosperous and politically
quiescent Japan, and he had none of Ikeda's ambition to diversify from
dependence on the United States. He wanted to avoid the acute embarrass-
ment experienced by his predecessor during a visit to France; today, no
doubt a French leader would be delighted to be referred to as a "transistor
salesman" on a visit to Japan, given France's almost desperate attempts to
compete with Japan in electronics.

This was, nevertheless, a crucial period in Japan's economic development. Like a chrysalis in a cocoon which is turning from a dull worm into a
new form which will suddenly emerge as a butterfly, Japan's new industries
were taking shape, protected by quotas, tariffs, and stringent investment
curbs, even stricter than anything attempted under Canada's new Foreign
Investment Review Agency. Japan was no longer a poor underdeveloped
country; it was rapidly becoming an affluent consumer society which would

soon burst forth, brandishing its new export products with which to conquer the markets of other developed and developing countries. Its high productivity was to be an impenetrable armor, enabling it easily to fling off much of the protective cocoon of quotas, tariffs, and investment barriers, as it now moved unscathed among its competitors, who were burdened down with obsolete equipment, low productivity, restrictive labor practices, and heavy taxes and defence expenditures or social welfare payments.

At the same time Japan's economy was growing in size to surpass Britain, France, and Germany, leaving Canada far behind, while its trade also expanded to global proportions. When Japan emerged fully in the seventies, it was as though Canada had receded in size and importance to Japan at the very moment that Japan's attraction was beginning to hold Canada's attention and dazzle it with its splendid metamorphosis. Japan was ready to meet the seventies and surmount the challenge of the oil crises with a leaner and even more sharply-honed economy, as it absorbed the new high cost of energy and scrapped large segments of several leading industries.

The new Liberal government of Trudeau was never content simply to inherit the policies of Pearson's Liberals. The prime minister himself has always delighted in foreign affairs. Projecting a distinctive image as Canada's leading spokesman abroad throughout his tenure in office, he has sought a larger and more independent role for Canada in keeping with its potential as a major developed country. Not satisfied with remaining as mere peace keeper in close cooperation with the United States and the other NATO allies in Europe, he looks toward the Third World for a new role for Canada. Perhaps because Canada can sympathize with the desire of other ex-colonies to escape subordination to the former colonial powers, it is a logical sphere in which to emphasize a new initiative; Canada still strives to be even more independent of both the United States and Britain. Soon after taking office, Trudeau moved to take the lead in recognizing the Peking government—a move followed by more and more countries, that eventually carried the People's Republic into China's seat in the United Nations against the opposition of the United States, which was backed only by the compliant Sato government in Japan among the major powers.

As a practitioner of judo and an admirer of Japanese cuisine, Pierre Trudeau had an appreciation of Japanese culture which may have helped to spur a political interest as well. He visited Japan as many times as his three predecessors. In pursuit of the "third option" policy to escape somewhat from American influence, he visited both Europe and Japan to carry through the "contractual link" and the Framework for Economic Cooperation. In emphasizing the Pacific Rim countries, Trudeau gave considerable attention to Japan as our principal partner in what he called "Canada's New West." From the signing of the Framework agreement in 1976, Ottawa hoped to attract more Japanese investment and technology, as well as a more satisfactory trading pattern with Japan in the competition with Australia and Brazil which vied for Japanese business as leading suppliers of essential raw materials.

This second initiative, after Pépin's failure to change the trading pattern in 1971, was dampened by the almost immediate imposition of a severe sanction in the form of the 1977 uranium ban. The adverse report of the Makita mission simultaneously with the signing of the Framework document also revealed Japanese disenchantment with Canadian economic nationalist policies, federal-provincial rivalries, and difficult labor conditions and tax policies. Meanwhile, the "second external affairs department," CIDA, was active with its large aid budget in the Third World, paying considerable attention to francophone countries where a role was provided for Québec. Thus, to some extent, what Canada was offering with one hand to the developing countries, it was seeking with the other from the newly developed major power of Japan.

Foreign policy initiatives toward Japan, then, have tended to be subordinated to other foreign or domestic objectives. For the Trudeau Liberals, from whom the western provinces became increasingly alienated, emphasis on the Pacific Rim and Japan was a way to express support for the interests of those provinces most closely involved with Pacific relations, just as the emphasis on CIDA activities in francophone Africa or Haiti supported the cultural and economic interests of Québec. The demand for greater entry for Canadian manufactured products to Japan has since become a hallmark of Trudeau's Japan policy, one with special relevance to Ontario and Québec as the Canadian manufacturing provinces and the heartland of Liberal electoral support. There can be no doubt that the federal Liberals care deeply about this objective, despite the lack of effective response or the difficulty inherent in it. When Pépin attended the Canada-Japan Joint Ministerial Committee meeting in Tokyo in 1969 and again in Toronto in 1971, he criticized Japanese barriers to Canadian products. The mission he led to Tokyo in January 1972 pointed out the availability of a vast array of high technology and finished goods such as the STOL aircraft, pollution control equipment, and prefabricated housing. He also induced the five largest Japanese trading companies to send special buying missions to Canada to import goods of this kind. Despite careful consideration by the big Japanese traders of the purchase and importing of those products, there was no significant change in Canadian exports of them, a matter which Canadian cabinet ministers complained about when they visited Japan thereafter.[1]

Japan drastically reduced the quotas and high tariffs protecting its market about that time, and encouraged foreign traders to enter what it proclaimed as an open market. It is possible that these barriers are now considerably lower than those of Canada, as Canadian importers often assert, yet the trade pattern still has not altered. The chief obstacle to change probably lies in Canada itself, as it does in the United States and Europe which have subsequently had the same difficulty in gaining greater entry to the Japanese market which in the past they dominated. The main problem is that their products are too costly in comparison with similar Japanese goods, or else are not adapted to the tastes or needs of Japanese consumers. Nor have the western makers or traders made sufficient marketing efforts to introduce their wares to Japan.

Canadian spokesmen customarily point to the tiny percentage of fully manufactured Canadian exports to Japan, but a more appropriate category would include other finished or fabricated items which together constitute close to twenty or more per cent of the total; it is an oversimplification to imply that more than ninety per cent are virtually raw materials. However, there are Canadian products which are unique, or at least not produced in Japan, such as the water bomber for fighting forest fires or the CANDU nuclear reactor, which have been turned down after careful consideration by the Japanese who wished to produce these items themselves for the sake of technological independence, or in hopes of eventually becoming exporters of such products. The Japanese goal is reasonable, but it perpetuates a pattern in which Japan does not accept from other advanced countries the exchange of many manufactured or high technology items that it expects to export freely to them in the future. Japan certainly differs from the other advanced countries in the relatively lesser degree to which it is willing to accept fully manufactured products.

Another very important motive on the Canadian side, behind the emphasis on the export of high technology goods, is its pride in achieving a unique item like the CANDU reactor, together with the fear that Canada cannot escape its historical role as primarily an exporter of raw or partially processed materials. Perhaps Canadian sensitivity is involved too, which derives from always standing in the shadow of its greater neighbor and from the natural desire to win recognition for its own achievements which are too easily overlooked in these circumstances. Central Canada has developed as the manufacturing centre in an often protected or restricted market, and with its champion, the federal government, has stronger feelings on this score than the outer provinces which often chafe under the historical economic policies. The purchase of the CANDU reactor or STOL aircraft, through government instrumentalities, would be a vote of confidence from Japan which would satisfy much more than just an economic or trading objective. It would be an acknowledgement by an important world power of Canada's achievement as a major developed country, and would reduce some of the domestic strains and uneasy feelings that trouble the Canadian psyche. It would not only reverse the failure of a deeply held foreign policy objective toward Japan, but it would also vindicate some of the policy around which Canada is constituted both economically and politically under the present Liberal government.

It is in broadening and deepening the relationship with Japan that Trudeau's government has seen a certain amount of success. This has been applied to exchanges of officials, businessmen, academics, and scientists, as well as to journalists and broadcasters. Although cabinet ministers no longer attempt to exchange group visits as in the sixties, individual ministers, particularly of external affairs and trade, confer frequently both in Canada and Japan as well as at international meetings in New York, Paris, and Geneva. Perhaps equally important are the now more frequent consultations, both formal and ad hoc, of lesser officials. This parallels a similar initiative with respect to the EEC, and diversifies and balances to some extent the tendency to depend too readily on the United States in economic, diplomatic, and cultural affairs. While it has not changed our relations with Japan to any marked degree, it does help to smooth the relations that we have, and to benefit the individuals and groups that are in direct contact.

The National Research Council of Canada initiated exchange visits of scientists and engineers between our two countries as early as 1960, and many Japanese scientists have worked in Canadian laboratories for a generation. In 1972 the governments of Canada and Japan began consultations in science and technology, with formal meetings every two years. In the June 1980 meeting in Tokyo, new programs in agriculture, transportation, space satellite applications, coal liquefaction, and heavy oil research were set up.

Prime Minister Kakuei Tanaka's visit to North and South America in 1974 was intended to improve relations with Brazil, Mexico, and Canada which are major sources of raw materials for Japanese industry; however, the outward emphasis of his tour was on cultural aspects rather than on primary economic needs. The prime minister dedicated the unfinished Asian Centre at the University of British Columbia and spoke at the Japanese-Canadian Cultural Centre in Toronto. He also gave a million dollars on behalf of his government for visiting Japanese professors to teach in Canada about their country and culture. Not to be outdone, the Canadian government put up a like amount to send Canadian professors to Japan, where their lectures on Canada have been very well received and have stimulated the study of Canadian affairs by Japanese professors and students. A similar grant to the University of British Columbia was made by Prime Minister Ohira on his visit to Vancouver in 1980, just before his untimely death.

When Prime Minister Trudeau visited Tokyo in 1976 to sign the Framework agreement, he set in motion a new Canada-Japan Joint Economic Committee to meet alternately in each country under the terms of the framework, and the two foreign ministers meet to discuss economic problems. On 26 October 1976, the last day of the Trudeau visit, the ambassador, Bruce Rankin, and the Japanese foreign minister, Zentaro Kosaka, signed a cultural agreement for exchanges of students, teachers, researchers, and youth and sporting organizations; these have been carried out on a wider and more regularized fashion ever since.[2] Under it, not only Canadian studies, but art exhibitions and performances by musicians and orchestras have taken place.

It was at the suggestion of Finance Minister Jean Chrétien that the Canada-Japan Business Cooperation Committee (noted in Chapter Five) was set up in 1977. The forty-five Canadian members from a cross-section of Canadian industry have met yearly with a corresponding group of Japanese businessmen. This provides an important regularized forum in the private sector for continued consultation among those who are actively involved in trade and investment between the two countries, and it enables them to plan and offer guidance to the economic relationship in a direct and practical way that often lies beyond the reach of the two governments.[3] A working group on resource processing was set up in 1980 to study further processing of Canadian resources for Japan. Since 1979 Canadian manufacturers have held dozens of exhibitions in Tokyo of Canadian products such as aerospace and ocean industries equipment, sportswear, sports equipment, and electronic components.

To summarize federal government policy aims, the emphasis of the earlier postwar governments was upon: (1) market entry to Japan for Canadian resource products, (2) protection of fishing off Canada, and (3) protection of Canadian manufactured products. Under Prime Minister Trudeau, policy aims included in addition: (4) entrée to Japan for Canadian manufactured and high technology products, (5) increased Japanese investment in joint processing of resources in Canada, (6) transfer of technology in manufacturing, and (7) broadening and deepening the ties with Japan to diversify from excessive dependence on the United States.

The provincial governments have also taken considerable interest themselves in pursuing similar policies, with the emphasis upon sales of the products of greatest importance to their provinces, and encouraging Japanese investment in processing and manufacturing there. Québec, Ontario, and Alberta have established their own permanent offices in Tokyo to facilitate their policy aims, while British Columbia has relied upon frequent visits of top provincial officials, including the premier. Nearly all provinces have sent visiting trade and investment missions to contact government officials and businessmen alike in Japan.

Provincial officials have sought to help medium and small businesses seeking to enter the Japanese market, as well as to encourage Japanese manufacturers to locate in Canada. They have also welcomed the big trading companies and manufacturers who need no introduction to Canada. Like the manufacturing provinces of Québec and Ontario, British Columbia has long sought Japanese manufacturing investment. Under the New Democrats the provincial government planned a copper smelter, and under the Social Credit government it is obtaining an automobile wheel plant. Both private and government corporations in Japan have participated in the development of tar sands and heavy oil in Alberta, as well as taking part in oil and gas drilling in the Beaufort Sea. Eight Japanese steel-makers, one gas company, and a trading company are partners with the British Columbia Resource Investment Corporation in Westar Mining Ltd. (formerly B.C. Coal), which owns mines in the southeastern part of the province; they also supply buyers for coal from the new mines opening up in the northeast. Other provinces have also been active in seeking Japanese manufacturing investment and technology.

FUTURE ECONOMIC PROBLEMS

Future problems and trends might best be considered in terms of the Canadian aims categorized above. Probably the most disappointing for the federal government and central provinces has been the limited progress in long-held hopes of gaining a market for manufactured and high technology goods to Japan. The latter are at present restricted to those that are cost-competitive with similar Japanese products or else unique, as noted above. Despite the Japanese preference to go for their own independent development of the same products, Ottawa has remained optimistic on future sales, even of the CANDU reactor. Of course, in mining and forestry equipment Canada has had some success in connection with its expertise in the resource sector, and any further significant shift in Canada's favor looks rather unlikely.

However, Canada's problem here is part of a broader one affecting the United States and Europe too, which have experienced the same difficulty in obtaining market entry to Japan despite their greater resources of funds, expertise, and worldwide reputation as exporters of the most advanced technology. Therefore, it seems likely that Canada's opportunities in the sales of manufactures will remain rather narrow. The removal of high tariffs and quotas, as we have seen, has not proved to make the Japanese market any more penetrable. Automobiles are now virtually tariff-free, but sales of foreign models are minuscule: in this case inspections as well as safety and pollution standards tend to price those models out of the market.

Some more competitively priced Canadian manufactured exports would eventually penetrate Japan further if expensive sales drives and advertising were instituted. Even Japanese buyers with strong ties to domestic suppliers will respond to favorably priced imports, but need convincing that they can depend on them for future supply and servicing. In the case of a product like Canadian whisky, which enjoys a worldwide reputation, the high tariff protection for domestic industry remains. An easing of restrictions on alcohol imports would be a gesture welcomed by Europe as well as Canada, but even then would probably not make a significant dent in the traditional trade pattern.

The problem of greater entrée for manufactures is likely to remain for an indefinite period as it was at the beginning of the Trudeau era. Any change will have to come from the Japanese side, when there is a major shift in their economic conditions or some special share of the Japanese market is opened up by an important initiative of government or business or both. Combined pressure from Canada, the United States, and Europe has been met by the Japanese assertion that their market is open and it is up to foreign traders to make the effort to develop it—knowing full well that there is no sign of a foreign effort comparable to that of Japanese businessmen in North America or Western Europe. Perhaps if such a concerted onslaught by foreign sales representatives or makers was made in Japan, it might be possible to test the real extent to which Japan is penetrable. There is some evolution within Japan of new supermarkets, reducing the chain of wholesalers and passing lower costs down to the consumer, and some of these stores buy directly from abroad. This process should aid any new foreign sales drive, but it will be a very slow process at best and may take decades.

The Pacific Rim Opportunities Conference in Vancouver in October 1981, sponsored by the federal Department of Industry, Trade, and Commerce, indicated that medium and small businesses might do better elsewhere in East Asia, particularly among the members of the Association of Southeast Asian Nations: Indonesia, Thailand, Malaysia, the Philippines, and Singapore. Attempts are being made on a joint business-government basis to improve government programs for opening up foreign business contacts for medium-sized Canadian firms which may enable them to make a better effort, but they cannot supply the funds needed for a small firm to open an office and undertake an expensive advertising and sales campaign in Japan. The Canada-Japan Business Cooperation Committee is a valuable new body, as is the Canadian Chamber of Commerce in Japan, but they are probably of most use for businessmen in the large companies and the already prosperous resource sector trade. Although some smaller-sized firms have done well in Japan, it is difficult to believe that the new programs now under consideration will greatly change the situation.

The future of our traditionally successful resource-based trade calls for caution even if the poor business conditions of the early 1980s change for the better. The developing countries are beginning to supply some of the same products as Canada, with the most modern technology and much lower wage costs; they will offer stiff competition unless Canada manages to upgrade its own facilities and keep costs down. The attempt by the United States, Japan, and other developed countries to undermine the new Law of the Sea Convention, which was championed by Canada, in order to corner the market for seabed minerals may further reduce the demand for important Canadian raw material exports. This is the area where Canada is most competitive now. It is also where some of Japan's protection is the strongest, particularly in agricultural trade. Canada has a substantial share of the grain trade, but the market for the export of beef is small, and the pork allocation is subject to frequent and arbitrary change as Japan tenaciously protects its uncompetitive farmers who provide a significant part of the ruling Liberal Democrats' voting support.[4] Perhaps this is analogous to the Canadian Liberals' tender feelings for the Québec and Ontario textile industry. Leather is also protected, for the sake of the minority of former outcastes or "burakumin" in Japan, and import of apples is burdened by health and inspection requirements.

The soybean export bans by Canada and the United States in 1973, as well as the American restrictions on grain sales to the Soviet Union in 1979 as a punishment for its Middle East policies, have reminded Japan how vulnerable is its foreign food supply. It has renewed its dedication to raising a substantial proportion of its own food requirements, to guard against starvation in case of interruptions of normal supply. When Canada enjoys such a favorable balance of trade with Japan due to its large exports of resource products, it is almost impossible to persuade Japan to relax quotas on beef and pork in the same general export sector. Most developed countries have similar agricultural protection; Canada has it on lamb, for example. The United States, with greater leverage against Japan, has pried open the beef allocation further and managed some relaxation on citrus fruits. Still, success in these industries for Canada might change the trade pattern only to a very minor extent.

With respect to fishing, it is likely that Canadian offshore waters will increasingly be reserved for Canadian fishermen, the fish in excess of Canadian requirements being exported to Japan and other foreign markets. Nontraditional fish such as pollock, hake, and squid are frequently caught under joint-venture arrangements with Japanese participation, but even these may be curtailed in favor of the Canadian industry.

Protection in the manufacturing sector will probably increase if the adverse economic conditions and unemployment of the early 1980s persist. In the sensitive case of automobiles, there may even be some regular arrangement for limiting the future Japanese market share in Canada, the Unitd States, and the EEC, as began to appear in 1981. There are doubts about the ability of the North American and European auto industries to become cost-competitive with that of Japan, even with the greater use of robots and Japanese-style management and technology. North American makers are also moving an increasing proportion of their production to Japan through joint arrangements. Japanese manufacturers may be compelled to carry on more production singly or jointly in North America, as some European makers are doing. In Australia and Mexico, a high domestic content is mandatory under laws to compel local Japanese production; this may be necessary to retain market entry for the Japanese, but will probably increase their costs and reduce their price differential vis-à-vis local makers. It will also increase the cost of both foreign and domestic cars to local buyers.

Only three Canadian auto-parts manufacturers, Duplate, Tridon, and Champion, have obtained modest parts sales in Japan, but at least seven Ontario auto-parts makers sought joint-venture and licensing agreements with Japanese firms in 1982. Those arrangements could lead to combining Japanese and Canadian technology in supplying the Japanese original equipment and after market in Canada, as well as some parts to the Japanese makers in Japan and eventually worldwide. The proviso was that, if Canadian firms were competitive and guaranteed quality and delivery, it would go through.[5] There is, however, more than a hint that the Canadian makers cannot fulfill the conditions of the proviso. Roy Bennett, formerly an executive of Ford Canada, proposed that any foreign company selling more than twenty-five thousand cars a year in Canada should buy or build a high proportion of the parts in the country, a policy similar to that enforced in Australia and Mexico. Professor Keith Hay of Carleton University suggested that prices should be kept down, for the sake of the Canadian consumer and the competitiveness of Canadian automobiles, by joint production with Japanese makers in Canada utilizing lower-cost Japanese management and production methods. He cautioned against an eighty-five per cent domestic content rule, as in Australia, that greatly increases costs.[6]

Japanese investment in production and processing in the resource industries will increase at least modestly, and perhaps even on a large scale. Nationalist policies in connection with the Foreign Investment Review Agency and the government's New Energy Policy have impinged more sharply on American and European investors, although Japanese businessmen have been greatly concerned about the manner of administration.

Japanese public and private companies have been especially interested in obtaining fuels. They have continued to own a substantial share of Westar Mining, as noted above, with some new investment in coal mines coming on-stream in Alberta. There is a promise of Japanese purchase of coal in the large northeast British Columbia coal development, where most of the investment cost falls on Canadian governmental and private companies. As also noted, Japanese firms have participated in Beaufort Sea oil and gas exploration, as well as in methods for extracting oil from tar sands and heavy oil deposits. Their disappointment there has been partially assuaged by the commencement of small shipments of oil to Japan by Dome Petroleum, of about 40,000 barrels a day of the 200,000 barrels per day surplus locked up in Alberta fields in 1983.

The amount of investment in petroleum will continue to be modest while there is little likelihood of substantially sharing the fuel in the near future. As long as the federal energy and tax policies aim at relatively narrow nationalist goals, or at maximizing revenues in conflict with the provinces, national self-sufficiency as well as export potential in oil is postponed or reduced. In gas, where there is a surplus, there is great export potential in the two-billion-dollar Dome-Nissho-Iwai LNG project. When that scheme goes through, there will be considerable change in Japan's share of our export trade, which will rise significantly for the very first time.[7]

The proposals for further investment and joint processing apply particularly to aluminum production, which has been cut back drastically in Japan due to the high cost of oil, and hence electricity, used in producing the metal. Moreover, the planned automobile plant to produce aluminum wheels in British Columbia will at least begin to upgrade the manufacture of components, as it becomes necessary for Japan to shift some of its auto production offshore to retain entry to the Canadian market. Volkswagen has already agreed to do this when it builds a new plant in Ontario.

Transfer of technology would also increase with any joint investment, especially in manufacturing but also in processing. The participation of the ten Japanese companies in what is now Westar Mining Ltd. involved their introduction of Russian hydraulic methods of mining in the open pit Sparwood coal mine. Similarly, increased management and technology transfer would probably accompany any joint production of autos and auto parts. However, upgraded production methods will probably not be sufficient to make the product competitive if labor costs are too high, as in the case of Bruck Mills which could not compensate for higher Canadian costs in textiles. Next to Japan, there may be Korean auto competition with even lower wages, and Korean steel is already underselling Japanese steel in Japan.

On 9 March 1983 Prime Minister Trudeau announced that the federal government would match provincial government and private sector funds for a Canada Asia Pacific Foundation to make Canada's involvement in Pacific affairs more effective and beneficial. The founding committee consists of executives, academics, labor representatives and others, chaired by John Bruk, a Vancouver businessman. In Canada as a whole there has been a strong interest among small- and medium-sized firms in export opportunities in the Asian Pacific region, as a result of the serious recession of 1981–1983, curtailing demand in their more traditional markets.[8] If successful, the foundation will spearhead the new interest in Canada not only to do more trade in the region but greatly to increase political and cultural contacts.

The new Canadian foundation comes at a time of rising interest in the Pacific region for some kind of greater regional integration. The initiative has been taken there by the Japanese and Australian prime ministers, who called a Pacific Community Seminar at the Australian National University, 15 to 18 September 1980, attended by academics, businessmen, and government officials in a private capacity from Canada, Japan, Australia, South Korea, Indonesia, Malaysia, New Zealand, the Philippines, Singapore, Thailand, the South Pacific (Papua-New Guinea, Tonga, the South Pacific Bureau), and the United States.[9] A similar group of sixty participants from the same three sectors of the twelve was convened in Bangkok, sponsored by the Thai government, 3 to 5 June 1982. A Pacific Economic Cooperation (PEC) Committee was set up to prepare for the conference to be held in Indonesia in 1983 and South Korea in 1984. Four task forces on trade in manufactures, agricultural products, minerals, and investment and technology transfer will report at the next consultative meeting.[10]

A Canadian-Pacific Cooperation Committee to coordinate with the regional group has been formed with fifteen Canadians from the same three sectors (business, academia, and government) under the chairmanship of Eric Trigg, the vice-chairman of Alcan Aluminum and a member of the Canberra and Bangkok groups. The similar interest in both Canada and the Asian Pacific region is a response to the acute downturn in world trade after nearly thirty years of continuous expansion. It is not confined to economic affairs, but includes concern for the social and political changes now going on which may be of considerable magnitude. Canada and the other market economies wish to be an integral part of any regional solutions to common problems. Japan is probably the most dynamic source of change in the region.

With respect to Japan, while any efforts at greater "people-to-people" contacts beyond trade and business are highly desirable and worthwhile in themselves, they will probably not lead to more than a moderate change in our relationship. On the other hand, greater public consciousness of Japan's achievements in the economic sphere, particularly as a consequence of the turmoil in the automobile industry, may result in greater cultural as well as economic influence from Japan. Both newspapers and television in Canada now include Japan in their definition of what is newsworthy.

The hope of lessening dependence on the United States under the so-called "third option" policy has still not been realized, even ten years after the idea was first given impetus by Mitchell Sharp and Pierre Trudeau. If there were a change in Canada's energy policies to encourage greater production and export of natural gas, at least, the trade increase might boost

Japan to the position of a major trading partner, as Britain had been before the Second World War even though the lion's share of the trade remained with the United States.

If more extensive exchanges of all sorts with Japan could produce a more independent, productive, and influential Canada, they would be eminently worthwhile. They would also produce their own problems. The federal government's dissatisfaction over its relations with Japan is due chiefly to the failure to obtain greater economic benefits from the new economic giant. That applies especially to the desire for greater employment and production in the central provinces of Ontario and Québec, which are not only the main population and manufacturing provinces but also the basis of the Liberal government's chief support which has shrunk in the western provinces.

As for Japan, it is not dependent upon Canada to the degree that it is on Australia for foods, fuels, and minerals, nor does it depend on either Canada or Australia to the extent it does upon the United States. It relies on the United States for some important raw materials, but is even more dependent on it for an enormous and rich consumer market as well as for military protection against Soviet or Chinese pressure and the security of its commerce in the world's oceans. Even toward the United States, Japan has not been willing to modify its trade pattern significantly after ten years of American pressure to do so. This situation may change if the current depression, unemployment, and inflation bring to a head the sort of Congressional protectionism that has been festering so long.

It is therefore not surprising that Ottawa has been somewhat less than successful in obtaining an entrée that even the United States has been denied in Japan. Canada lacks the leverage of being either an essential trading partner or a superpower to force greater concessions from Japan. Still, it remains a major partner, and pending some resolution of the trade issues with the United States and the EEC, it could well enter into more joint production in Canada which is an important automobile market for Japan. If some sort of trilateral or quadrilateral auto pact were tried, this might be a time when it would succeed and bring closer integration with Japan, but at higher costs.

COOPERATION AND CONFLICT

As our coverage of Canada's economic relations with Japan has indicated, they can be characterized as generally cooperative. Looking over the past, current, and future phases of those ties, there have also been conflicts of interest, or at least times when Canada has not been satisfied with them. The chief problems or issues were probably the immigration conflict culminating in the Lemieux agreement in 1907, the trade war of 1935, the China and Pacific Wars, and finally Canada's protection of its fisheries, textile production, and auto production since those wars. One other difficulty which Canada has in common with the United States and the EEC is greater market entry to Japan for manufactured products, a matter on which the Liberal government has pressed Japan for over a decade.

Compared to the prewar conflicts, those since the Pacific War have been mild and confined mainly to trade. Thus it seems proper to describe our relations as good, despite some disappointment that Japan's economic expansion and affluence has not been turned to greater Canadian advantage in the manufactured and processed goods trade.

The foregoing account has principally treated Canadian policies and activities with respect to Japan. Nevertheless, the Japanese side has not been neglected, since on some issues, such as the sale of the CANDU reactor, the Japanese political forces involved have been examined to get a better understanding of how Canada has been viewed by its partner. In addition, the official and unofficial missions which have gone between the two countries have left some enlightening comments that have been recounted in this story of our relations. This is, then, an account of intentions, policies, and activities interwoven to suggest the paths our two countries have taken together, and where they seem to be heading. Without belittling the desires of either country toward the other, the present course of the relationship is generally favorable to both.

There is considerable potential for conflict over the problem of automobiles, but also room for accommodation. As the matter is a concern of other countries besides Canada and Japan, its solution will inevitably be influenced by the resolution of the problem with the United States and the EEC, although this does not prevent some bilateral arrangement such as that already suggested. It is tied up with the whole problem of protectionism among the developed countries and the world trading system under GATT. Equally important for Japan is how it resolves the problem of greater entrée to its market. Like Canada, the United States and the European Common Market are demanding a greater degree of balance in the horizontal aspects of trade, in which Japan would buy much more in the way of manufactured goods from its chief partners when it depends on them for its export markets. This will put on Japan a strain probably as great as that required for its remarkable adaptation to the successive oil price increases of the past decade.

It is optimistic in the extreme to expect Japan's developed partners to achieve suddenly or even slowly more productive economies that could equal that of Japan. Under present conditions they even appear to be sinking ever deeper into the quagmire of uncompetitive production. The future is full of possibilities for trouble. Japan could yield to pressure to limit its share of foreign markets, or to participate in joint production there under less favorable conditions. It might also react in a negative way, and isolate itself in Asia with bad economic consequences for all concerned. If the international financial mechanism breaks down, there might even have to be some resort to barter trade.

Given the existence of the present GATT system and the successful global trading regime since the Second World War, as well as Japan's remarkable prosperity under it even at the present time, it seems more likely that Japan and its developed partners will come to some arrangement which will ease any buildup of great strain. If the developed countries, including Japan, can do this, they would create a better basis for some solution to more effective accommodation with the desires of the developing countries, which need to be given entry to the world trade of the developed countries under more favorable conditions.

To end on such an optimistic note, it is necessary for Japan to turn its remarkable adaptability and diligence to this accommodation with its trading partners, whereby both sides can salvage something perhaps better than exists at present. Canada's role could be similar to that which it has played before, not as a superpower, but as an important member of the leading world traders. It took that part at the beginning of Trudeau's premiership, when it helped to break the logjam over recognizing the Chinese People's Republic. It is probably not feasible for Canada to achieve its ambitions regarding entry to the Japanese market without much more individual effort by Canadians in Japan. Other ambitions with respect to attracting Japanese investment and technology are up to Canada itself.

The chief obstacles are twofold. One is the conflict within Canada between the federal and provincial governments. This has been exacerbated by the federal government's attempt to shift the balance of political power with the provinces more toward the centre, especially in the quarrel over the spoils of tax revenues from the oil and gas industry in the western provinces.

The second obstacle is the nationalist economic policies under the Foreign Investment Review Agency and the attempt to Canadianize the petroleum industry under the New Energy Policy, which attracted such unfavorable attention of the Reagan administration in 1981. While these policies had the commendable aims of ensuring greater economic benefits and national independence in Canadian development, they were introduced or amplified at an unfortunate time or in ways that have frightened off foreign investors. As far as the idea of careful screening of foreign investment is concerned, or ensuring that nationally owned firms dominate the chief industries, these are policies that Japan has followed for nearly a century and are not uncommon in other developed countries. When Canada needs foreign investment to increase its own domestic energy supplies and to weather adverse economic conditions, it may not be the best time to antagonize both the foreign and Canadian business community and provincial governments. If these obstacles are reduced, Japanese investors will be more eager to participate along the lines which the Liberal government has been urging in recent years.

Of all the conditions that inhibit the realization of Canadian desires toward Japan, it is the domestic ones that we can do the most about, and which will probably give us more influence or increase our attractiveness to Japan as a trading or investment partner. Let us hope that the patriation of the constitution and the reduction of federal-provincial tensions over developments in the petroleum industry will provide a better climate for the solution of problems in the areas of trade and the domestic economy.

Notes

PREFACE

1. Ken Adachi, *The Enemy That Never Was: A History of the Japanese Canadians* (Toronto: McClelland and Stewart, 1976). Barry Broadfoot, *Years of Sorrow, Years of Shame: The Story of the Japanese Canadians in World War II* (Toronto: Doubleday Canada, 1977). W. Peter Ward, *White Canada Forever: Popular Attitudes and Public Policy Toward Orientals in British Columbia* (Montreal: McGill-Queen's University Press, 1978). Rintaro Hayashi, *Kuroshio no Hate ni* [On the Shore by the Japan Current] (Tokyo: Nichieki Shuppan Sha, 1973, privately printed). Yuko Shibata, Shoji Matsumoto, Rintaro Hayashi, and Shotaro Iida, *The Forgotten History of the Japanese Canadians* (Vancouver: New Sun Books, 1977). Roy Ito, *The Japanese Canadians* (Toronto: Van Nostrand Reinhold, 1978), Multicultural Canada series.
2. Zavis Zeman, *Men with the Yen* (Montreal: Institute for Research on Public Policy, 1980), Occasional Paper no. 15. Keith Spicer, "The Samurai Are Coming," *Vancouver Sun*, 30 July 1980, p. 5. Toronto *Globe and Mail*, "Japan Aims to Dominate Canadian Economy, Study Warns," 24 July 1980, p. 1. Zavis Zeman, "The Men with Yen Aren't Conspirators," *Vancouver Sun*, 7 Aug. 1980, p. A 5.

3. *Kokusai Mondai*, "Shoten: Kanada Gendai to Kadai" [Focus: Canada Present Conditions and Problems], no. 203, Feb. 1977. *Kanada Kenkyu Nempo/The Annual Review of Canadian Studies*, "Ni-Ka Gakujutsu Kaigi Tokushū/Proceedings of Japan-Canada Conference 1979," no. 2, 1980. Keidanren [Federation of Economic Organizations], *Ni-Ka Keizai Kankei no Shomondai* [Problems of Japan-Canada Relations] (Tokyo: 1974), pamphlet no. 119.
4. Keith A. J. Hay, ed., *Canadian Perspectives on Economic Relations with Japan* (Montreal: Institute for Research on Public Policy, 1980). Keith A. J. Hay and S. R. Hill, *Canada-Japan Trade and Investment* (Ottawa: Canada-Japan Trade Council, 1979). Keith A. J. Hay and Peter Price, *Canada, Japan and the Pacific Community* (Ottawa: Canada-Japan Trade Council, Econolynx International, 1981).
5. Gérard Hervouet, *Le Canada face à l'Asie de l'est* (Ville Saint-Laurent: Éditions Nouvelle Optique, 1981), pp. 43–74.

CHAPTER 1

1. Charles J. Woodsworth, *Canada and the Orient* (Toronto: Macmillan Co. of Canada, 1941), p. 237. The author reports that

fully manufactured products made up 24.5 per cent of Canada's exports to Japan in 1935. Those included automobiles, automobile parts, electrical machinery and apparatus and films—all nowadays going from Japan to Canada.

2. Japan Trade Centre, *100 Years of Trade and Commerce between Canada and Japan* (Toronto: [1977]), p. 6.

3. Ibid., p. 3.

4. Jinshiro Nakayama, *Kanada Dōhō Hatten Taikan* [Complete Handbook of the Progress of Japanese in Canada], 3rd ed. (Tokyo: 1929; privately printed, copies in University of British Columbia Library), p. 13.

5. Woodsworth, *Canada and the Orient*, p. 213.

6. Japan Trade Centre, *100 Years of Trade*, p. 3.

7. Kazushi Ohkawa and Henry Rosovsky, *Japanese Economic Growth* (Stanford: Stanford University Press, 1973), p. 15.

8. Robert J. Gowen, "Canada and the Myth of the Japanese Market, 1896–1911," *Pacific Historical Review* 39, no. 1 (Feb. 1970), pp. 67–68.

9. Woodsworth, *Canada and the Orient*, pp. 217–18. Gowen, "Japanese Market," pp. 67–69, 75.

10. Gowen, "Japanese Market," p. 68. Woodsworth, *Canada and the Orient*, p. 68.

11. Gowen, "Japanese Market," p. 73.

12. W. Peter Ward, *White Canada Forever*, pp. 53–76. Woodsworth, *Canada and the Orient*, p. 76 ff.

13. Gowen, "Japanese Market," p. 76.

14. Woodsworth, *Canada and the Orient*, p. 80. Gowen, "Japanese Market," p. 78. William T. R. Preston, *My Generation of Politics and Politicians* (Toronto: D. A. Rose Publishing Co., 1927), pp. 272–87.

15. Preston, *My Generation*, ibid.

16. Ibid. Gowen, "Japanese Market," p. 80 and fn. 78.

17. Gowen, "Japanese Market," p. 79.

18. Woodsworth, *Canada and the Orient*, p. 219.

19. See table 1–1.

20. Woodsworth, *Canada and the Orient*, p. 224.

21. Michael W. Donnelly, Victor C. Falkenheim, *Canada and the Pacific Community*, Joint Centre on Modern East Asia, University of Toronto–York University, Working Paper series 4 (Toronto: [1981]).

22. Woodsworth, *Canada and the Orient*, p. 232.

23. Japan Trade Centre, *100 Years of Trade*, p. 8.

24. Kenneth W. Taylor, "The Canadian-Japanese Tariff War," *Pacific Affairs* 8, no. 1 (Dec. 1935), pp. 475–77. Woodsworth, *Canada and the Orient*, pp. 242–46. Government of Japan, "Imperial Ordinance No. 208, 1935," *Contemporary Japan* 4, no. 2 (Sept. 1935), pp. 315–17. Government of Japan, "Statement of the Spokesman of the Foreign Office Regarding the Above, July 20, 1935," *Contemporary Japan* 4 no. 2 (Sept. 1935), pp. 317–20.

25. Miriam S. Farley, "Japan Considering Retaliation Against Canada," *Far Eastern Survey* 4, no. 12 (19 June 1935), pp. 93–94. *The Oriental Economist*, "Flour Mills and Canadian Wheat," Aug. 1935, p. 19.

26. Miriam S. Farley, "Trends in Japan's Lumber and Wood Pulp Trade," *Far Eastern Survey* 4, no. 20 (9 Oct. 1935), p. 142.

27. Taylor, "Tariff War," p. 476. Woodsworth, *Canada and the Orient*, p. 245, fn. 45.

28. Michael Fry, "The Development of Canada's Relations with Japan, 1919–1947," *Canadian Perspectives on Economic Relations with Japan*, ed. Keith J. Hay (Montreal: Institute for Research on Public Policy, 1980), pp. 33–34.

29. Fry, "Relations with Japan," pp. 35–36.

30. Ibid., p. 38.

31. Ibid., p. 40.

CHAPTER 2

1. Canada, House of Commons, *Debates*, 1953–1954, pp. 4656–57, 4666.

2. Treaty of Peace with Japan, Article 12, sections (a) and (b).

3. Interview.

4. Ibid.

5. General Agreement on Tariffs and Trade (GATT), *Basic Instruments and Selected Documents*, vol. 3, Text of the General Agreement, 1958 (Geneva: Nov. 1958), Article 19, section 1(a), p. 41.

6. *New York Times*, "Dumping Protection on Ourselves," 29 Dec. 1979, p. 20.

7. Interview.
8. Asahi Shimbun Sha, *Asahi Nenkan*, 1954 (Tokyo: 1953), p. 150.
9. Asahi Shimbun Sha, *Asahi Nenkan*, 1955 (Tokyo: 1955), p. 244.
10. Interview.
11. *Nihon Keizai Shimbun*, "Gatto Kakanyu, Gyokai wa Kokan, Boeki Fushin Menkai no Koki" [Business Happy over Temporary Accession to GATT, Opportunity to Turn Back Trade Depression], 25 Oct. 1953, p. 2.
12. Exchange of Notes 5 and 6, Ottawa, 31 March 1954; Canada, Treaties, *Treaty Series*, 1954, no. 3, "Agreement on Commerce Between Canada and Japan," pp. 12–15. *Nihon Keizai Shimbun*, "Nikka Tsusho Kyotei Choin Sogo ni Saikekoku Taigu" [Canada-Japan Commercial Agreement Signed, Mutual Most-Favored Nation Treatment], 1 April 1954, p. 2. Toronto *Globe and Mail*, "Slash Tariffs Under Pact with Japan," 24 Oct. 1953, pp. 1, 2.
13. Interview.
14. Canada, Treaties, "Agreement on Commerce . . . ," Article 1, p. 2.
15. Canada, Dept. of External Affairs, press release, 31 March 1954. Canada, Treaties, "Agreement on Commerce . . . ," Notes 2 and 3, pp. 8–11.
16. Canada, House of Commons, *Debates*, 1953–1954, vol. 5, 12 May 1954, pp. 4647–71.
17. *Financial Post*, "New Pact with Japan Protects our Market, Major Exports to be Free from Discrimination at All Times—Japanese Imports Subject to Special Valuation to Stop Unfair Competition," 3 April 1954, pp. 1–2. *Financial Post*, "The Japanese Trade Dilemma," 10 April 1954, p. 6. Toronto *Globe and Mail*, "Our Late Awakening," 2 April 1954, p. 6.
18. *Nihon Keizai Shimbun*, "Nihonhin e no Kazeiken Horyu, Nikka Kyotei, Kagyokai Kokan" [Tariff Control over Japanese Products Retained, Japan-Canada Agreement, Canadian Business Favorable], 3 April 1954, p. 2. *Nihon Keizai Shimbun*, "Seni Sangyo wa Hinan" [Textile Producers Criticize], 3 April 1954.
19. Canada, House of Commons, *Debates*, 1953–1954, vol. 5, pp. 4647–71; the debate of the resolution.
20. GATT, Article 35, section 1, paragraphs (a) and (b), 1958, pp. 58–59: text.
21. Interview.
22. Interview.
23. Interview.

CHAPTER 3

1. Aaron J. Sarna, "Safeguards Against Market Disruption—The Canadian View," *Journal of World Trade Law* 10, no. 4 (July–Aug. 1976), p. 357.
2. David B. Yoffie and Robert O. Keohane, "Responding to the 'New Protectionism': Strategies for the Advanced Developing Countries in the Pacific Basin," paper prepared for Eleventh Pacific Trade and Development Conference (Canberra: Sept. 1980), p. 4.
3. Canada, Textile and Clothing Board, *Clothing Inquiry: A Report to the Minister of Industry, Trade & Commerce* (Ottawa: 29 May 1977), p. 2–2. Leslie Wilson, "Japan Talks Drag, Fear Quota Boost," *Financial Post*, 30 April 1960, p. 35.
4. *Financial Post*, "Japan Clamps Quotas on Exports to Canada," 25 July 1959, p. 13.
5. Canada, Consultative Task Force on Textiles and Clothing, *Report to the Minister of Industry, Trade & Commerce* (Montreal: 22 June 1978), table, p. 53.
6. *Financial Post*, "We're on the GATT Spot: Ask Japan for New Quotas," 21 Nov. 1959, p. 23.
7. William F. Bull, "Greater Total Trade," *Financial Post*, 27 Aug. 1960, p. J 4. Sarna, "Safeguards," p. 38.
8. Toru Hagiwara (Japanese ambassador), "We Seek Better Balance of our Mutual Trade," *Financial Post*, 27 Aug. 1960, p. J 4. Mitsujiro Ishii (Japanese minister of trade), "Mutual Understanding Basis of Sound Trade," *Financial Post*, 27 Aug. 1960, p. J 4.
9. *Daily Colonist*, "Canada to Open Door to Japanese Industry," 27 June 1961, p. 1.
10. *Vancouver Sun*, "Japan 'Flooding' Canadian Market, Fleming Threatens Action to Protect Domestic Trade," 12 Jan. 1961, p. 1.
11. Chris Young, "Japan Clamps Tight Curb on Its Exports to Canada, Textiles, Transistors, Wide Range of Goods Covered by Agreement," *Vancouver Sun*, 20 May 1961, p. 1.
12. *Financial Post*, "Trade Quotas May Linger," 18 Aug. 1962, p. 50.

13. *Financial Post*, "Japan Looks for Quality Sales in Canadian Textile Markets," 18 Aug. 1962, p. J 40.

14. *Financial Post*, "How Asahi Views Surcharges," 18 Aug. 1962, p. 50.

15. *Financial Post*, "It's Hard Horse-Trading Over Quotas, Despite Restriction Penetration Here Rising," 17 Aug. 1963, p. 51, text and table.

16. *Financial Post*, "What Raised Quotas on Japanese Goods Mean," 5 Sept. 1964, p. 27.

17. Alan Fotheringham, "'Cheap Labor' No Excuse, Japanese Envoy Protests Canadian Trade Barriers," *Vancouver Sun*, 15 May 1964, p. 29.

18. *Vancouver Sun*, "Japan-B.C. Trade Crisis Predicted, Loffmark Says Japanese Worried About Canada's Dumping Laws," 25 Sept. 1964, p. 29.

19. *Financial Post*, "Battle of Exports Getting Rough, Tough," 14 Aug. 1965, p. 41.

20. Keith A. J. Hay, "Canada's Economic Ties with Japan," *Foremost Nation, Canadian Foreign Policy and a Changing World*, ed. Norman Hillmer and Garth Stevenson (Toronto: McClelland and Stewart, 1977), pp. 275–77.

21. *Financial Post*, "Weavers, Spinners Fight Slump with Higher Quality Products," 14 Aug. 1965, p. 41.

22. *Financial Post*, "Japan Pulls Silk Curtain on Export-Quota Parley, No Reply from Tokyo Since Canada sent Its Counter-Proposal. Both Countries Appear to be Digging In," 4 June 1966, p. 21.

23. Clive Baxter, "Can Row Be Avoided? Ottawa Asks Japan to Slow Exports," *Financial Post*, 9 Sept. 1967, pp. 1, 2.

24. Canada, House of Commons, *Debates*, 24 Oct. 1967, pp. 3418–19. Letter and annex with the quotas printed in *Votes and Proceedings* after item 64.

25. Sarna, "Safeguards," p. 367.

26. Patrick Durrant, "B.C. Gets Short Shrift in Free Trade Plea," 27 April 1978, p. 23. *Vancouver Sun*, "Gov't Removes Duty, Steel Importers Delighted," 4 July 1978, p. B 8.

27. Rodney de C. Grey, *The Development of the Canadian Anti-Dumping System* (Montreal: Private Planning Association of Canada, The Canadian Economic Policy Committee, 1973).

28. I. M. Destler, Haruhiro Fukui, and Hideo Sato, *The Textile Wrangle, Conflict in Japanese-American Relations 1969–1971* (Ithaca and London: Cornell University Press, 1979).

29. Canada, House of Commons, *Debates*, 21 Nov. 1968, p. 3004.

30. Canada, House of Commons, *Appendix to Votes and Proceedings*, 1968, letter and annex respecting Japanese quotas, after no. 48, p. 380.

31. Sarna, "Safeguards," pp. 367–68. Caroline Pestieau, *The Canadian Textile Policy: A Sectoral Trade Adjustment Strategy?* (Montreal: C. D. Howe Research Institute, Canadian Economic Policy Committee, 1976), chap. 6. David R. Protheroe, *Imports and Politics* (Montreal: Institute for Research on Public Policy, 1980), pp. 59–63.

32. Pestieau, *Canadian Textile Policy*, pp. 30–31.

33. *Financial Post*, "Textiles Bring Out Fierce Talk from Trade Experts," 23 Aug. 1969, p. J 10.

34. Hyman Solomon, "Guard Up Against Influx of Diverted Japanese Textiles," *Financial Post*, 8 Sept. 1971, p. 9.

35. Hyman Solomon, "More 'Voluntary' Curbs for Japanese Textiles?" *Financial Post*, 22 May 1971, p. 1.

36. John Rolfe, "Japan Extends Curbs of Exports to Canada," Toronto *Globe and Mail*, 6 Oct. 1971, p. B 6. Harvey Shepherd, "Textile Group Wants Import Cuts," Toronto *Globe and Mail*, 6 Oct. 1971, p. B 6. Canada, Dept. of External Affairs, Information Division, *Statements and Speeches*, no. 72/4, "The State of Canada's Trade with Japan," address by Jean-Luc Pépin to Japanese Press Club, Tokyo, 1 Jan. 1972.

37. Aaron J. Sarna, "GATT Agreement Provides Hope for Textiles," *Canada Commerce*, June 1974, p. 10.

38. Destler, Fukui, and Sato, *The Textile Wrangle*, pp. 189–91.

39. Interview.

40. Sarna, "Safeguards," p. 360.

41. Albert Sigurdson, "Ottawa Reviewing Textile Policy Established in '70," Toronto *Globe and Mail*, 21 Nov. 1975, p. B 4.

42. Canada, Consultative Task Force on Textiles and Clothing, *Report to the Minister*, p. 52.

43. The Wabasso Ltd. program: Canada, Senate, Standing Committee on Banking, Trade and Commerce, *Proceedings*, 1st session, 30th Parliament, issue 76, p. 21.
44. Sarna, "Safeguards," pp. 366–67.
45. *Canada Commerce*, "Restraint Measures," July 1978, p. 13.
46. See testimony of President T. Yamaguchi: Senate, Standing Committee on Banking, *Proceedings*, issue 75, 11 Feb. 1976, p. 19.
47. Protheroe, *Imports and Politics*, p. 119.
48. Ibid., p. 121.
49. Ibid., p. 124.
50. Canada, Privy Council, Federal-Provincial Relations Office, *The Textile Industry—A Canadian Challenge*, 1978, pp. 53–59.
51. Peter Cook, "A Quota Is Imposed, A Pact Is Shattered," *Financial Times*, 10 Jan. 1977, p. 7.
52. Canada, Textile and Clothing Board, *Clothing Inquiry*.
53. Toronto *Globe and Mail*, "Global Clothing Quotas Extended," 24 Dec. 1977, p. B 3.
54. *Financial Post, Special Report: Japan, Land of the Rising Sun*, "Overcapacity and Rising Labor Costs Wear Down Textile Producers," 23 Sept. 1978, p. 3.
55. *Financial Post, Special Report*, 23 Sept. 1978, p. 3.
56. Caroline Pestieau, *The Quebec Textile Industry in Canada* (Montreal: C. D. Howe Research Institute, 1978). Barbara Keddy, "Howe Research Study Asks Re-Examination of Textiles Policies," Toronto *Globe and Mail*, 11 July 1978, p. B 6.
57. *Canada Commerce*, "Restraint Measures," July 1978, p. 13.
58. Alan D. Gray, "Clothing Makers Face New Threat, Although Shrinking Dollar Has Improved Sales, Higher Cost of Materials Will Outweigh Gains," *Financial Times of Canada*, 9 Oct. 1978, p. 27.
59. Interview.
60. Interview.
61. Toronto *Globe and Mail*, "Pact with Japan Approved to Limit Textile Exports," 18 Oct. 1978, p. B 7.
62. Interview.
63. Keith A. J. Hay and S. R. Hill, *Canada-Japan: The Export-Import Picture 1979* (Ottawa: Canada-Japan Trade Council, 1980), tables 5 and 6.
64. R. A. Matthews and A. R. Moroz, "The Impact of Imports from Japan on Canadian Manufacturing, Part 2: A Case Study: Competition for Manufacturers of Television Sets," paper for the conference on Canadian Perspectives on Economic Relations with Japan, 9–11 May 1979, Joint Centre on Modern East Asia, University of Toronto–York University, and Institute for Research on Public Policy, Montreal.
65. Hay and Hill, *Export-Import Picture*, section on Canadian imports of television sets from Japan.
66. Matthews and Moroz, "The Impact of Imports," pt. 2, table 2.
67. *Financial Post*, "Industry Expects 33% Gain over 1967 in Color TV Sets," 15 June 1968, p. 27.
68. *Vancouver Province*, "Brakes Put on Import of Japanese TV Sets," 28 Aug. 1968, p. 13.
69. Matthews and Moroz, "The Impact of Imports," pt. 2, p. 10.
70. Ibid., pt. 1, p. 18.
71. Ibid., pt. 1, p. 14.
72. Canada, Dept. of Industry, Trade & Commerce, "Government Five Year Plan to Aid Television Manufacturers," news release 24/79, 23 March 1979.
73. Source: Transportation Industries Branch, Motor Vehicles Division of Dept. of Industry, Trade & Commerce in Ottawa, given in Matthews and Moroz, "The Impact of Imports," pt. 1, table 8.
74. Hay and Hill, *Export-Import Picture*, chart 24.
75. *Vancouver Sun*, "Japan, Canada Discuss Possible Auto Export Cuts," 16 April 1981, p. G 3.
76. *Vancouver Province*, "Car 'Dumping' Charged," Midweek Report, 13 Aug. 1980, p. D 7.
77. Toronto *Globe and Mail*, "Gray to Warn Japan of Mounting Concern over Imports," 25 July 1980, p. 11. *Japan Times Weekly*, "Canada Industry Minister Asks Car Firms to Invest," 9 Aug. 1980, p. 8.
78. *Japan Times Weekly*, "Canada Encouraged After Auto Trade Tour," 4 Oct. 1980, p. 4.
79. *Japan Times*, "Toyota Plans to Set Up Parts Plant in Canada," 10 May 1981, p. 5.
80. Hyman Solomon and Patricia Best, "Car Import Talks Blow a Gasket," *Financial Times*, 18 April 1981, pp. 1–2.
81. *Vancouver Sun*, "Japan, Canada Discuss Possible Auto Export Cuts," 16 April

Introduction: One Minute to Midnight

Had you told me 10 years ago that I would become a financial author and one of the leading voices in the world on the subject of gold and the global economy, I would have said you were absolutely crazy. Ten years ago, my life looked entirely different than it does today. Back then, my life was consumed with pursuits in the entertainment industry. I had spent the first 20 years after college making my way up the ranks in Hollywood—from "actor," to "writer," to "director," and eventually to "producer." I am a storyteller at heart. It is what I am most passionate about.

But seven years ago I came across a story that caused me to leave the entertainment business altogether. The more I learned about this story, the more I realized it was a story that very few people knew, that no one else was telling, and everyone needed to hear. It's one I have become so passionate about that I have made it my life's mission to share it with as many people around the world as I can. Candidly, I was initially unsure that I was the right person to share this story, but have since come to view it as my obligation to share the enlightenment I have obtained with as many people around the world as I know need it. I have written books and newsletters, produced award-winning videos, helmed multiple documentaries and webinars, and even created animations and children's stories. I have given talks around the world, and my presentations have been subscribed to by tens of thousands of people.

So what is this story I've been telling? Told in its simplest form, it is the title of my first book, *Gold Is A Better Way—and Other Secrets Wall Street Doesn't Want You to Know*. The purpose of that book was to challenge the way people viewed investing. It explains how the Wall Street model is broken and why gold is among the most misunderstood assets in the world. It became a national bestseller.

I believe *Gold Is A Better Way* resonated for a few main reasons, the first of which is that I am not an insider writing about markets in a boring way, but rather, looking at and telling the story from a fresh perspective. The second is that I was right. *Gold Is A Better Way* was published on August 14, 2018. Since that time, the price of gold has risen from $1192 to $1498 today, an increase of 25 percent. The Dow Jones in the same span is down 25 percent. This spread is just the beginning and will widen significantly in the coming decade. I predict that gold will outperform equities *eight* to *one* over the next decade. It's why I have put every investment dollar I have into physical gold.

What makes me so sure? I believe that mankind is on the verge of making the same mistakes we did 90 years ago. Mark Twain famously said, "History may not repeat itself, but it sure does rhyme." The Great Depression that happened in the 1930s must have seemed impossible to comprehend to those in the peak of the roaring 1920s. But what happened then is an excellent roadmap for what's coming next. The order will come similarly; first we will have a stock market collapse, followed by recession, followed by global depression, all of which will end in a monetary reset. This book is about how that will transpire and why mankind will continue to keep making the same mistakes in the future. *The Great Devaluation* was chosen as a title for this very reason, to remind people, and to forewarn the risks.

You should know from the outset that this book is unlike any other you will find on investing, gold, and the global economy. It is intentionally designed that way. I am a storyteller. That is my unique talent. My goal is to tell you this story in ways that will make sense, that will allow you a real understanding and to do so in a compelling way. This way you will receive the maximum benefit and can take actions that will improve your wealth. I will try not to use the complicated language found in most books of this kind. Rather, I will use pictures and imagery, children's stories, and easy-to-understand analogies, all in an effort to simplify the story. I will provide a new lens from which to view the world that will finally allow you to see things clearly.

I believe this story will amaze you, and once you hear it you'll be even more amazed that you've never heard it before. It features heroes and villains and danger and risk. It's the story of power, who controls it, and the tremendous efforts being made to keep it. Like every great story, this one has a beginning, a middle, and an end. While everyone is impacted by this story, very few people are aware that it's even taking place. That's why it's a story I am compelled to tell.

This is the story of the world economy, the US dollar, the Federal Reserve, and their arch-nemesis, gold.

From the beginning, the story was *designed* to be confusing. The Federal Reserve was created by powerful men who invented new words and ideas that regular people couldn't understand. In fact, the more confusing the terms were, the less questions that were asked. Over time, as the story has unfolded the terms have become more and more confusing, the rules ever changing, and the citizens more confused than ever.

Why the importance for complexity? Because the stakes were too high and the reality was too obvious. The Federal Reserve is an institution that was initially designed to enrich a few wealthy bankers and titans of industry. These were the Rockefellers, the Vanderbilts, the Carnegies, and the Morgans. It was imperative that their true motives for the institution forever remain a secret. In order for the scheme to work, it had to *appear* that it was created for the benefit of the people. So long as these men could keep their true motives private, they could amass tremendous wealth and power, more than the greatest monarchs of history, all while claiming to be the benefactors of the people.

How did it all work? The creation of the Federal Reserve allowed the central bank to legally seize the money of the citizens. It's design allowed for the expansion of the money supply and for the funneling of the real money of gold from the masses to the few.

These men got away with it, at least for a while. That is, until greed and corruption became too much and they caused a debt crisis that led to a global economic collapse known as the Great Depression. By then, the institution was too powerful to be dissolved. It was too integral to the monetary system. Rather than become extinct after it failed, it was then taken over by the government and the politicians. Over the last 90 years, control of the institution of the Federal Reserve has been passed back and forth between the bankers and politicians. Control by the politicians has allowed for the expansion of tremendous unpayable debts. Control by the bankers has allowed for massive financial asset bubbles that enrich the investor class. Over time, bankers and governments have been complicit. Today we have both—asset bubbles and unpayable debts.

While it's still alive, neither side will ever admit the true nature of the institution. This is why as the story of the dollar has unfolded, the words used to define the rules have become even more complicated—*quantitative easing, federal funds rate, real interest rates, overnight repo operations, swap lines, foreign currency exchanges, inflation, deflation,* and now *negative interest rates and yield curve control.* The terms and ideas are so confusing that most people don't even try to understand. Those that do are insiders who continue to benefit from the obfuscation.

It's been said that power corrupts and absolute power corrupts absolutely. The power wielded by controlling the US dollar has been too much for either side to maintain. Each time they've abused their power, each time causing a massive debt crisis. Each crisis permits the wrestling of power from the other side. We are at that crisis stage once again, only this time the Federal Reserve will not continue on. *The Great Devaluation* will be its end.

The Great Depression of the 1930s occurred on the heels of the roaring twenties at a time when inequality had created a polarized world. The debt crisis that caused the Depression looks in many ways identical to what we are witnessing today. I believe we have come full circle from where we were 90 years ago. We have seen this movie before. My purpose is now to share with you the similarities so that we may be aware of the risks and evaluate the best way to prepare.

I recently flew to Canada, where I was invited to give a 20-minute presentation at the Vancouver Resource Investment Conference. The annual event was held on January 20, 2020, and was attended by over 10,000 people. The attendees came from all over the world to learn the most up-to-date information about precious metals, mining, and the world economy.

My talk that weekend was on the fragility of the monetary system and how the global economy is in the midst of an unprecedented debt crisis, one that could be knocked out by the most unpredictable of catalysts.

I argued that these events happen roughly every 90 years or so and that when they do, mankind endures an event so big it changes the entirety of human perspective moving forward. I argued that the world was on the verge of such an event, and due to the weakness of the global economy, the event would lead to a reset of the entire monetary system. I titled the presentation *The Black Swan.*

The presentation I gave was intended to highlight how the exponential growth of the world's debt was akin to an unseen deadly virus. I had prepared a video sequence that showed a virus growing in a glass. The question I posed to the audience was, if we began an experiment at 11 pm with one deadly bacteria inside a glass, that doubled every minute so that by midnight the glass would be completely full, what time would it be when the glass was half full?

The point of the exercise was to highlight why mankind continues to make the same mistakes over and over again. The reason is that we are not very good at recognizing exponential growth as it is occurring. To prove the concept, most people guess the glass would be half full at 11:30 pm. The correct answer is that the glass doesn't become half full until one minute to midnight. Of course, by then, it's too late to stop.

I believed the demonstration was a good way to describe the problem with the United States national debt that had been growing exponentially over the past 20 years. Trump is on pace to double the debt of Obama, who doubled the debt of Bush, who doubled the debt of Clinton. The exponential growth of our debt has caused an asymptote. When that occurs, the curve then shoots straight up in a 90-degree angle toward infinity. My conclusion was that our national debt has become an uncontrollable deadly virus that was already growing too rapidly to contain. Little did I know as I wrapped the presentation that an *actual* deadly virus called COVID-19 was spreading exponentially across the globe. As I was giving my talk, mankind was in the midst of underestimating the deadly coronavirus, a real-world black swan.

It is incredible to consider, but the economic tsunami caused by the coronavirus pandemic is *not* the crash *the Great Devaluation* predicts. Think of it, rather, as the "check engine" light on the dashboard of the world economy. I could not have asked for a more timely (or terrible) warning to confirm the importance of the message of this book. As everyone now knows all too well, our economy is not the "best ever" and it is not in any sense "strong." It is a house of cards constructed on out-of-control debt and fiscal trickery. The COVID-19 virus, of course, was unpredictable. I did not predict the crisis. I predicted the *response*.

In that presentation I highlighted how economic shocks are inevitable and can come from out of nowhere. The conclusion of the *Black Swan* presentation was that the next economic shock would cause a serious recession that would force the Federal Reserve to expand its balance sheet $20 trillion and that the national debt of our country would soon hit $50 trillion. I predicted that this all would all occur by the year 2027. This presentation has since gone viral across the internet.

Thus far our government's response to this crisis, lowering rates to zero percent and an immediate $6 trillion bailout, is further evidence of the accuracy of that prediction. We can be certain there are trillions and trillions more stimulus to come. It's the only thing they can think of to do. It may well get the economic engine of the world to last a few more miles down the road, but as we all know, you can only ignore that check engine light for so long before it dies altogether.

There used to be two things in life that were guarantees: death and taxes. I believe we can now add a third guarantee to that list. Government debt is going to continue to explode higher globally. The only solution moving forward is to *print more money*. It is for this reason I am compelled to continue the story. *The Great Devaluation* picks up the story where *Gold Is A Better Way* left off. This story, however, is so much bigger than simply recommending investors to buy gold. The story of *The Great Devaluation* is a story about the state of today's polarized world, why we are all so angry, who has caused that anger, and the inevitable next steps facing the world.

The former movie producer in me wants to summarize the story in the most impactful and efficient way. In the entertainment business, this description is called a *logline* and is a brief summary (one to two sentences) of what the movie, TV show, or, in this case, book is about that hooks the reader in and describes the central conflict of the story. For example, the pitch for the movie *Speed* starring Sandra Bullock and Keanu Reeves was "*Die Hard* on a bus." Following this formula, I would say the story you are about to read in *The Great Devaluation* is "The movie *Groundhog Day* meets the Great Depression."

The Great Depression in the 1930s that ultimately led to that global monetary reset lasted more than a decade and witnessed the largest transfer of wealth the world has ever seen. *The Great Devaluation* coming in the 2020s could be even more painful and will witness an even larger transfer of wealth. This book highlights the similarities, explains why a massive devaluation of currencies is inevitable, and offers a solution that would allow for the necessary restructuring to transpire without another world war.

I am an outsider who became an insider. I've dedicated the last seven year of my life to learning insiders language so I could interpret it all for you. I doubt that this book will ever be taught at Harvard Business School, but it should. The good news is, you do not need a degree from an Ivy League school to position yourself for tremendous wealth in the coming decade. You simply need to remember history.

George Santanaya famously said, "Those who cannot remember the past are condemned to repeat it." Anyone wanting to predict the future need only understand and remember the past. *The Great Devaluation* therefore seeks to remind investors of the mistakes of the past, not in an effort to alarm, but rather, to offer a tremendous advantage in preparation for what's coming in the future and the inevitable global monetary reset. That time has come, we are now only one minute to midnight.

Author's Note:

Today is Mother's Day, May 10, 2020. **The final draft of *The Great Devaluation* was submitted 11 weeks ago on February 14, 2020. Due to the size and speed of the economic shock presented by the coronavirus, I have been permitted by the publisher to add a new Chapter 1 and an addendum to the chapters in Parts One and Two, called "28 Trading Days Later (More or Less)." These addendums will highlight the most up-to-date data points and offer a rare opportunity for the reader to weigh the logic and predictions made within each chapter.**

The Great Devaluation is a prophecy unfolding in real time. While the impact of the Covid-19 coronavirus has only just begun and remains unknown at this moment, I believe it will turn out to be the *ultimate* black swan and will change everything about our future. As a writer, I'm challenged by the speed of change. As a forward thinker, I'm blown away by the early accuracy of the predictions. This rare combination allows the reader a clearer window into the future that should add deeper insight to the evaluation.

PART

I

The System is Broken

1 | Parasite

On Tuesday, March 3, 2020, the world's financial markets watched in stunned silence as Federal Reserve Chairman Jerome Powell announced an emergency interest rate cut of 50 basis points to the Federal Funds overnight interbank lending rate. At the time the Fed Funds rate was at 1.75 percent and Dow Jones was trading at 26,703 points.

> "My colleagues and I took this action to help the US economy keep strong in the face of new risks to the economic outlook. The fundamentals of the US economy remain strong."
>
> —*Jerome Powell*

Within minutes, the Dow Jones would sink over 1000 points. Powell's emergency move would ignite the most volatile few weeks in stock market history, causing the market whipsaw in 1000-point swings up and down in the coming days. As the week ended, what had been the highest flying stock market in history was monkey-hammered down over 10 percent and the rate on the "risk-free" 10-year Treasury had fallen to its lowest yield in history at nearly 0.3 percent. Unfortunately, this was just the beginning of a very long month.

President Trump, who for the first three years of his presidency had ridden the equity boom for all it was worth and had pinned his entire re-election campaign to the success of the economy in general and the height of the stock market specifically, seemed aloof to the situation. Weeks before, in February, he had enjoyed his highest ratings while in office as the stock market had boomed to all-time highs. On the night before the Fed's emergency announcement, Trump touted the American economy as the strongest economy in history and tweeted the following.

"This is an incredible time for our nation—we are in the midst of the Great American Comeback! Jobs are booming, incomes are soaring, poverty is plummeting, confidence is surging, and we have completely rebuilt the awesome power of the U.S Military. PROMISES MADE, PROMISES KEPT!"

Actual tweet, March 2nd

What did the Federal Reserve know that the president didn't seem to? An outbreak of a virus in China called Covid-19 had spread in pandemic fashion globally. While the virus had originated and expanded quickly in China, causing government leaders to shut down much of their country and disrupting the global supply chain, it was initially viewed by most of the rest of the world as remote and temporary. That perception soon changed as the coronavirus spread across Europe, Japan, South Korea, and the United States.

The Fed understood the severity of the moment. This was less because of the medical science and more because they quickly realized the virus could be the catalyst they'd long feared. The coronavirus could be the black swan that could expose the entire global economy for what it was—a house of cards built on a mountain of debt, one that could collapse at any moment.

The immediate problem for the Fed was that the smart money was very aware of the economy's underlying weaknesses. For over a decade, the Fed had pumped liquidity into the system through a series of interest rate cuts and balance sheet expansions. Wall Street had taken full advantage. For over 10 years, CEOs and corporate executives had ridden the free-money elevator to the very top by taking on massive leverage and through stock buyback programs. The effect was a stock market that had risen to nosebleed valuations, completely untethered to underlying economic conditions. Stock prices had risen nearly 30 percent in the prior year while corporate earnings growth had turned negative for seven consecutive quarters. The annual chart displaying the trend lines between equities and earnings represented an "alligator jaw" that could collapse shut at any moment. The Federal Reserve hoped that the emergency cut announcement would signal calm to the market. The opposite occurred. On the announcement, Wall Street insiders, who had been looking for an excuse to exit, fled in unison.

This was definitely new territory. Over the course of the previous decade, the stock market had always reacted positively to additional Federal Reserve liquidity. What had often been bad news for the economy had been good news for Wall Street. The money changers realized that the worse the real numbers were, the more free candy the Fed would give away. The more "easy money," the bigger the sugar high and the higher the equity markets would rise. Anyone doubting that truth needed only look at the balance sheet of the central bank. Since 2009 anytime the Fed expanded their balance sheet, stocks soared higher. Any time their balance sheet contracted, stocks dropped precipitously. During this time, the phrase "Don't fight the Fed," once a Wall Street insider secret, became the popular investment strategy for Main Street investors.

This time, however, was different. Immediately after their emergency cut, the economy began seizing. Anyone expecting markets to soar on the lower interest rate news was made violently aware that the game was over. The rate cut didn't help to soothe the market. Instead, the paper markets dropped like a rock. The Fed's next regular meeting wasn't scheduled for another two weeks, which meant that markets would likely have to wait for more sugar. Those who believed the underlying economy was strong were surprised by the speed of the selloff. Those aware of the massive debt bubble underlying the economy turned immediately bearish. They understood that markets could drop much, much further.

The term *liquidity* as it relates to the paper investment markets means that assets have both buyers and sellers on either side of a transaction. When there are more buyers than sellers, asset values rise; when there are more sellers than buyers, asset values drop. When *everyone* is selling and *no one* is buying, it's called a *liquidity crisis*. As markets cratered in the days after the Fed's emergency rate cut, liquidity in the credit markets completely dried up. The spreads between the *bid* and the *ask* on paper assets widened massively. The lack of liquidity meant greater volatility. The VIX, an index that measures volatility and had hovered at a price of $15 for much of the past five years, rose to $82. This violent move wiped out multiple hedge funds who had been shorting volatility and using massive leverage. Within days, stocks dropped over 20 percent, their fastest fall into a bear market in history. The move ended an 11-year bull run, the longest running bull market in history. Markets that had been roaring just weeks earlier plummeted. Further emergency actions would be necessary, and sooner than the Fed's next scheduled meeting.

Adding literal fuel to the fire of the liquidity crisis was what was simultaneously happening in the oil markets. A game of chicken had broken out between former OPEC partners Russia and Saudi Arabia in the form of a price war. Rather than agree to oil cuts, a standard policy tool of the oil cartel during a demand shock, the Saudi's decided to increase production and flood the world oil markets with supply. In one week, oil prices dropped 50 percent from $44 to $22 per barrel. The Saudi's upped their daily production from 10 million barrels a day to nearly 13 million. This increase in supply was happening as the world's travel industry was shutting down. The combination equated to a terrible shock in both supply and demand. The oil collapse put additional pressure on the world's equity markets. Conspiracy theorists wondered if the price war in oil wasn't an indirect attack on the United States by Russian President Vladimir Putin.

Whatever the underlying reality in oil, it was clear that the Federal Reserve would need to step in with far more aggressive action. A second emergency press conference would take place on Sunday, March 15, and was intentionally presented *before* the premarket opened. In a live conference call, a jittery Jerome Powell announced that the Federal Reserve had officially cut interest rates to zero percent. In addition, he announced that the Fed had taken several other measures to ensure that the credit markets would continue to function. Powell continued to insist that these actions were being taken to "keep" the economy strong.

The actions contradicted the rhetoric of a strong and well-functioning economy. Over the course of several press conferences and additional Fed statements after their first emergency action on March 3, the central bank offered a bazooka of liquidity. In addition to pushing rates down to zero, the Fed also announced the restarting of 2008 crisis-era policy asset purchases. It offered US dollar swap lines and eased banking rules to encourage lending. It announced longer-term Treasury purchases and repurchase operations amounting to more than $1 trillion to address what was deemed "highly unusual disruptions in the Treasury financing markets associated with the coronavirus outbreak." The moves did nothing to help the market. In fact, they further ushered in the collapse, as investors wondered what the Fed was seeing that they weren't.

The extreme actions were signaling a much deeper problem to Wall Street. The following day, the stock market endured its largest one-day drop since the 1987 Black Monday collapse, falling 12 percent in one trading session.

By March 23, the Dow Jones had fallen 37 percent from its highs just six weeks earlier. According to Bloomberg, the collapse would wipe out $26 trillion from the equity markets from their February highs, nearly triple the wealth lost during the housing crisis in 2008. Despite assurances from the administration and the talking heads on TV, investors sold first and asked questions later. As investors fled the markets, the plumbing of the entire system got clogged.

The stock market exchanges have "shut-off" switches designed to stop the bleeding in a selloff. The action is called *limit down* and anytime the market drops 7 percent or more during regular trading, or 5 percent in the after-hours market, trading is halted for 15 minutes. This collapse protection mechanism was added after Black Monday in 1987 when stocks dropped 27 percent in one day. They were put in place to eliminate mass hysteria selling. Since being introduced, the markets had only gone "limit down" in active trading twice in 33 years. In the two weeks following the Fed's first emergency cut, stocks would be sold so aggressively the market was turned off a record five different times in both regular and overnight trading sessions. The carnage was so deep that even safe havens like gold were sold as investors raced for the exits and liquidated anything with a bid.

The epic collapse would mark the fastest bear market in US stock market history. Unfortunately, news from the rest of the global economy was just as bad. Italy and France, who had already been suffering through economic recessions, both went into country-wide lockdown in an effort to stem the curve of the virus. Stock markets around the world collapsed in unison.

Central bankers from Australia, to Japan, to the European Union all held emergency press conferences and all slashed what had been record low rates even lower and into negative territory. They universally promised to unleash every "tool" at their disposal to fend off the economic collapse. They begged for fiscal support from governments in the form of tax cuts and stimulus packages.

On Tuesday, March 17, President Donald Trump, along with his Treasury Secretary Steve Mnuchin, announced plans for over $1 trillion in fiscal stimulus. The Treasury made it clear they were also prepared to pull out all of the stops. Their press conferences called for measures that were by far the most extreme ideas ever considered, especially by a Republican administration. In two weeks since touting "the best economy in American history," the president of the United States was proposing that the Treasury write checks to every adult American citizen for $1000 and delay the tax deadline indefinitely. In two weeks, the country went from capitalism to socialism. The act alone if approved meant that the Treasury would need to spend $1 trillion in the form of direct payments. They would also be short the $400 billion they had been budgeted to collect in April, the biggest month of the year for tax collection. By Sunday, March 22, the proposed stimulus package had risen from $1 trillion to a total of $4 trillion in emergency liquidity. Of course any fiscal stimulus would need the approval of Congress.

On Sunday night, March 22, Minneapolis Federal Reserve Governor Neil Kaskari was interviewed on prime time on the longest-running show in television, *60 Minutes*. In an orchestrated interview, Kashkari sent a message to the markets. The Fed would print as much new money as was necessary and wouldn't stop. It was as close to a hammer and nail as you'll ever hear from a central banker. The message was clear. The Federal Reserve was going to do everything in its power to weaken the dollar. By Tuesday, the price of gold surged over $200 per ounce, it's largest two-day move in history.

The actions of the Federal Reserve and other central banks around the globe, coupled with the promises of fiscal relief from the US government, represented an historic onslaught of never-before-seen monetary and fiscal stimulus. These stimulus packages would be unleashed everywhere around the globe. *The Great Devaluation* had officially begun.

While these actions were shocking to most investors in the world, some were prepared. I was among them. These were events that I had been predicting for over two years. I not only expected what was coming,

I had also game planned what was coming next. These events occurred as I submitting the final manuscript for *The Great Devaluation* to the publisher. While I wasn't certain what was going to happen in the short term, I felt confident that the road ahead was going to be a long and painful depression that would witness the largest transfer of wealth in human history. The Great Devaluation coming in the 2020s could prove to be more painful than the Great Depression of the 1930s.

The main question that no one seemed to be asking was, "Where was all of this money going to come from? Governments around the world were all broke. Over the previous 20 years, global debt had risen sevenfold. No country in the world was solvent. Even Germany, which had since the days of the Weimar Republic been stoic defenders of sound money, caved. Germany announced it would issue over $400 billion in new debt, amounting to 10 percent of its entire GDP. Making matters all the more real, on Sunday March, 22, German Chancellor Angela Merkel announced she was undergoing a 14-day self-quarantine due to concerns she had contracted the virus.

The combination of the oil shock and coronavirus presented a black swan. A *black swan* is an event so big it changes the entirety of mankind's perspective. These events are characterized by their extreme rarity. They cause catastrophic damage to the economy and cannot be predicted by any standard forecasting tool. A black swan event by definition is unpredictable.

The coronavirus was a medical black swan that was spreading globally. The virus attacked the human respiratory system and was highly contagious. Early reports were that the mortality rate was nearly 3 percent. For the young and the strong, the virus wasn't deadly. This reality only further enhanced the true danger for those most at risk. Signs for most people often went unnoticed. Many who contracted the virus showed no symptoms whatsoever. Those who did often were unaware until as many as 14 days after contracting the virus. This fact made the virus much harder to contain, since individuals carrying and transmitting the virus often were unaware that they were even infected.

Early on, the president called the virus a "hoax from the left." He argued the virus was a political football being used by Democrats to make the administration look bad. Even after the emergency cut from the central bank Trump seemed disconnected to the gravity of the situation. He continued to tell the country that the pandemic was "under control." While the governors of New York, California, Illinois, Ohio, and Pennsylvania had all ordered statewide lockdowns, Trump refused to admit the nation needed to be shut down. His dismissive tone in the early stages only further enhanced the chaos that was to come. Trump and his chosen scientists held press conferences nearly every day. While his top scientist Anthony Fauci warned of the true danger, Trump insisted it would all quickly blow over and that there was little for most Americans to worry about. He seemed far more concerned about the stock market than the impending health crisis. By St. Patrick's Day the president had changed his tune. There was no denying the reality of the health crisis. People were dying.

In the course of just two weeks, the Federal Reserve would unleash an alphabet soup of monetary stimulus. On Tuesday, March 17, the Fed relaunched CPFF, a Commercial Paper Funding Facility offering liquidity to businesses and households, and PDCF, which supports primary dealers stuck with large inventories of commercial paper. On Wednesday, the Fed established MMLF, the Money Market Mutual Fund Liquidity facility, an emergency liquidity program to back the money markets. On Thursday the Fed opened up USD liquidity swap lines with a wide set of central banks. The Federal Reserve had taken on the responsibility of lender of last resort to unthinkable levels. What few people would understand is that these extreme measures became necessary because of the actions taken over decades by the central banks of the world. The central banks were the arsonists and were being called on to put out the fire of their own making.

By March 22, just six weeks after the highest stock market of all time, central banks and governments around the globe had added an additional $3 trillion in liquidity and were proposing another estimated $7 trillion in the coming weeks.

The coronavirus, it turned out, was also an *economic* black swan. The term *underlying conditions* refers to structural issues beneath a surface that impact the foundation. These two words quickly became a part of the world's vernacular. Medically, they referred to the dangers that the virus imposed on weaker individuals suffering from health conditions. While the virus was sometimes unpleasant for the strong, it was proving deadly for those with high blood pressure, diabetes, heart disease, cancer, asthma, and other chronic illnesses.

The words *underlying conditions* perfectly applied economically as well. No two words better described the world economy. The reality was that the economy that had been touted as the strongest in American history was a mirage—something that looked strong from the outside but suffered from serious underlying conditions. The entire foundation of the global economy had been built on a pile of cheap and leveraged debt. The coronavirus could very well prove deadly to the entire monetary system that had stood for more than 75 years. Not only was the system old, it stood on a broken foundation suffered from underlying conditions of insolvency too big to overcome.

The problems facing the world were so much greater than just the financial insolvency. An underlying condition of polarization and anger had grown rapidly amongst the people of the entire world. It was an anger derived from inequality suffered by decades of monetary manipulation. The culprits were the central banks themselves, most especially the Federal Reserve, and their response to the crisis would put a spotlight on their culpability.

2

Trading Places

Are rich people smarter than they were 30 years ago? Are they more talented or massively more productive? Do they add dramatically more value to society? What about the middle class? Are the middle class less intelligent today? Does the average person contribute substantially less value to society than they did just three decades ago?

In the last 30 years, the top 1 percent has gained $21 trillion in wealth. This may sound like a lot until it's measured against the bottom 50 percent, who have *lost* $900 billion in wealth during the same period, which exposes the numbers as obscene. Today the top *1 percent* owns more than 50 percent of the wealth of the country. The bottom *80 percent* own only 7 percent of the pie. The rich are getting richer and everyone else is getting poorer, literally.

Today, the average CEO makes *360 times* more than the *average* employee. This means that for every month of work performed by a middle-class employee, the CEO only has to work one hour. These lucky few are considered rich and make up the top 1 percent of the population in the United States. Qualifications for membership in this elite status require an average income of over $1.3 million annually and ownership of assets that are worth more than $10 million. The next *60 percent* of Americans are considered middle class. These individuals share an average income of

13

$57,000 with a total net worth of $97,000. The remaining population in America are considered poor, make an average of $25,000, and have less than $5000 in net worth.

Unfortunately, this is not only an American problem but one shared globally. Income inequality has spread like a virus around the globe. The recent disparity between the rich and the poor has never been greater in human history. According to the St. Louis Federal Reserve, the bottom 50 percent of the world's population, amounting to *3.75 billion* people, are worth a total of $1.3 trillion. The top *20* billionaires in the world, according to *Forbes* magazine, have a combined net worth of over $1.31 trillion. This means that 20 people in the world are worth more than the bottom half of the entire world *combined*. If these numbers don't scare you, they should. Not because the accumulation of enormous wealth is a bad thing but because the gross disparity very simply represents an *unstable* math problem that history has taught us over and over again cannot be sustained.

America was built on a system of capitalism. A place where anyone, regardless of color or creed, could find success through hard work, resourcefulness, and ingenuity. For this reason, America has long been considered the land of opportunity. People from all over the world envied our system. The "American dream" identified the United States as the best place to live, and the whole world was aware of it. While that may still be true in some ways today, we are in rapid decline. *Hope* is the major ingredient of dreams. Unfortunately, there is less to be hopeful about than ever before.

Opportunities for young people are dramatically different today than they were for young baby boomers 50 years ago. The millennial generation is the first generation in American history that will not exceed the wealth of its parents. This is a reality that young people are acutely aware of. When asked their number-one strategy for achieving future wealth, the most popular answer among millennials is "inherit it."

Student loan debt has kept the millennial generation from investing. They have put off buying homes. They have put off buying cars. They have put off getting married. All because they are too busy paying off their debts. Keep in mind that the costs for college tuition have more than doubled since the turn of the century. Keep in mind as well that more Americans today than at any time in history are going to college. A college degree is as necessary today as a high school diploma was a few generations ago. This means that not only do more millennials have more college degrees than any generation, they have also taken on 300 percent more debt than their grandparents, all *before* entering the workforce.

The weight of this debt is a problem for the future of investment and should scare the heck out of everyone with real money. Millennials have now all reached adulthood. The class of 2019 was the last graduating college class of their generation. This generation will be the main drivers of the economy over the next 30 years, and they are facing a mountain of debt.

I recently had a discussion with a 33-year-old doctor. He specializes in sports rehabilitation and served as the doctor to the Olympic team. He's an exceptional young man. His personal scenario summarizes the problems facing our younger generation. He told me about how he and his wife are working to pay off their student debt. He graduated with over $250,000 in loans that he is working to pay down. He was excited that he was finally earning good money and in the last year had been able to pay down his student debt by $40,000. I was quite impressed by the young man's responsibility and curiously asked him what interest rate his loans were costing. He said, I am very lucky; my rate is 6.5 percent, but my wife and friends are paying closer to 8 percent.

This number may not jolt you the way it did me. One of the primary premises of *Gold Is A Better Way* is that it's not just the amount of money that has been printed, it's *who has had access to it* and *at what rate* that has driven financial assets. Wall Street has borrowed money for free and then bought back their stock. Students, who are the future of America, are paying 8 percent interest rates and are trying to pay down their debt. This one example summarizes the divide between today's older and younger generations.

"Borrow and invest" in a rigged game has been the plan for the established and the wealthy. For those starting out it's the opposite: "Earn more than I spend so I can pay off my debt." The young are being forced to be more responsible than the supposedly mature. This is backward. The young are supposed to take risks. The elderly are meant to play it safer since they have less time to recover should things turn south.

My young doctor friend and the other members of his generation are faced with terrible options. If they don't pay their debts, their credit ratings will collapse. If they do pay off their debts, they must forgo investing entirely to do so. It's lopsided math. Why invest and make even 5 percent a year when loan costs are 8 percent? In order for it to make sense for my doctor friend to invest, he would need to ensure he receives a higher return through investment than the costs on his loan. This, by the way, is precisely what Wall Street has done over the past decade. They've borrowed and bought stock, and they've done that at far better rates and inside a rigged game.

If you don't believe the game is rigged toward the wealthy, consider the following story of 42-year-old Daniel Sundheim. Mr Sundheim is a hedge fund manager and fine art collector who, according to Bloomberg, has recently purchased a $28 million Warhol, a $35 million Basquiat, and a $70 million Tumbly. The first thing that may cross your mind is, "Wow, that guy sure has a lot of money; this financial management business sure is lucrative!" But that's not the point. The point is to highlight *what is being done* with these fine art assets. They are being *leveraged*. Sundheim is not alone. This has taken place across the entire fine art space. The wealthy are borrowing up to 50 percent against their art collections. Steve Wynn, the casino magnate, has also been playing this leverage game. What interest rate he is paying, you may ask? According to Bloomberg, Wynn has been paying 1.25 percent interest rates as far back as 2015. And what are these wealthy investors doing with all this borrowed money? They are using it to invest in stocks and other financial assets. This is leverage that will blow up when the bubble pops and fine art prices collapse and loans are called. Of course, while the casino is open, it's a license to steal.

The cage at the casino is where the cash is held. Dozens of movies have been made, *Oceans 11* among many others, that dream of getting past the security systems of the casino in order to walk away with the cash. In the movies, it takes 11 people, all of whom take on tremendous risk and danger to avoid being caught, in order to walk away with the tens of millions from the big casino heist. But due to the Fed, one no longer has to be a criminal to steal millions of dollars.

Last year, five individual hedge fund managers earned more than $1 billion personally. According to Bloomberg this number adds up to more than the total annual gambling losses in Las Vegas in 2019. What massive risks have these five men taken to achieve such a tremendous feat? None at all. They didn't put their lives in danger and crack some impossible code to escape with the loot. Nope. And nobody is threatening to lock these men up for fleecing the system because they did nothing illegal. The Federal Reserve *handed them* the keys to the vault.

That it's legal doesn't make it less outrageous. The wealthy have been able to arbitrage and borrow for next to nothing and invest in the rigged paper markets, while the students who have no money cannot afford their rent. According to *Business Insider,* 45 percent of all millennials have student debt hanging over their heads. This keeps them from buying homes and purchasing items that drive economies. Making matters even worse, millennials are paying eight times the rent their grandparents paid as young adults 60 years ago. In 1960, the median gross rent was $71. Today that number is $1700. Even when factoring for inflation, millennials are paying four times the rent their grandparents paid.

This one mismatch crystalizes the political situation our country faces, and why socialism has so much support from younger generations. Millennials do not associate socialism with the same stigma as their grandparents. The Cold War that boomers remember and that labeled socialism a disease no longer resonates today. Socialism starts to look like a far better option for those beginning their careers today, especially when one realizes that the Federal Reserve policy of ZIRP is actually "socialism for the wealthy." When the central bank lowers rates they are giving handouts of money to the wealthy.

Even if younger people had the capacity to invest, why would they invest in the things Wall Street recommends? The price-to-earnings multiple of the stock market in the early 1980s when the 35-year-old baby boomer was hitting their peak earning years was *six times* earnings. Today, 35-year-old millennials are entering their peak earning years with the P/E multiple of the stock market at *32* times earnings. Worse yet, the average interest rate isn't 9 percent like it was back then. Long-term interest rates today are closer to 1.5 percent. This means the boomers had five times greater advantage over millennials today when it comes to investing. How can we expect the younger generation to continue to play the same capitalism game and buy stocks and bonds at these nosebleed and risky levels?

When looking at the Shiller P/E over the last 140 years, long-term investors who invest when multiples are above 24 times earnings *lose* an average of 10 percent per year over time—and the P/E multiple today is 32 times earnings. This means that a young investors doing this math can virtually guarantee they will lose. Why would any young investor do that? Why is any investor doing that?

There is only one reason. Wall Street has continued to attempt to convince everyone with their clichés of "You can't time the market," and "You must stay invested for the long term," and "The market always goes higher over time," hoping these clichés will keep older investors invested and get younger investors interested in joining the game. Believing these lies are the only reason any rational long-term investor would invest in today's markets. And what does Wall Street do with the money? They leverage it and take advantage of the system.

Millennials that have capacity are not investing the way their grandparents did. Millennials today are investing in crypto currencies and other things that offer the opportunity to "get rich quick." What they absolutely are *not investing* in is the stock market. According to a survey from Bankrate, only 23 percent of people between the ages of 18 and 37 say that stocks are the best place to invest money they won't need for 10 years. By contrast, 52 percent of baby boomers have more than 70 percent of their money invested in stocks! This is an incredible mismatch, and bad math for baby boomers.

This reality couldn't come at a worse time. While the average millennial is facing a mountain of debt and higher costs of living, their boomer grandparents are also in trouble. Only one in four baby boomers has more than enough money to last their life expectancy. This means that they will be needing additional entitlements from a social security system that will be insolvent within the next decade and from a country that is accruing debt at a faster rate than at any time since World War II. If this situation sounds dire, don't forget to add into the equation that the boomers who *do have money* are going to be withdrawing that money from the stock and bond markets to live on as they no longer generate income after retirement. Every day, 10,000 boomers hit retirement age, and this will continue through 2031. This means old money is coming out while no new money is going in. This is the number-one killer of all Ponzi schemes and debt bubbles.

The system is broken and guarantees our rapid decline. This math is becoming obvious to the younger generation and exactly why extreme socialist ideas in politics are gaining support, mostly from younger voters. The responsibility for the decline in confidence in the system is directly attributable to the central banks.

As has ever been the case, the rich have been greedy. But their selfish distortions and manipulations on the price of money have met their limits and are now being questioned by the masses. When their greed caused a financial collapse in 2008, the true protectorate of the Federal Reserve was exposed. Despite the criminal activity that took place amongst bankers who sold toxic investments they knew were worthless, no major criminal convictions ensued. Rather than allow these bankers to fail, Congress bailed them out. Doing so required a massive money-printing campaign by the Fed, and here we are once again. A decade later, the bankers that collapsed the system have fleeced it once again. They have gotten mind-numbingly rich at the expense of the masses. Unfortunately for the banker class, they're about to give it all back. This time, I predict they won't be bailed out again.

The 2020 election will be a referendum on inequality. Before we can appreciate the massive mindset shift *The Great Devaluation* predicts, we must have a deeper understanding of how capitalism has changed over the last 40 years and how the actions of the Federal Reserve have led to "social-ism for the wealthy." Only then will it become obvious that these policies will become politically unfeasible in the future. The supercycle has run its course; a new cycle will soon begin.

28 Trading Days Later (More or Less)

1. Rather than address specific changes within the original manuscript submitted on February 14, 2020, the decision was made to handle updates in these chapter postscripts.
2. The coronavirus itself has become a referendum on the divide between boomers and millennials. Because the disease is especially deadly for older people, it has become known as the Boomer Killer among angry millennials and an unfortunate and insensitive social media rallying cry for some of these disheartened youth.
3. On Wednesday, March 18, as the pace of the stock market selloff increased, Jeffrey Gundlach, DoubleLine Capital CEO and chief investment officer, tweeted that he had received "panic offers of blue chip (though not all trophy) art at slashed prices"—evidence he said in the tweet of a liquidity crunch. Gundlach's tweet highlights the risks that the wealthy have been permitted to take on, and how quickly

these leveraged bets can create economic pain. As asset valuations on these art works drop in earnest during the next recession, bailouts will become all the more necessary. Perhaps not coincidentally, on March 16, 2020, the Casino Industry requested aid from Congress in the form of a comprehensive bailout package. These bailouts will surely be labeled handouts to the wealthy in the coming 2020 election.

4. While the Fed Funds Rate was at 1.5 percent in February, it has since been slashed to 0 percent.

5. While the selloff in stocks saw the P/E multiple of the market decline, it today stands at a historically elevated 28 times earnings.

3

For a Few Dollars More

According to usdebtclock.org the national debt of the United States is currently $23.25 trillion. It is growing at a speed of $2 million per minute, $120 million per hour, $2.9 billion per day, and $88 billion per month. In 2019, the United States ran a deficit of over $1 trillion. Believe it or not, this runaway national debt *understates* the actual problem. When factoring in *unfunded liabilities*, the total debt of the United States is over $122 trillion today.

What exactly is an unfunded liability, you may ask? These are "promises to pay" made by our government, mostly in the form of Social Security and Medicare. An old statute requires the Treasury to issue an annual financial statement. According to the 2018 financial statement of the US Treasury, Social Security insurance alone is currently underfunded by $53.8 trillion. This level of underfunding has grown from $41.9 trillion in 2014. In the last five years, the deficit in Social Security funding has grown over $10 trillion. While our national debt is growing at $1 trillion per year, our "promises to pay" deficit is growing more than twice as fast.

We have continued to borrow from the future to pay for today. That burden has been made easier by central bank policies. Interest rates that have been manipulated to the floor allow governments to borrow even more at even lower costs. Unfortunately, this doesn't incentivize fiscal responsibility, it incentivizes the opposite. With interest rates at the zero lower bound, governments can borrow at little or no cost. In much of the world where rates are negative, they can even get paid to borrow. Rather than be rational and save, we do the exact opposite. We spend as if there is no tomorrow and a never-ending source of revenue.

In 2019, the United States brought in $3.2 trillion in taxes against expenditures of $4.4 trillion. This amounts to a deficit of $1.2 trillion. We spend 30 percent more annually than what we bring in through revenues and taxes. But these percentages barely register because the numbers have become too big to comprehend. In the 1960s, Senator Everett Dirkson famously said, "A billion here and a billion there and pretty soon you're talking about real money." Little did he know that 50 years later the problem would literally be 1000 times worse.

Can anyone truly understand what one trillion of anything is? These numbers are impossible to get our minds around. Perhaps it helps to consider this another way. One million seconds is equal to *11 days* of time. One billion seconds equals *32* years. One trillion seconds equals *32,000* years. They say time equals money, and this amount of time offers a clue to the amount of money we can never repay and the amount of time it may take us to pay it back.

If you are reading this right now thinking, "This sounds like an old story, why should I care? Clearly this is not a problem. We are in the greatest economy in history. Unemployment is at historic lows, the stock market is at all-time highs, and the dollar is the strongest it's been in nearly 25 years," and you would be completely correct. However, the line of reasoning that these peaks *equate to* the best times ever begs a few obvious questions.

Was the best year you ever had the year you *borrowed* the most money? We typically define our *worst* years as the years we needed to borrow to stay afloat. Our *best* years are those in which we make far more money than we spend. In our best years, we run surpluses, not deficits.

Further, if this is the best economy ever, and the United States is running $1.2 trillion annual deficits, what will happen in the next inevitable downturn? If we have budget deficits of over $1 trillion when the economy is this strong, can't we expect $2 trillion and even $3 trillion deficits in the next recession?

Lastly, and most critically, *Why* is this the "best" economy? It certainly isn't because we are booming in growth. GDP in the United States is averaging just over 2 percent and has remained stagnant for nearly 20 years. By contrast, in the years from 1980–2000 our GDP averaged 4 percent per year. Clearly, based on GDP, we are nowhere near the best running economy ever. In fact, our economy is barely slugging along at about 50 percent the speed of it was just 20 years ago.

So what's the deal? Why the all-time highs, if things aren't the best? The reality is that this is not the best economy ever. The reason for these skewed numbers is that we no longer have an economy built on growth. The world economy is built entirely on debt. This is the fundamental problem. The world is living high on the hog on borrowed money. Our debt crisis has reached epidemic proportions, and we are so infected that we accept the disease as normal. We've focused entirely on the height of the tree, not the depth of the roots.

The debt disease has become a pandemic, and every major country is treating it with the same drug as the United States. We here in America happen to be enjoying the best of it because we control the chips in the game. This hardly means we are doing well. We are simply the winner of the ugly contest. We are the prettiest mare at the slaughterhouse.

In the midst of the biggest debt bubble in human history, we have fooled ourselves into thinking everything is great. Our intentional ignorance is the guarantee that it's only going to get far worse. Over the past 50 years, the United States budget deficit has averaged 2.9 percent of GDP. The Congressional Budget Office projects that larger budget deficits over the next 30 years will drive this number to over 6.5 percent of GDP. Keep in mind that the CBO does not factor in recessions to their projections, which means we can virtually guarantee this *underestimates* the eventual reality. The CBO continues to readjust these numbers annually, and its projections keep getting worse and worse. The prognosis today will assuredly get worse tomorrow.

Let's not forget that this debt epidemic is occurring in the midst of the stock market returning its best performance in decades. In 2019, the Dow Jones rose *27 percent*. This explosion in value happened at the same time corporate earnings were flat. In other words, we have seen a massive expansion in the equity valuations of public companies without any actual underlying growth. Those who argue that we are at all-time highs because the economy is booming are ignoring the fact that these gains have exclusively been due to the loose monetary policies of the Federal Reserve through its creation of more and more credit and the expansion of their balance sheet. This is a Ponzi scheme. It is the definition of a bubble.

Unfortunately, the disease is too advanced to cure. We will not grow our way out of our problems. We will not pay down these debts, at least not with dollars that have any value. The United States has not had a budget surplus in over 20 years. During the last two decades of budget deficits, our national debt has grown more than *six times*, from $3.5 trillion in the year 2000 to over $23 trillion today. During that same time, our GDP has only doubled. Our debt is growing three times faster than our growth, and no one seems interested in slowing that lopsided rate down. A five-year-old can see this is bad math.

The whole idea that this is the "best economy ever" is what makes it all so confusing for so many people. Relative to every other country in the world today? Perhaps. Relative to where we were five years ago? Maybe. But saying this is the best economy ever literally means that the entire economic system must be broken. More and more people are beginning to recognize this reality. How have things become so distorted? What underlying systemic issue has allowed for this ridiculous explosion of debt? Who is responsible for this?

There is one institution alone to blame. The Federal Reserve. Since its creation, the Fed has manipulated the price of money. It's the Fed's job to do so. For the last 40 years, however, it has manipulated it in virtually only one direction, *lower*. As a result, investors have learned one valuable lesson: Don't fight the Fed. Investors no longer worry about the fundamentals of capitalism and its underlying structure. Why bother maintaining a corporate balance sheet when the entire market moves higher on liquidity guaranteed to be pumped in by the Fed?

For 40 years the Federal Reserve has continued to push interest rates lower and lower, from highs of nearly 20 percent in 1980 to today, where they are the lowest in human history. Interest rates today are on the floor and are negative in much of the world. This one ongoing action by the Federal Reserve has created the disparate world in which we live, the massive asset bubble within which we currently sit, and the populist movements that have arisen around the globe. In order to understand *why* this has occurred, it is essential to understand how the price of money directly affects *where* capital flows. It's even more important to understand that the flow is coming on full steam.

28 Trading Days Later (More or Less)

1. The official US debt according to usdebtclock.org rose from $23 trillion to over $25 trillion in a matter of eight weeks.
2. According to Forbes the United States budget deficit will exceed $4 trillion in 2020.
3. The annual budget deficit and its expected total of over $4 trillion presents an interesting and growing challenge. We collected $3.2 trillion in taxes in 2019. If we can simply print the money by going further into debt, why do we need to pay taxes at all? In fact, isn't one of the main principles behind the paying of taxes is that the government will continue to be responsible and practice sound money policies? At what point do the people revolt against these unplayable debts?
4. How are we going to pay for it? That was the main question being asked of Bernie Sanders on his proposal to wipe out student debt. The one question not being asked by anyone in Congress today is, "How are we going to pay for it?" If the government can simply create $4 trillion out of thin air to try to halt a crashing economy, why is a $1.6 trillion student debt total something to argue about? If the overarching goal is to "stimulate" the economy (see bailout language for programs 1, 2, 3 and the soon to be proposed "infrastructure" bill that will exceed $2 trillion), why couldn't student debt become a proposal from the right as well? What could be more stimulative than having the largest consumer generation in history having the newfound capital to consume rather than pay off debt? The one question that is no longer relevant is, "How would we pay for it?" Don't be surprised to see the Trump campaign float this idea in the runup to the 2020 election. Remember, what looks "crazy" in normal times becomes "necessary" in a crisis.
5. The US budget deficit will hit 19 percent of GDP in 2020 according to fxstreet.com. This is a worldwide effort—stimulus added around the globe in eight weeks has added up to more than 20 percent of world GDP.

4 | Hustle and Flow

Pretend for a moment that money had its own mind. Let's also pretend that money had its own goal, which is to find the very best place to flow in order to maximize its growth. When interest rates rise, money flows out of financial assets and into investments that pay fixed returns and physical tangible assets. Interest rates that rise indicate growth and encourage money to deleverage and pay down debts before costs become too great. When interest rates are lowered, the opposite occurs, and rather than flow into saving, money flows into borrowing as money takes advantage of the lower rates. This ebb and flow happens organically in a healthy environment. In a healthy economy this rise and fall of rates is organic and is called the *business cycle*.

In times of economic strife, central banks manipulate the price of money lower in an effort to stimulate. Lowering interest rates allows more money to be borrowed and the ability to refinance debts at lower costs. In the past, these manipulations by central banks have worked to generate enough liquidity to lubricate the system and get it functioning at a higher level. This only works when there is *demand* for more borrowing. In times of great uncertainty, even free money will be shunned.

Historically, when faced with an economic downturn, the Federal Reserve immediately lowers interest rates *five hundred basis points.*

27

The financial collapse in 2008 was so big that the standard action of lowering rates by 5 percent wasn't enough. Lower rates did very little to stimulate and the economy continued in recession. It was only after the Fed began *quantitative easing* (QE) and printed trillions of dollars that things begin to pick up. But understanding where all of this newly printed money flowed is the key to comprehending how big today's problems really are. It has all flowed to the top. The Federal Reserve has manipulated the financial system. It has become so distorted that all of the benefits of new money have flowed to the top at the expense of everyone else.

A quick explanation of QE and how it works is useful. The Fed "buys bonds" and then deposits cash into the banking system. Banks are then able to lend the money. This action of bond buying increases the money supply and the overall supply of credit. For every dollar that is created, 10 times more credit is added to the system. When the Fed "sells bonds," the opposite occurs. The money supply shrinks and interest rates rise.

Make sense? It's not supposed to. The rational person will ask, "Where does the Fed get the money to buy the bonds?" And while that is a fabulous question, the answer is less so because the answer is, *the Fed creates it out of thin air*. OK, you may say to yourself, but where does all the newly created money go? The money goes to Wall Street banks.

OK, you say, then what do the banks do with this money? They lend it, of course, because that's what banks do. But they don't lend it to you and me. Virtually all of the free money from QE was lent by Wall Street banks to major corporations. This money did not go to the average American making $50,000 per year. In fact, anyone attempting to get a loan in the last decade needed to have more money than they were looking to borrow, because only the best credit risks had access to this "free money." If you had anything less than perfect credit, if you were a student, or a regular Joe, loans weren't free. These types of borrowers have been forced to pay higher rates. No, only the wealthy and corporations have had access to the "free money." So rather than stimulating the economy and distributing the new money to people who would actually spend it within the real economy, the banks have lent it to major corporations and big businesses, which have not deployed it to anyone's advantage but their own.

But then the problem got even worse. With interest rates so low, banks needed borrowers who would pay higher rates. They found their clients in subprime corporate borrowers. According to *Forbes* magazine, the total corporate bond market totals $15.5 trillion. Of that total, roughly one-third, or $5 trillion, has been lent to those with *less than* investment grade credit. When a higher-risk corporation wants to borrow, it can borrow in the corporate debt market. Lending to less-worthy creditors allows the bankers to receive a higher rate. When these subprime corporations borrow, their debt is called *junk bonds*.

As the Fed dumped liquidity into the banking system, more and more banks had available cash to lend. Bankers chased after the junk bond market. The risky subprime borrowers were at an advantage, since more and more banks sought their business. As this occurred, junk bond interest rates came down and the covenants lenders demand weakened. The result is that firms with crappy credit have received trillions of borrowed money at rates lower than a financially responsible young graduate receives, while the investors lending to them have less protections than at any time in history.

A BBB bond is called junk because it has a higher risk of default. The average junk bond interest rate historically has been 12 percent. This high rate makes sense. Lenders demand higher rates of return to get compensated for the risks taken lending to these types of institutions. Due to the manipulated system and distorted incentives, banks have loosened lending standards and are taking on more risk than at any time in history. According to Jeffrey Gundlach of Doubleline Capital, 45 percent of all corporate debt should be rated BBB, or junk. Gundlach adds that the corporate subprime debt market is five times the size of the subprime mortgage market prior to the housing collapse. The comparison is one that investors would do well to pay attention to heed. The exact same setup that happened with subprime mortgage borrowers has happened in the corporate debt world. Greedy bankers making bad loans that the average citizen will wind up paying for when it all turns south. We are headed back to the future.

But why do bankers keep putting us "all-in" on this jackpot? It's all about their incentives. The more loans a banker makes the more fees they can generate. When the Fed lowered interest rates to 0 percent, banks started chasing the subprime corporate borrowers willing to pay more. As more and more banks went after this business, the field became tilted in favor of the borrowers because there was far more money available to lend than there were worthy creditors to lend to.

This reality causes two things to occur. Banks lower lending standards, and also lower rates to compete with other banks. Today the average subprime corporate loan rate isn't 12 percent as one would expect for such credit risks. Today, the corporate bond market average rate is less than 4 percent. Worse still, these loans are *covenant lite,* meaning they have less stringent terms. These loans are to the corporate world what "stated income" loans were to the housing boom.

Well OK, you may say, I get all that, but haven't the corporations that borrowed all this free money used it to hire new employees, raise wages, and invest in infrastructure investments that drive the real economy? No, is the simple answer. They didn't. That was what they were *supposed* to do. That is what had happened in the past when the Fed manipulated interest rates lower and the economy *wasn't broken.* Unfortunately, that didn't happen this time. Over the last decade, Wall Street has not invested this money. Instead, public companies borrowed trillions of dollars of free money made possible by the Federal Reserve and did something else almost entirely with the money—they bought back their stock.

Let's roleplay the job of the CEO who can borrow money for free so we can get a better sense of what has occurred. We have been offered zero percent interest rates. The question is, what should we do with the money after we borrow it? We have a couple of choices. We can *invest* it and try to grow the business. We can hire new people, expand marketing efforts, build new plants, and expand operations. Our problem with this option is that there isn't much demand and the real people who would normally purchase our products aren't doing very well financially and cannot afford to buy more of them. Attempting to grow the business in this scenario through *investment* is therefore a very risky proposition. The likelihood is we will waste this borrowed money by investing it. As CEO, we decide this is not the best use of the capital, even if it's free.

We also have a second, and ultimately far more appealing option. We could borrow the money for free, and *rather than risk it* by investing and attempting to grow the business, we can use the borrowed money a different way. We can *buy back* our company's stock. This, it turns out, is a beautiful option. Keep in mind that our entire job as members of the C-suite (CEO, CFO, etc.) is to increase shareholder value. This program is bulletproof for the stockholders.

Buying back the stock is simple math. Suppose there are 1,000,000 shares of our company outstanding and each share is worth $50. This means our company has a market capitalization of $50 million. Now, if we buy back our stock, we will reduce the number of shares outstanding. In this example, let's say we buy back half the stock with borrowed free money. What we have just accomplished without having to do any work at all is incredible. After buying back the stock, there are now only 500,000 shares of stock outstanding, all sharing in a $50 million company. Magically, each share is worth $100 instead of $50. This is a win–win–win. As the CEO, we did *nothing* to increase the overall value of the company, *and* we just made the shareholders rich, *and* they love us. We have also made ourselves rich, because our compensation and bonus are based on our share price. In fact, as corporate executives, we own lots of shares of the firm. So borrowing money for free and buying back our stock is the best thing for the shareholders and for us personally, too. We make millions of dollars more individually by making them more money. Our shareholders are all happy and nobody gets hurt. At least, that's what we tell ourselves.

Corporate buybacks have amounted to more than 50 percent of stock market returns over the past decade. This fabulous new byproduct of QE created by the Federal Reserve has stimulated only one thing, paper assets owned by the investor class. This is what has driven stocks to historic all-time highs. These are highs that have been built on debt, not growth. The Federal Reserve has funded the stock market boom while our nation's debt has launched into the stratosphere.

As the CEO we understand this, but hey, that's not our problem. If the people get stuck with all of this debt, so be it. As the CEO, we have a responsibility to our shareholders, right? Even if we were a highly moral CEO who understood the risks and negative impact of this process, we couldn't do anything about it anyway. We have competitors. As our competition plays this game, their share prices will go higher and they will have a competitive advantage over us. For this reason, even if we don't like the reality, as the CEO we have a *responsibility* to maximize shareholder return. Right?

Sound familiar? This was the exact excuse of the banks that knew they were taking on toxic loans in the housing crisis that inevitably blew up and forced a taxpayer bailout. The banks and CEOs all understand how risky this is but rationalize their destructive behavior by arguing they have no choice. When it all blows up again, it won't impact us as CEO because we'll have fleeced the system for tens of millions of personal dollars we "earned" by providing shareholders value. The Fed has created the Wild West. Their policy action has changed the entire mindset and flow of investment capital.

28 Trading Days Later (More or Less)

1. Inserted within the Federal Reserve's bazooka of liquidity following the coronavirus crisis was an extreme move that will assuredly be a sensitive point of future criticism. In a matter of weeks, and in an alphabet soup of new fiscal and monetary policies that nobody understands, Congress nearly unanimously passed a stimulus package to bail out Wall Street again, and the Federal Reserve rode right alongside. This time it's not only mortgage-backed securities, it's corporate bonds, and not only companies with good credit, but the junk bonds of the zombies they've kept in business with their ZIRP over the last decade. It's even worse than it sounds. Not only is the Fed buying the underlying bonds directly, they are also buying the ETFs that own the junk bonds. JNK, the ETF that tracks subprime corporate credit, is up 20 percent since the announcement. Anyone against it is against America. This takes "don't fight the Fed" to a new extreme. Who cares if most of these companies are insolvent? If the Fed is buying, we should, too! The only asset that is not officially propped up currently are stocks, and now that the buyback boom is officially dead, we will soon see the Fed buying these, too. If you are getting excited, you may want to see how well this idea of a managed economy has worked in Japan for the last 30 years. When the Fed and other central banks "buy everything," true supply and demand are eliminated. Determining the real value of paper assets in the future will be impossible. Governments have only one thing they can do. Print more money. As they do, asset prices could rise. The sad part is that most people won't recognize they are losing their shirts because they'll focus on the height of the tree, not the depth of the roots.

2. The airline industry has been among the biggest beneficiaries of the Fed's policies. From 2009 through 2019, the share prices of every major airline had increased an average of eight times. What's essential to consider about that massive valuation increase is that the vast majority of free

cash flow from the industry went toward stock buybacks. Bloomberg reported that 96 percent of all free cash flow from the biggest US airlines went toward their buyback programs. The average compensation for CEOs of the major airlines was more than $12 million in 2019. Now that the airline industry is suffering, they are getting bailed out with a $50 billion plan approved by Congress. This screams of the inequality that will be the lightning rod of division sure to become the focus of the 2020 election.

3. Warren Buffett famously refused to buy back more shares of his own company because the valuation was too high. Had more CEOs followed the Berkshire Hathaway CEOs example, they would have had cash on hand to endure the downturn. Through the last two years, Buffett has been widely criticized for not buying back more Berkshire Hathaway shares. The stock price has suffered as a result. On the flip side Buffett currently sits on over $125 billion in cash and has the dry powder available to sustain the next economic downturn.

4. The decade-long buyback binge is now over. Congress has mandated that the companies receiving stimulus will not be eligible to buy back shares for one year after the loan has been repaid. This one trend is a reason to be bearish for the 2020s. The main driver of financial asset valuations will be removed from the toolkits of CEOs and will make the job of increasing share price significantly more difficult over the coming years.

5 | Free Willy

Free money has changed the way all investors invest. At one time it made sense for investors to have a balanced portfolio that held stocks and bonds. The stocks offered growth with dividend income. The bonds offered diversification, protection, and a guaranteed income stream. Since the creation of QE, investor mindset has radically transitioned to "nothing pays a meaningful dividend and therefore *everything* is about growth," even including assets that are supposed to be considered the safest investments." The strategy for even the smallest investors has been to buy up the stocks of major corporations who buy back their shares and catch a ride on the free money train.

The distortions of the Federal Reserve have changed the fundamentals of even the safest asset classes. The only way to win as an investor has been to play the game. If you can't beat them, join them.

With everyone playing the same stock buyback game, investing is no longer about capitalism and building the best companies. Capitalism has become about having access to free money. So now the only thing for investors to do is to buy the stocks of *every* company. The system now ensures that everyone will win. Index investing is the rage. In fact, the more discerning investors have been punished. The risk-taking cowboys have been incentivized more than ever to take on more risk. The only way to win is to join the risk frenzy and buy. Who cares if it's safe?

Treasuries have long been considered the safest asset class of all to own. Are you excited to lend to the US government for a return of 1.5 percent on a 10-year loan? If you are, it's likely *not* because the 1.5 percent rate is appealing. At a 1.5 percent rate, it'll take 48 years of compounded returns to double your money. How about a 2 percent return for 30 years? Does that get you any more fired up? A 2 percent rate allows you to double your money in only 36 years with compounded returns. Pretty exciting, right?

Remember the days when the average return on government debt was 7 percent? A 7 percent return on Treasuries allowed investors to double their money every 10 years. Investors who were willing to take on a 20-year time horizon could expect *four times* gains through compound interest in that short period of time. At 1.5 percent interest rates, one needs to wait over 100 years to get the same *four times* compounded returns. Wow!

For comparison, over the last 90 years the price of gold has increased in value 78 times. Which would you rather receive after 90 years, *4 times* your money or *78* times your money? The answer is so obvious it's amazing everybody isn't moving every penny into gold. Today, bond investors are taking on even more risk for dramatically less return. The Federal Reserve has turned every investor into a gambler. The odds *used to be* favorable for those willing to take a long-term approach. Savers who were willing to forgo short-term pleasure were rewarded for the *time value of money*. The longer they were willing to lend for, the less the risk, and the higher the rate. The Federal Reserve has eliminated that incentive.

What investors are probably more interested in when buying Treasuries today is front-running the Federal Reserve. Investors today are banking on the fact that as the Fed is forced to continue buying more and more Treasuries, that rates will go lower and that these bonds will increase in value as they do. For those holding bonds, their entire growth strategy is that "something bad is going to happen in the future, and when it does interest rates will be forced even lower and these bonds will be more valuable." Treasury holders aren't therefore holding these assets for the itty bitty returns. No, bondholders today expect the house to burn down and are buying Treasuries as fire insurance.

Well, at least Treasuries are safe, right? This is an old reputation that has turned into an investment cliché that is no longer applicable to today's environment. Do you think it's safe to lend money to someone who is certain to never be able to pay you back? That is what you are doing when buying Treasuries. You are lending to an insolvent government. There is only *one guarantee* when you lend money to the government today. That guarantee is simple. The US government will pay you back the only way it can, with *diluted dollars*. Anyone who tells you otherwise is either lying or completely uninformed of the future risks.

We run $1 trillion deficits in the best of times, and that number exploded in 2020. Trump's newest budget proposal sought twice the deficit he projected in his first budget proposal. At what point will interest rates surge higher because investors demand higher reward for the increasing risks being taken to lend insolvent governments more money? That time is coming far sooner than you might think.

The Federal Reserve has broken the economic system. Savers are now punished. Companies' stock prices are no longer based on performance. What used to be up is now down, and vice versa. With interest rates on the ground, investors have had to rethink everything. This policy action has led to massive distortions and created a new paradigm. Historically when the Fed lowers rates, that action has driven economic activity. The last decade of borrowing has only flowed into financial assets. This has led to a bond bubble that is even bigger than the stock market bubble, and *that* bubble is the fattest it's ever been. These moves have forced investors into financial assets at some of the highest overvaluations in history.

The market cap to GDP ratio was made famous by Warren Buffett in 2001 while doing an interview with *Fortune* magazine. He explained it as his number-one metric and allowed him to determine if markets were overvalued. It measures the amount of cash in the market and compares it to the GDP of the country. When this ratio is less than 75 percent, he argued that the market was significantly undervalued. When this ratio was over 115 percent, he believed the market was significantly overvalued and thus a terrible time for long-term investors to be investing. Interestingly this ratio has only been above 115% three times in history. In 1929, it hit 141 percent. In 2000 it hit 151 percent, and today the ratio sits at 156 percent. This means according to the Warren Buffett Indicator, this the most overvalued market in history.

A second well-known metric for measuring stock valuations was made famous by Yale economist Robert Shiller. The CAPE Shiller P/E ratio measures corporate earnings over the last 10 years adjusted for inflation. This formula is different from the rigged P/E multiple Wall Street uses based on future projections. The CAPE measures real data of the last decade. Shiller did the math going all the way back to the 1880s. What he found is that the historical average of this metric is 17 times earnings. When this number has reached over 30, it has witnessed the biggest stock market collapses in history. It hit 41 times earnings in 2000 before the dot-coms collapsed. It hit 31 in 1929 before the Great Depression. The CAPE Shiller P/E multiple stands at 32 times earnings today.

The stock and bond bubbles have reached epic proportions. This is not opinion, this is according to the most consistent long-term indicators. Massive undertaking of debts have tilted the field in favor of the investor class. Those lucky enough to have held financial assets over the last decade have seen significant gains. Everyone else has suffered. The investor class has binged on debt and bought financial assets. They've won at everyone else's expense.

President Trump can say, "This is the best economy we have ever had" because stocks are at all-time highs. But he understands the true reality as well as anyone. While he may be entitled to argue that things look better economically than they did before he took office, his words during the presidential debate in 2016 remain true. He said then, "The only thing that looks good is the stock market, and if interest rates go up even a little bit, that's gonna come crashing down. We are in a big fat ugly bubble."

But what's so bad about a bubble? The good news is that debt bubbles are awesome before they pop. And if you're enjoying the ride that's great—just make sure it's a ride you can get off. When the roller coaster declines, it will do so with such rapid speed that exiting might be far more painful than you may be planning for. If you are on the ride because you are stuck and don't know where else to go, understand that there are other choices you'll find far more appealing.

Do you love the idea of owning risky assets and investing in fixed income that pay next to nothing? Or have you been forced to marry TINA (There Is No Alternative)? It's been said that this is the least-loved stock market boom in history. Investors are not eager about nosebleed valuations. They aren't excited about risky fixed investments that pay no return. Investors simply have nowhere else to go. This fact alone is a signal that the end is near. We are being forced into relationships with things we don't even like. Unfortunately, the divorce is going to be very messy.

28 Trading Days Later (More or Less)

1. The market cap to GDP ratio stands at 134 percent, as of May 10, 2020. While this is lower than the highs hit in February 2020 of 156 percent, it still represents a market that is "significantly" overvalued and offers a likely explanation as to why Warren Buffett has remained in cash.
2. The CAPE/SHILLER P/E ratio for the stock market currently stands at 27. The historical average is 17 times earnings.
3. Evidence that the main strategy for investors is to "front run" the Federal Reserve can be seen in the explosion in the junk bond ETF—JNK. Interestingly, as of this writing on May 7, 2020, the Fed has yet to begin buying JNK. This was duly noted by Charles Schwab analyst Kathy Jones, who remarked, "Spreads have come in a lot just based on the Fed's announcement, so they haven't had to buy anything." This is forward guidance at its best. Don't worry, the Fed won't disappoint, and buying will inevitably begin later in May.

9 | Prometheus

The central bank of the United States is over 100 years old. Unlike many other government agencies, the Federal Reserve was not created for the benefit of the citizens. It was an entity created solely to protect the interests of a few rich and powerful men. These men included steel magnate Andrew Carnegie, philanthropist John D. Rockefeller—the wealthiest man in the world at the time—railroad baron Cornelius Vanderbilt, the Warburgs of Hamburg, and the Rothchilds of Paris and London. These men remained silent behind the most powerful man of them all, J.P. Morgan, the secret father of the Federal Reserve.

Prior to 1913, when the Federal Reserve was founded, the United States had never succeeded in maintaining a central banking system. Banking institutions were controlled by state chartered banks and unchartered "free banks" that issued their own notes, redeemable in gold. Gold served as the one constant. This localized formation of independent regional banks, however, presented regulatory challenges for the federal government.

The J.P. Morgan & Co. is a commercial and banking institution officially founded in 1871. It is the predecessor of the three largest banking institutions in the world today, JP Morgan Chase, Morgan Stanley, and Drexel Burnham Lambert. Insiders refer to it as the *House of Morgan*. The banks origins trace back to 1854, when patriarch Junius Morgan

79

joined George Peabody & Co, a London based banking institution. "J.P." Morgan, the son of Junius, would grow the House of Morgan into the largest banking institution in the world.

Morgan's business thrived without the benefit of a central bank. The inevitable recessions and bank runs caused by a fractured system required a survival of the fittest environment. They were excellent bankers, and when other banks failed over time, the Morgans' empire expanded. By the early 1890s J.P. Morgan and Co. had become the de facto central bank of the United States.

The House of Morgan would be responsible for putting together the capital to fund a rapidly growing America and led the funding of the transcontinental railroad. The bank catered to the Astors, DuPonts, Guggenheims, Vanderbilts, and Rockefellers. The tentacles of Morgan's financial octopus wrapped around the globe and financed the launch and operations of many of America's greatest companies, General Motors, General Electric, and DuPont, to name just a small few.

The Morgan company kept offices abroad and maintained essential banking relationships with the global banking center in London. By the early 1890s, the House of Morgan was considered the premier bank in the United States, with power that reached around the globe.

In 1893, a financial panic triggered the greatest depression the United States had ever seen. The collapse of the country's largest employers, the *Philadelphia and Reading Railroad* and the *National Cordage Company*, caused a run on the banks that then led to the collapse of the stock market. Businesses and independent depositors raced to remove gold from their accounts. By 1895, the nation's gold reserves had been heavily depleted. With no central bank to rely on for liquidity, Morgan would be forced to personally save his bank from disaster. In the process, he wound up finding himself the rescuer of the gold standard and the savior of the American economy.

Morgan went to Washington and promised to form an international syndicate that would buy gold and protect the Treasury from additional gold withdrawals. President Grover Cleveland was assured by Morgan that the gold being purchased would not join the flow out of the country. Morgan and Company led a US bond offering to buy gold back from foreign investors. The firm presented the bonds for sale at $112.25 and sold out the issue in New York within 22 minutes. Stability was soon restored. The action rescued the United States from the severe two-year depression.

Banking is based on faith. Depositors are incentivized to leave their deposits with a bank to receive interest on their money. Two things are necessary for this to work. The depositor must be offered a worthwhile rate, and they must have faith that the bank they leave their money will remain solvent. Depositors must always have confidence that the bank with whom they leave their money will return that money upon "demand." Without *faith,* the system ultimately will fail.

By 1906, and still with no central bank backing the nation, Morgan found himself in the position of *savior* once again. The San Francisco earthquake would be the cause of the next major crisis. The earthquake killed nearly 3,000 people and devastated a large part of the city. The domino effects and chain reaction this unexpected event had on the banking system is a lesson in the fragility of economic systems, and how one event completely unrelated to banking can cause a ripple effect that then undermines faith in the entire system.

Most of the buildings that suffered damage were insured. The insurance companies that covered the disaster were mostly located in Great Britain. London at the time was the banking center of the world. As claims were paid, gold flowed from London to San Francisco. The sudden outflow of gold caused bank runs in London from depositors seeking to remove their gold from the system.

To defend against the outflow of gold leaving its coffers, the Bank of England decided to raise interest rates and incentivize depositors. The tightening of monetary policy turned out to be a mistake and added additional pressure on the money markets in England. As liquidity dried up, account holders became worried that they would be unable to withdraw their funds. A deeper run on the banks ensued.

A second issue exacerbated this financial crisis. A group of New York traders had been trying to corner the market on copper. They had leveraged up and borrowed sizable amounts on margin from the Knickerbocker Trust Company of New York. The copper corner failed, though, and when the loans were called, the Knickerbocker didn't have the capital to cover. It started a chain reaction of bank runs. The run on the Knickerbocker spread to other trusts, which were tied to the major banks, Citibank and Chase bank. The combination of the San Francisco earthquake and the copper corner caused a chain reaction and a prolonged banking crisis.

Morgan was in Virginia when he received news of the crisis. He was 70 years old at the time and the most powerful man in the world. He wasted no time and boarded his private locomotive and traveled on his private railroad and was in New York within 48 hours to address the crisis.

Morgan instructed his team of partners to review the books of the major banks and trusts that were under the most pressure. Fortunately, most of the issues were with short-term liquidity challenges, a mere short-term mismatch of assets and liabilities. While the majority of banks had limited cash on hand, they were still stable. Morgan stepped in and agreed to add the necessary liquidity for the banks that were solvent. He let the insolvent institutions fail. In the process, Morgan acted as a one-man central bank who's self-preservation saved the entire banking system. The crisis abated and vital lessons were learned.

Through a system of collectives and trusts, the House of Morgan was further fortified, and by then held equity in a large portion of the economy. Through the process, Morgan personally became the de facto *owner* of the system. Once virtually all assets were owned by his personal banking cartel, having an insurance policy to protect the assets was essential.

Twice in less than 15 years, Morgan had been forced to save the banking system and vowed never to be put into the same position again. He had learned his lessons well. Morgan understood that lack of liquidity in stressful times would continue to pressure the largest banks and that a central, reliable institution that could provide emergency funding in the future serving as a lender of last resort was necessary.

Morgan began planning a central bank that would serve as that lender. How that bank was designed and capitalized would be integral to Morgan's and the rest of the power elites' future fortunes. The central bank needed to be a government institution that would offer the complete backing and credit of the United States, while at the same time remaining entirely independent and free of government oversight. The *independence* of this new central bank was of the highest priority. Independence would allow the government institution to remain loyal to its true benefactors, Morgan and the wealthiest families in the world.

Morgan understood the need to have full control of the central bank. It was a control that must be held privately and never to be taken over by politicians and the government. Loss of that control could mean the loss of everything. The plotting and planning of the institution that would be both public and private at the same time took Morgan several years, and was only shared with the most powerful and wealthy individuals in the world.

On November 22, 1910, a private delegation representing a quarter of the world's wealth left on a train from Hoboken, New Jersey. The group traveled in secrecy, dropping their last names in favor of code names so that no one would discover who they were or the true purpose of their mission. Among the group was Senator Nelson Aldrich, the chairman of the *National Monetary Commission,* and Benjamin Strong, a Morgan man, and the first chairman of the soon to be created Federal Reserve.

The *Jekyll Island Club* was a private club on the Atlantic Coast of Georgia. Its original members had purchased the island for a sum of $125,000 The members of the club came from the United States' wealthiest families, most notably the Morgans, the Rockefellers, and the Vanderbilts. The club had only 100 members, and these men were the world's true power elite.

On that evening in November, Aldrich met with five other men at Jekyll Island to set about restructuring the US banking system. Aldrich was joined by A.P. Andrews, the assistant secretary of the United States Treasury Department, Paul Warburg, representing the investment bank Kuhn, Loeb & Co, Frank Vanderlip, president of National City Bank of New York, Henry P. Davidson, senior partner of J.P. Morgan Company, Charles D. Norton, president of the Morgan-dominated First National Bank of New York, and Benjamin Strong, representing J.P. Morgan.

Forbes magazine founder, Bertie Charles Forbes, wrote the following about the clandestine meeting years later:

Picture a party of the nation's greatest bankers stealing out of New York on a private railroad car under cover of darkness, stealthily riding hundreds of miles South, embarking on a mysterious launch, sneaking onto an island deserted by all but a few servants, living there a full week under such rigid secrecy that the names of not one of them was once mentioned, lest the servants learn the identity and disclose to the world this strangest, most secret expedition in the history of American finance. I am not romancing; I am giving to the world, for the first time, the real story of how the famous Aldrich currency report, the foundation of our new currency system, was written . . . The utmost secrecy was enjoined upon all. The public must not glean a hint of what was to be done. Senator Aldrich notified each one to go quietly into a private car of which the railroad had received orders to draw up on an unfrequented platform. Off the party set. New York's ubiquitous reporters had been foiled . . . Nelson (Aldrich) had confided to Henry, Frank, Paul and Piatt that he was to keep them locked up at Jekyll Island, out of the rest of the world, until they had evolved and compiled a scientific currency system for the United States, the real birth of the present Federal Reserve System, the plan was completed on Jekyll Island.

That the meeting to reframe the US banking system would take place at the exclusive Jekyll Island Club is an indication of the priorities for whom the new institution was meant to protect. The secret temple of the Federal Reserve was created to protect the wealth and power of this elite group. It was born from the plan Aldrich and his cohorts at Jekyll Island drew up at this meeting.

The plan called for the creation of a central institution, the *National Reserve Association,* that would have branches across the country and would have the power to issue currency. It would be controlled by a board of directors, primarily composed of bankers. These bankers would not answer to any government institution and would act together to control the new money supply.

Initially, Congress was quite suspicious of the plan, contending that it would enhance the power of the larger banks and the power and influence of Wall Street. It would eventually be called the Federal Reserve Act. Despite its detractors, it was approved by Congress in 1913.

The final resolution called for a centralized bank with *a dozen* regional Reserve Banks and a central Federal Reserve Board. The most important of all of the 12 regional banks was to always remain in New York City. The plan allowed a board of commercial bankers to be empowered by the federal government to act like a central bank that could create money and lend reserves to private banks. Idle reserves would be consolidated in strategic locations where they could be distributed quickly to illiquid banks. This created an *elastic currency* that could grow or shrink in response to credit demands. The new national currency (eventually called Federal Reserve notes) would be automatically interchangeable with demand deposits and gold.

The Federal Reserve Bank's longevity and success can be attributed to its ability to thread the fine needle between private and public institutions. It became an important prototype for the modern liberal state. As a result, the Federal Reserve would be "independent" of politics. That independence has long allowed the institution to retain its murky and secretive practices.

The charter allowed the Federal Reserve to create and issue new currency. The central bank allowed for a more pliable solution than offered by a true gold standard which limited the ability to expand the money supply. The gold standard, however, was of paramount importance and was built into the framework of the Federal Reserve. The Federal Reserve Act required the Federal Reserve to hold gold "equal to 40 percent of the value of the currency it issued." It also mandated that Federal Reserve notes would convert into gold at a fixed price of $20.67 per ounce of pure gold. The mandate intended that gold and Federal Reserve notes would be interchangeable.

This aspect of the original design and its ties to gold have been forgotten over time. Morgan himself insisted that the new currency be backed by gold. As the owner of a majority of the assets the bank would ultimately issue credit for, it was essential to Morgan that the currency have a constant in gold against which to be measured. According to Morgan, "the only true form of money was gold," and he made certain that gold served as the foundation of the new monetary act. As initially designed, the Federal

Reserve was meant to always have enough gold sufficient to satisfy any and all requests for redemption.

The Federal Reserve could increase its holdings of gold by raising interest rates, encouraging Americans to deposit gold in the banking system and encouraging foreign investment into the United States. This would shift the flows of gold from the public here and abroad to Federal Reserve vaults and member banks. Conversely, when the Federal Reserve lowered interest rates, gold would flow out of the coffers of the Federal Reserve vaults and into the hands of the public. This construct would protect an orchestrated institution from issuing far more credit than gold backing. While the exact amount of credit in the system would float and go through periods of expansion and contraction, a 40 percent reserve holding remained essential for the long-term health of the institution.

Back to the Future

Today, more than 100 years after the institution's creation, the heads of the Federal Reserve would argue that gold has zero place in the system other than "tradition." Morgan understood the risks associated with extending too much credit and the devaluation of currencies that occurs through runaway government debts. It was essential for the bank's original framework that it stay out of the hands of politicians, while always being backed by gold. For Morgan, the secret father of the Federal Reserve, gold was the only true form of money. While central banks around the world *verbally claim* gold has no meaning, their actions speak otherwise. The one true asset every major central bank in the world owns is gold. Most major central banks have been net buyers of gold over the last decade and have added several thousand tonnes since 2008.

28 Trading Days Later (More or Less)

One of the most important aspects about the newly constructed central bank was that it would become a "lender of last resort." Of particular note is that in the recession of 1893, and the recession of 1906, then in the recession of

1920, and finally in the Great Depression, the role of lender of last resort was meant for only the most solvent institutions. The weaker banks who had taken on too much leverage were allowed to fail. This was a constant mantra for qualification for bailout loans. What's fascinating today is how dramatically that idea has been flipped. In March, the Federal Reserve decided to buy corporate bonds and those of the lowest-rated firms and even junk bonds, becoming a "lender of first resort." This action further incentivizes a moral hazard and careless leverage because everyone gets bailed out. I believe we can call it corporate socialism. Howard Marks recently repeated a famous line; "Capitalism without default is like Catholicism without hell." When nobody is allowed to fail, the system can no longer be considered capitalism.

10 | The Banker

Times of crisis and war are the times when a country most needs to expand its credit facility. On June 14, 1914, when a Bosnian revolutionary named Gavrilo Princip assassinated Archduke of Austria Franz Ferdinand and his wife, such a crisis was sparked. The event would trigger the first world war and confront the six-month-old Federal Reserve with its first true test. The world was about to see the need for credit explode.

The war was initially known as the European war. The fight pitted the Central Powers of Germany, Austria-Hungary, and Turkey against the Allies, mainly France, Great Britain, Russia, Italy, and Japan. The United States stayed out of the war during its first two and a half years, openly debating whether it was our war to fight. President Woodrow Wilson declared that the United States would remain neutral.

Remaining neutral in the conflict turned out to be a windfall to the United States' bottom line. The American economy would boom while we sold materials, munitions, commodities, and other goods to both sides. As supplies headed out, gold flowed in. The war effort caused England and France to go heavily into debt. Once their local central banks had been tapped to exhaustion, these governments turned to the Americans. The largest lender in the crisis was the House of Morgan. Despite the formal "neutrality" of the United States, Morgan's deep relationships in England inclined the private Morgan bank to lend to the side of the Allies. John Moody, in his book the *Masters of Capital,* explained Morgan's involvement in the war following way:

> Not only did England and France pay for their supplies with money furnished by Wall Street, but they made their purchases through the same medium. Inevitably the house of Morgan was selected for this important task. Thus the war had given Wall Street an entirely new role. Hitherto it had been exclusively the headquarters of finance; now it became the greatest industrial mart the world had ever known. In addition to selling stocks and bonds, financing railroads, and perform-ing the other tasks of a banking center, Wall Street began to deal in shells, cannons, submarines, blankets, clothing, shoes, canned meats, wheat, and the thousands of other articles needed for the prosecution of a great war.

The money would flow to the British. The House of Morgan and the *British Army Council and Admiralty* signed a contract whose purchases would ultimately amount to an astronomical $3 billion. As the war raged on, the House of Morgan would preside over purchases each month that were equal to the annual gross national product of the entire world just a generation before. While Morgan publicly proclaimed to be a pacifist, his firm made tremendous fees being the broker to the Allied forces.

Morgan's loyalties nearly put his entire House of Morgan operation at risk. The Allied forces were losing the war. Between 1914, and 1918, Ger-man U-boats, a fleet that totaled a mere *21* submarines, sank 5,700 surface ships. One out of every four British steamers that left harbor never returned. The incredible German submarines were able to cut off the supplies to half of Great Britain, and it looked dire for the Allies. Treasury Secretary William McAdoo wrote in his memoirs:

> Across the sea came the dismay of the British—a dismay that carried a deepening note of disaster. There was a fear, and a well-grounded one, that England may be starved into abject surrender . . . On April 27, 2017, Ambassador Walter H. Page reported confidentially to the President that the food of the British Isles was not more than enough to feed the population for six weeks or two months.

The news reports of the impending defeat was cause for great alarm in New York. If the Germans were to win the war, the losses for J.P. Morgan and company would be catastrophic. Over $1.5 billion in loans had been executed to Britain and France. These loans would become a complete write-off to the House of Morgan and the power elite's interests they represented.

As the battle raged on, it was clear the Allies were on the losing side and were in dire need of reinforcements. The only chance the Allies had of winning the fight was if the Americans were to enter the war on their behalf. The House of Morgan needed the *neutral* United States to join the fray. A German submarine's sinking of the civilian vessel, the *Lusitania,* accomplished exactly that and tilted the balance of American emotion in that direction.

The ship was a British passenger ship built to compete for the lucrative transatlantic passenger trade and was equal in size to the *Titanic,* which had sunk three years earlier. On Friday, May 7, 1915, the ship was hit by a German torpedo and would sink within 18 minutes, killing 1,198 civilian passengers, 128 of whom were American.

The attack on a civilian ship and killing of innocent Americans would shift the tide of emotion towards support for the Allies against the Germans. The sinking of the *Lusitania* would serve as the momentum necessary to push the United States into the war.

Edward G. Griffin, in his epic tale *The Creature from Jekyll Island,* makes the case that the banking cartel from the House of Morgan pushed President Wilson to join the war in order to protect the loans that had been made to the Allies. These men, he claims, understood the need to get the American people behind the Allied war effort and that they would need an emotional trigger to accomplish. The death of innocent Americans would provide exactly that.

The *Lusitania* would eventually be discovered to have held 600 tons of pyroxline (gun cotton), six-million rounds of ammunition, and 1,248 cases of shrapnel shells, which bolstered the argument that the Germans were not in fact sinking a civilian ship, but rather a *secret warship.* The Germans were outraged, claiming the sinking of the ship was justified and that they had a right to sink the ship, regardless that the vessel carried civilian passengers, which the Germans likened to putting women and children at the front lines. The German argument fell on deaf ears. American emotion was too great to overcome and Congress could not deny the groundswell of support. On April, 6, 1917, the United States officially declared war on Imperial Germany. The clear beneficiary of the sinking of the *Lusitania* was the Morgan company and the power elite that they represented.

Once the hands of the United States were forced into joining the war effort, the next trick for the banking cartel would be to get Congress to cover all of the loans that they had made to the Allied forces. One week after President Wilson made the official Declaration of War, Congress passed the *War Loan Act*, extending $1 billion in credit to the Allied nations. The first $200 million went to the British who, in turn, immediately applied it as payment of debt they owed the bank of Morgan. This payment fell far short of the outstanding balance owed. The overdraft to Morgan by the Allies was still $400 million short. The Treasury was unwilling to cover the deficit.

Benjamin Strong, serving as the first president of the newly created Federal Reserve, had a solution. He would simply *create* the money out of thin air. Author Griffin calls Strong's solution *the Mandrake method,* referring to Mandrake the Magician, and the trick of creating money out of debt. It's the same method the Federal Reserve would use in World War II, and still uses today more than 100 years later. The Federal Reserve would "buy bonds" and create the money and add it to the supply.

The massive gold reserves that had flowed to the Americans over the early course of the war was tremendous collateral and meant that the House of Morgan could ultimately convert the newly created money for gold. This would serve to further enrich the power elite, and would create challenges for the Federal Reserve years later.

The first 14,000 American infantry troops arrived in France to begin training for combat on June 14, 1917. More than 2 million soldiers would eventually be sent to the battlefields of the western front in the coming months. The tremendous American momentum so deep into the battle was too great for the Germans to overcome. The war would finally end 18 months later on November 11, 1918.

The story of the financing of World War I is relevant to understanding the genesis, evolution, and extreme power of the newly created central bank. The ability to *create* money had forever been reserved for God. That power was now in the hands of the Federal Reserve, and a group of men effectively acting as bag men for the House of Morgan and the banking cartel. The Fed had created the money to give to England and France, who, in turn, paid back the American bank. All of this would be paid for by the world's consumers in the form of higher prices and inflation.

The outcome of World War I brought tremendous new wealth and power to the United States, which had gone from debtor nation prior to the start of the conflict to the world's largest creditor. The fight also depleted the superpowers of Europe and did more than shift the balance of power—it also shifted the balance of gold holdings, allowing for the United States to build larger reserves of gold than any other country in the world.

The House of Morgan was perhaps the greatest beneficiary. Winning the war allowed a boom in the power of the bank as well whose tentacles were now deeply entrenched on a global scale. The House of Morgan controlled the Federal Reserve, making the power elite of bankers the most powerful group of individuals the world would ever know. Over the next decade, while Europe struggled to recover, the United States would literally roar.

Back to the Future

The "Mandrake method" of creating money through the buying bonds continues today. In the last decade, the Federal Reserve has continued to make new money appear out of thin air. Since 2008 the Federal Reserve has expanded its balance sheet more than five times from $800 billion to $4.1 trillion. While we are no longer on a gold standard, gold is still the standard by which our currency is measured and why gold prices have hit all-time high in every major currency outside the United States. While our currencies will forever continue to be devalued, gold will always serve as the barometer for the true value of money. Gold will always serve as the true foundation of the monetary system.

28 Trading Days Later (More or Less)

1. What struck me when thinking through this chapter since the Covid-19 outbreak were the ideas and the importance of "the balance of American emotion," an "emotional trigger," and the power of "the death of innocent Americans." Politically today, just as it was over 100 years ago, it is imperative that the American people have a unified enemy to coalesce against. Today there is concerted effort from the right and the left, that will certainly only heat up as the 2020 election campaign nears, to label China the evil nation that created and allowed the coronavirus to be unleashed on an innocent and unsuspecting world.

2. In the last two months, the central bank's balance sheet has exploded higher, rising from $4.1 trillion to over $6.7 trillion today. This action is a more than a 50 percent increase in the supply of new money creation. The unfortunate aspect for the Federal Reserve is that the tricks of the magician are now easily identified. Henry Ford cautioned that the people would revolt if they really understood how our monetary system worked. That revolt is a serious risk to the existing structure of the Federal Reserve.

11 | The Lion King

The mindset of the United States following the first world war may well be summed up by the words of writer William Ernest Henley. His poem *Invictus,* whose title means "undefeated" or "unconquerable," ends with the powerful and optimistic words, *I am the master of my fate: I am the captain of my soul.* This became the mindset of the country following the war. Americans felt invincible.

The war had been a test of American power on the world stage. Similar to a young lion first realizing his unbeatable strength, while simultaneously becoming aware of his royal status as king of the jungle, America had come of age and was now the heir to the throne of world power. The crowning wasn't only ceremonial. It was spiritual, tangible and globally accepted. America was the new and undisputed king.

While World War I would claim casualties of 40 million, killing 17 million and wounding 23 million more, American casualties were relatively modest. Of the nearly 5 million who served in the war from the American side, there were only 116,516 deaths, and of those more were due to illness rather than battle. While the United States survived virtually unharmed, Europe had been decimated. Four empires collapsed. Old world countries were abolished and new ones were formed.

For hundreds of years, the center of power for international finance had been located in London, England. That torch was passed across the Atlantic. New York City would become the new center of international finance. Back at home, an American energy and optimism pervaded and the afterparty raged. It was a party that would be promoted and funded by the most powerful bankers in the world, the House of Morgan.

The bank's patriarch, J.P. Morgan, died in 1913. The central bank he secretly worked so hard to create wouldn't be ratified by Congress until six months after his death. His creation endures today. If their power had been great prior to the conflict, the wealth of the banking cartel exploded after the war. To the victor go the spoils. Morgan and his cabal of bankers had backed the winning Allied side, whose newfound wealth allowed them to live like royalty. They were American kings.

The Morgan-designed Federal Reserve, which by 1920 was only seven years old, was rarely tested in its early years. Once the Treasury of the United States created the money to pay back the Morgan loans in 1917, there was little need for any interference or support from the central bank in the boom years following the war. The newly captained bankers of the world set their sails on expansion. The world was embracing change, and the youthful American spirit would lead the charge. The House of Morgan's bankers would be there to provide the *credit* needed for the expansion.

The war had led to tremendous innovations in mass production. The transformation occurred across multiple industries, including film, radio, and the chemical industry. Of course, the industry that had the greatest impact on the future was the automobile. For the first time ever, travel outside of one's local town reshaped the American landscape. Prior to the war, automobiles had been considered a luxury item available only to the wealthy. Henry Ford's assembly line brought down the costs of production, making the automobile affordable to the everyman.

What had taken 12 hours to produce a decade earlier now took just *90 minutes*, allowing Ford to mass produce vehicles while simultaneously bringing down their average price to $290. This amounted to less than three months' salary for the average worker. The automobile, of course, also ignited the rubber, glass, steel, and oil industries. Business was booming for everyone.

But cheaper as they might be, buyers of these cars still needed *financing*, and the bankers and car companies found themselves at the forefront of an entirely new financial market, *consumer lending*. Consumer credit exploded in the 1920s. Alongside the automobile, the technologies of *electricity* and the *telephone* would become emblematic of the new consumer economy. By 1930, half of all American households had a telephone. As electricity became commonplace, appliances—refrigerators, washing machines, toasters, and vacuum cleaners—quickly found their way into homes across the country. The luxuries of life were now within reach for the middle class, and the House of Morgan bankers were there to provide the credit average Americans needed in order to participate.

Another major aftereffect of the war was the global women's suffrage movement. Women of the world had come together during the fight. American women participated in defense industry work and munitions production, performing jobs traditionally reserved for men. Their support and involvement made the case and convinced Americans that the female citizens deserve the right to vote.

The American woman would become a major player in the growth of the booming US economy. Appliances were bought on credit and were sold to a whole new market that had seemingly overnight doubled in size as women were added to the pools of borrowers. Women especially loved the ready-to-wear clothing that mass production had made more affordable. Department stores allowed women to finance the entire purchase prices of appliances and clothing. The First Women's Bank of Tennessee opened in 1919 catered exclusively to women.

"Buy now, pay later" became the new credo for the middle class. Installment plans were blithely offered to virtually any buyers. As credit expanded, lending standards loosened. Large down payments, which at one time were required for most large purchases, were now reduced to "12 easy payments." No item was more financed than the automobile. Half of all cars sold annually were sold on credit by the end of the decade.

Laws prior to the 1920s had capped the abilities of bankers to extend credit by limiting the interest rates they could charge on debt. *Usury laws* were common in most states and capped the rates that banks could charge consumers at an average of 10 percent. In 1916, the passing of the *Uniform*

Small Loan Act allowed specially licensed lenders to charge higher interest rates of up to 36 percent. The regulatory changes in lending coincided with the innovations of the roaring twenties and permitted the amount of credit offered to *double* throughout the decade.

These new laws were a gift to Wall Street. All of the newly created credit produced new money out of thin air. It was money that would ultimately flow almost exclusively into the pockets of the growing trusts and corporations. As the economy boomed and credit exploded, the fortunes on Wall Street skyrocketed and the wealth of the House of Morgan and the power elite rose to unimaginable heights.

Jack Morgan, heir to the J.P. Morgan throne, moved through the decade like a monarch, and he relished his position. When gifting Pope Pius XI with restored Coptic texts in 1922, he made the following comment: "My special job is the most interesting I know anywhere. More fun than being King, Pope, or Prime Minister anywhere—for no one can turn me out of it and I don't have to make any compromises with principles."

These high times were a wonderful example that when growth and ingenuity are combined, true prosperity is the result. Unfortunately, too much of a good thing usually becomes a bad thing. The credit explosion of the roaring twenties that facilitated the nation's greedily growing desires, witnessed a stock market that would increase *400 percent* throughout the decade. While the regular worker was going into debt to afford the trappings of automobiles and new big-ticket consumer products, the titans of Wall Street watched their fortunes balloon. The divide between the wealthy and the working class grew in ways the world had never seen.

While America was booming, Europe was suffering. The finances of Great Britain were left in tatters after the war. The Brits were dependent on commodities produced in the States and the pound sterling had lost much of its value relative to the dollar, making American commodities more expensive to English consumers. This further propelled American growth at the expense of the overindebted Europeans.

Great Britain had always had close ties to the House of Morgan and thus the early Federal Reserve. Not only did the banking cartel privately fund the Allies during World War I, the institution thereafter prioritized the rehabilitation of Great Britain over the rest of Europe. Benjamin

Strong, the first chairman of the Fed, had deep connections in London, and spent a great deal of time abroad. He had developed a great friendship with Montagu Norman, the new Governor of the Bank of England. Of paramount importance for the two men was how to assist Great Britain in her recovery after the war.

Of particular concern was that the British economy had witnessed a massive outflow of gold as a result of the war effort. The two central bankers spent a great deal of time planning how to resuscitate the weakening English superpower, and agreed that gold held the key. It was determined by Strong and Norman that in order for the flow of gold to reverse, interest rates in the United States would need to drop. Carroll Quigley, in his book *Tragedy and Hope, A History of the World in Our Time,* wrote the following:

> Norman had a devoted colleague in Benjamin Strong. In the 1920s they were determined to use the financial power of Britain and of the United States to force all of the major countries of the world to go on the gold standard (with an artificial value set for the benefit of England) and to operate it through the central banks free from all political control. . .without interference from governments.

In 1924, Secretary of the Treasury Andrew Mellon wrote about the importance of lowering interest rates with the objective of raising American prices relative to Great Britain:

> At the present time it is probably true that British prices for goods internationally dealt are, as a whole, roughly 10 percent above our prices, and one of the preliminaries to the re-establishment of gold payment by Great Britain will be to facilitate a gradual readjustment of these price levels before monetary reform is undertaken. . . . The burden of this readjustment must fall largely upon us than upon them. It will be difficult politically and socially for the Bank of England to face the price liquidation in England. . .in the fact that trade is poor and they have over a million people receiving government aid.

The means by which the Federal Reserve would accomplish this "read-justment" would be through the purchasing of government bonds and, as a result, driving down interest rates. These bond purchases increased the Federal Reserve balance sheet by a total of $445 million. At the same time, the discount rate was lowered from 4 percent to 3.5 percent. This further allowed American banks to issue even more credit. When totaled, the amount of new money created would be $10 billion from 1924 to 1930. (For comparison, The Federal Reserve added $73 billion in *one day* to its balance sheet in November 2019.)

As intended, the effect of the Fed's monetary policy saw the American hoard of gold begin to move abroad. Low interest rates and easy credit only further fueled speculation in the paper securities markets, as more and more leverage was created because of the dropping costs of money. Parker Willis, the disillusioned first secretary of the board of governors, wrote in the *North Atlantic Review* in 1929:

> By the autumn of 1926, a group of bankers, among whom was one with a famous name, were sitting at a table in Washington hotel. One of them raised the question whether the low discount rates of the system were not likely to encourage speculation. "Yes," replied the conspicuous figure referred to, "they will, but that cannot be helped. It is the price we must pay for helping Europe."

The banker in question was Jack Morgan, who spent half the year in London. There can be no doubt that the Federal Reserve, which was under the control of Strong, was working at the direction of Jack Morgan, who was more concerned about the fortunes of the British than the moral hazards created from loose monetary policies here at home. It is important to note that these interests were not charitable. The looser monetary policy became, the higher the speculation on Wall Street, the more the pockets of the power elite were lined.

Profits from the debt that financed Americans consumption, as well as the leverage that fueled the massive asset bubble of the stock market, flowed almost exclusively to the banker class on Wall Street. The American worker was leveraged to the hilt. These new consumers of the growing middle class were unfamiliar with the negative side of debt expansion, and the drain on future production. They would be the unwitting fall guys when it all imploded.

The creation of the Federal Reserve permitted the tremendous expansion of credit. For every dollar added to the money supply, 10 times that amount was created by the banks. This expansion of credit was a boon for banking. In the dozen years after the end of the war, securities dealers had grown from a group of about 250 to more than 6500 by 1929. It wasn't only the most powerful bankers who enjoyed the fruits of central bank policies. Smaller dealers and banking institutions sprouted up like weeds—weeds that would later strangle the entire system.

The active securities markets, coupled with the cheap money rates made possible by the Federal Reserve, made it easier for corporations to borrow and fuel their stocks through repurchases built on more and more borrowed money. Cash flooded the market.

Morgan invented the scheme, the Federal Reserve and its banks ran with it. They created a new Monster of Credit, and, with nobody reining them in, allowed the monster to uncontrollably grow. The new playground of risk fueled by cheap money witnessed an explosion in smaller retail banks and private lenders. Cheaper and cheaper money throughout the 1920s allowed these new bankers to create more credit. This credit directly contributed to the stock market speculation. As stocks and bonds boomed, the new bankers were eager to get in on more of the action.

The bailout of Great Britain, which had caused the Fed to lower rates to begin with, had now led to a self-replicating loop of easy money, which led to more leverage, more borrowing on margin, and more bad debt. Money fled hard assets and poured into financial markets. Stocks and bonds soared while commodities and tangible assets suffered.

For analysts at the time, the amount of cash available was a signal of strength, not as an omen of the dwindling opportunities for productive investments. *The day before the crash* the *Wall Street Journal* reported, "There is a vast amount of money awaiting investment, thousands of investors have been waiting for an opportunity to buy stocks."

The market boom enjoyed by the United States in the late 1920s was not matched by other markets. Germany's market peaked in 1927, Britain's in 1928, and France's in early 1929. Shortly before the crash, economist Irving Fisher, in what would later become a famous quote for his incredibly poor timing, offered, "*Stock prices have reached what looks like a permanently high plateau.*" The market had been lulled to sleep by a seemingly never-ending rise. And then it all collapsed.

The selling began on the US stock market in October 24, 1929, famously known as Black Thursday. The self-replicating loop of leverage that drives markets higher in the boom time becomes a noose that strangles as stocks sell off. The market collapse of 1929 is an abject lesson in liquidity risk. Margin calls forced those who had bought on leverage to sell more to create the necessary liquidity. Selling led to more selling, which led to panic and even more selling, and a further drying up of liquidity. The day would end with a record 16 million shares traded on the day. Unfortunately, the selling continued on the following Monday and Tuesday. The Dow Jones, which had been trading at 381 points in September, had dropped to 230 points by Tuesday, October 29, a fall of 40 percent.

While the market collapse of 1929 is credited with causing the Great Depression, and is an easy target due to its drama, the pain didn't come all at once. The true cause developed over the next several years as consumer spending and investment would drop, causing steep declines in production from industrial output. The Depression hit its low in 1933. By then, nearly half of the nation's banks had failed and over 15 million Americans were unemployed.

The dark side of debt expansion is widespread default. The growth in debt allows for the perception that things are stronger than they actually are. As production invariably slows, the debt becomes a major headwind. Debt payments cannot be maintained, leading to default. It was a default on the massive amounts of global debt that led to the Great Depression.

The even darker underbelly of a loose monetary policy is that it speeds up an inequality of wealth. As rates are lowered and money is expanded and more and more money flows to the investor class, the rich get richer at the expense of the poor.

Every revolution in history is founded on inequality. Revolutions are born out of pain. The pain of the recession caused a collective mindset shift and eventually the power elite suffered from their own mismanagement. The collapse of the market, and then the underlying economy in the ensuing years, hastened the disappearance of the all-powerful banker. If the roaring twenties promoted the banker boom, the pain that endured through the depressed thirties witnessed their demise. An angry electorate blamed Wall Street, and the money changers lost control of the original design. As the anger and suffering from the Great Depression intensified, the Federal Reserve lost its most important asset: *independence*. It would be nearly 50 years before it gained it back.

Back to the Future

History repeats. Where we stand today is nearly identical to where the world stood 90 years ago. The equity markets, which boomed *four times* during the 1920s, have similarly increased *four times* in the last decade. Notice that while American prosperity continued in the late 1920s, other nations were suffering. This exact situation has played out in recent years as the global economy has struggled while the American market has continued to rise. When the next recession hits in earnest, we can expect Wall Street to be blamed.

28 Trading Days Later (More or Less)

I'm fascinated by the idea of the "collective mindset." After World War I, the mindset of Americans was one of young strength. It was both spiritual and tangible. The foundation of that strength was that the United States was the creditor to the world. From February 26 to May 6, 2020, the Federal Reserve expanded its balance sheet by $2.6 trillion. Our national debt and deficit are exploding. The new collective mindset is built on the idea that debt and deficits don't matter. It's why the Great Devaluation will make us so insecure. We innately understand that being debt free offers tremendous freedom; swimming in debt makes us feel enslaved and trapped.

12 | The Money Pit

The Federal Reserve's response to the 1929 collapse has often been criticized by today's central bankers. In a conference honoring Milton Friedman in 2002, future Federal Reserve Chairman Ben Bernanke said, "You're right, we did it. We are very sorry, but thanks to you we won't do it again," referring to Friedman's claim that it was the mistakes of the central bank that caused the Great Depression.

What the Fed missed most in 1929 was the direction of Benjamin Strong, the Fed's first chairman, who died in 1928, leaving the institution (literally) without strong leadership. Strong had understood the risks coming from the viral growth of the lending business and often lobbied to raise rates to stem the tide of speculators and speculation.

The Federal Reserve system, which was designed to provide the banking industry a lender of last resort, failed miserably in that function. Over 5000 banks would fail by 1933. At the time, the weeding out of weaker banks was considered a necessary function of the system. The House of Morgan, whom the Fed was specifically built to protect, was not a big participant in the Wall Street speculation. In fact, the larger banks, while damaged, were still in decent shape throughout the crisis. The feeling at the Fed was that the smaller institutions were casualties that were to be expected and not to be saved.

For this reason, the collapse was initially tolerable on Wall Street. While the banking cartel lost fortunes, they still maintained significant wealth. Their tragic mistake, though, was allowing the smaller retail banks that had grown like a fungus at their feet, to die. Along with these bank failures came the dissipation of the savings of millions of unsuspecting Americans. The average worker kept his savings in the local banks, and bank runs came fast and furious. The resulting economic hardship caused a massive shift in the social collective mindset. Regardless of the cause, the effect was one that would ultimately end the Federal Reserve's *independence.*

At the core of the crisis was the growing difference in value between the dollar and gold. They were intended to be the same. Federal Reserve rules mandated that the dollar be backed and maintained as good as gold. However, the explosion of credit in the 1920s caused substantial growth in the overall money supply without a corresponding growth in the supply of gold. As the dollar became devalued, more depositors turned in their cash for gold. With less gold on hand than was being withdrawn, banks were unable to meet demand withdrawals, and one by one around the country they began folding.

Debt bubbles and collapses are nothing new. Mankind has continued to make the same mistakes over and over throughout the course of history. The problem has faced central planners for thousands of years. In 405 BC, in his play *The Frogs*, Aristophenes preached about the dangers of bad money "chasing out" the good:

> It has often struck our notice that the course our city runs
> Is the same towards men and money. She has true and worthy sons:
> She has good and ancient silver, she has good and recent gold.
> These are coins untouched with alloys; everywhere their fame is told.
> Not all Hellas holds their equal, not all Barbary far and near.
> Gold or silver, each well minted, tested each and ringing clear.
> Yet, we never use them! Others always pass from hand to hand.
> Sorry brass just struck last week and branded with a wretched brand.
> So with men we know for upright, blameless lives and noble names.
> Trained in music and palestra, freemen's choirs and freemen's games.
> These we spurn for men of brass. . .

This idea that "bad money will always chase out the good" was presented to Queen Elizabeth I by Sir Thomas Gresham, a sixteenth-century advisor to the royal court, to explain the issues with the English currency, the shilling, after debasements by her father Henry VIII. The king had debased the silver in the coinage by *40 percent* as a way to increase the government's revenue without raising taxes. The idea has since become known as *Gresham's law*.

King Henry VIII ordered that the silver in the coinage be reduced from 92.5 percent purity to 25 percent purity, the difference replaced with other cheap base metals. The Great Debasement of 1544, also saw the amount of gold in coinage to be reduced from 23 carats to 20 carats.

King Henry's trick had been used often in the course of history. The Roman Empire's downfall is partially attributed to the ongoing debasement of its gold and silver coinage. The major silver coin for the first 220 years of the Roman Empire was the *denarius*. In the early days, the coin had 4.5 grams of silver. A finite supply of silver limited the amount of denari that could be minted. The way the Romans worked their way around this issue was to continually reduce the amount of silver in each coin. By the time of Marcus Arelius in 175 AD, the amount of silver in each coin had dropped from 99 percent to 75 percent. By the time of Emperor Galinius in 265 AD, the amount of silver in each coin would be reduced down to 5 percent, with a thin layer of silver covering a bronze core. Three years later, the amount of silver in the coinage was reduced to 0.5 percent.

The ultimate blow to the Roman Empire was when the soldiers demanded higher wages as the coinage was debased, ultimately refusing to accept it as payment from the Empire.

(Pay special note to the speed of the debasement at the end. In three years at the end of the Empire, the Roman currency lost 90 percent of its value. A similar debasement today would put the price of gold at $15,000 per ounce.)

Currency debasement transfers wealth away from the citizens. Gresham's point to the queen was that with various purity of coins in circulation, the one with the least purity would drive out the more pure metals. Citizens would "hoard" the more pure coinage, and only the debased metals would circulate. These metals would ultimately be the one used to pay taxes. In the end, only the bad currency would remain.

The early 1930s witnessed Gresham's law in action. Bank depositors turned in their dollars for gold. Bank runs became prevalent as citizens hoarded their gold. This hoarding of gold created a massive headwind for the economy. Economies need money to circulate. As gold was being withdrawn and hoarded, the economy ground to a halt and the Depression deepened. The ongoing depression witnessed a loss of the most important key to any banking system: *faith*.

Back to the Future

It is unpayable debt that drives governments to debase the currency. This has been the way since the beginning of time. Every great empire in history has eventually fallen due to their unpayable debts. What governments count on while this is occurring is that the citizens won't notice. How many of us have been focused on investing our money in the stock market over the last 20 years? While we have all been focused on the stock market, which has hit all-time highs and offers a glorious mountain that only surges higher, almost everyone has missed the true mountain of debt growing alongside it—gold has outperformed the highest-flying market in history *two to one* during this time. Stocks have gone up 250 percent in 20 years. Gold has increased 500 percent in the same time, which means our currency has weakened dramatically. While the number on the Dow is higher, our wealth has decreased by 50 percent.

28 Trading Days Later (More or Less)

The idea of inflation is one that for the last decade has seemed a far-off reality. The worry over that time hasn't been inflation, it has been deflation. That is, until the last couple months. When we add to the balance sheet of the central bank by 50 percent in a matter of weeks, the real and new concern must be that inflation will soon rear its head. When the central banks become a lender of "first" resort, inflation is the desired outcome.

13 | It's a Wonderful Life

The backdrop of the Great Depression led to the landslide victory of Democrat Franklin Delano Roosevelt over incumbent President Hoover in 1932. Roosevelt carried every state outside the northeast and won 57 percent of the popular vote, a record for the Democratic party at the time.

Roosevelt's campaign promised reforms of a *New Deal* for the American people, which were the opposite of Hoover's protectionist policies. When Roosevelt accepted the Democratic nomination, he stated, "Ours must be a party of liberal thought, of planned action, of enlightened international outlook, and of the greatest good to the greatest number of our citizens." His New Deal offered financial reforms, public works, and regulations designed around what he called the three *R*s—relief, recovery, and reform—as the solution to the Great Depression.

The ideas of the New Deal had been considered radical just four years prior. Then, Republican candidate Herbert Hoover had also won in his own landslide in 1928, on the exact opposite platform. Hoover had been elected on an agenda of *protectionism* and putting the American worker "first." These promises by Hoover were followed through with the *Smoot-Hawley tariffs* in 1930, which placed a tax on over 125,000 imported goods. These protectionist policies, at first anyway, kept America prospering above other countries. We had boom years in 1928 and 1929 while the rest of the world was in recession. These same policies, however, later hastened the downturn.

Beginning in February 1933, Michigan closed its banks for an eight-day banking holiday. The action caused widespread fears that other banks would follow. On the day of Roosevelt's inauguration, Delaware became the 48th, and last, state to close its banks.

FDR was inaugurated on March 4, 1933. He spent his first week in office addressing the bank closures that had been sweeping the nation. Two days after the inauguration, Roosevelt called for a *national bank holiday* of four days that would keep all banks shut until Congress could act. The *Emergency Banking Act*, passed on March 9 stipulated that the Federal Reserve would issue unlimited amounts of currency to reopened banks, and that all deposits would be backed by a *100 percent* deposit insurance. The proposal was made amidst chaos. Over 100 newly elected Democrats were also serving in their first days in Congress and were eager to pass legislation that addressed the banking collapse. The urgency of the crisis was such that only one copy of the bill was prepared. Henry Steagall, chairman of the banking committee, read aloud the contents of the bill to the newly formed Congress.

The new technology of radio allowed Roosevelt to speak directly to the American population like no previous president had in what would become known as "fireside chats." The radio allowed Roosevelt to explain his policies directly to the people and quell rumors. His apparent calm and self-assurance in the face of crisis became an identifying trait of the Roosevelt legacy. His talks were effective and soothed the nation. Even better, his emergency policy worked. The depositors who had withdrawn their cash and gold lined up to redeposit more than half of what they had removed when the banks opened on March 9, 1933. The stock market posted its best one-day increase ever, rising 15 percent in one day.

While the banking institutions showed early signs of recovery, an underlying fundamental issue remained. Depositors had removed their gold and continued to hoard the yellow metal. Gresham's law was still in effect. The "bad money" of the dollar had pushed out the "sound money" of gold from the economy. Something dramatic needed to be done about gold.

One month later, by *Executive Order 6102*, Roosevelt did just that by making gold ownership by private citizens illegal (Figure 13.1).

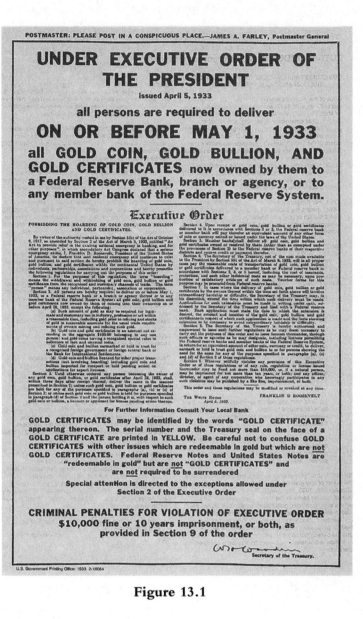

Figure 13.1

The reasons provided were that "gold hoarding" was slowing the economy, stalling economic growth, and deepening the recession. Roosevelt labeled the activity "un-American," essentially making faith in the economy an act of patriotism. The order was deemed law with no outside oversight or approval from Congress or the Judiciary.

The true purpose of Roosevelt's action was to remove the restriction on the Federal Reserve's ability to increase the money supply. The order required that all gold bullion and gold certificates be turned into any member bank of the Federal Reserve system, which, in effect, bailed out the Federal Reserve. But the bailout came at a cost. The Federal Reserve was forced to give up its "independence" as a result.

But not all at once. Initially, few were calling for a complete overhaul of the system. It wasn't until the results of the Pecora Commission, a Senate investigation led by Judge Ferdinand Pecora into the cause of the Wall Street crash, that the tide of sentiment turned against the bankers of Wall Street and the Federal Reserve. The Pecora commission found a wide array of abuses by banks and their affiliates, including *conflicts of interest, underwriting of unsound securities*, and *pool operations* that were falsely supporting the price of bank stocks. The hearings ended on May 4, 1934. Pecora was thereafter appointed the first commissioner of the Securities and Exchange Commission (SEC).

It was also uncovered by the commission that bankers had taken on debts from loans made to Latin America, then bundled these loans into bonds and sold the toxic assets as securities to their clients. The exposed "rigging" of the stock market lead to sweeping reform of the American finance system through new financial laws put in place by FDR's *New Deal*.

Glass-Steagall was one such piece of legislation. Its name refers to its sponsors, Carter Glass and Henry Steagall. This legislation separated banking into two forms, commercial and investment banking, prevented investment banks and securities firms from taking deposits, and discontinued the ability of reserve member banks to trade and purchase securities for themselves or their clients. The law effectively ended the ability of public lending institutions to also be speculators in the stock market. Its passage was a huge blow to Wall Street and the House of Morgan.

(The repeal of Glass-Steagall legislation in 1999 is widely credited with the explosive boom in banking profits and the root cause of the housing crisis.)

What followed after Glass-Steagall was effectively a *universal currency debasement*. In 1934, Congress passed the *Gold Reserve Act,* which summarily raised the price of gold from $20 to $35. Moving the price of gold meant an overnight devaluation of the currencies of the world. While many decried the policy as illegal, the devaluation allowed for the reflation of the world's economy. The stock market would go on to rally 200 percent from its 1933 low over the next three years.

Roosevelt's executive order recalling gold constructed a core pillar of America's future dominance on the world economic stage. Gold pouring in from her citizens meant that the United States became the dominant holder of the world's gold supply, with over 20,000 tonnes, three-fourths of the world's total. It prepared the United States for Bretton Woods and enabled us to flex our Golden Rule of power. Remember, "He who has the gold makes the rules." Since that time, America's dominance on the world stage above all others has continued uninterrupted.

The Federal Reserve's favorable image was substantially and dramatically impacted as a result of the Great Depression. In fact, the central bank was blamed for the collapse. The public anger directed at Wall Street and the Reserve Bank led to sweeping changes. The central bank as an institution was taken over by Congress with the passing of the Emergency Banking Act of 1933.

This meant that in just the few short years since its creation, the Federal Reserve Bank lost the very thing that J.P. Morgan and the Jekyll Island Club had understood to be the essential element of its power—independence from government control. The impact of the Great Depression was too great even for the fat-cat bankers to overcome.

Back to the Future

The benefit of understanding history is that it can offer insight into the present. Mark Twain said, "History may not repeat itself, but it sure does rhyme." The populist protectionist movement of Hoover and his

Smoot-Hawley tariffs on 125,000 American goods in the late 1920s sure rhymes with today's political environment. Hoover then looks a lot like Donald Trump today.

History teaches that extreme times call for extreme measures. The policies adopted in the New Deal had been considered crazy to people in 1929 at the peak of the boom. But just three years later, what had seemed so crazy before suddenly became urgently necessary. FDR's policies sure look a lot like those proposed by Bernie Sanders and Elizabeth Warren today. (So similar, in fact, that the platform of the left is called the *Green New Deal*.)

28 Trading Days Later (More or Less)

As historians looking for clues to what might happen next, we should pay particular attention to the potential erosion of the *independence* of the Federal Reserve. The entire system was designed by Morgan to remain independent. Losing that independence to the politicians encouraged debasement and the transfer of wealth away from the power elite back toward the masses. The Great Depression was a crisis too dire to permit the continued independence of the Fed. Monetary policy was taken over by the executive branch and Congress, and was not returned to the Federal Reserve until 1951. The Federal Reserve was *labeled* the culprit and positioned as the cause of the problem. Does any of this seem familiar? Trump's attacks against the Federal Reserve have positioned the Fed to take the blame as the next recession hits in earnest.

14

Signs

Going back in time to review the early foundation of the Federal Reserve allows for a comparison between *then* and *now*. We would all do well to heed the wisdom espoused by Mark Twain, who wrote, "History may not repeat itself, but it sure does rhyme." We have come full circle and sit exactly where we were 90 years ago. Only by recognizing a problem can we attempt to address it or predict its natural next progression. Everything in life is cyclical, which means that all things have a beginning, a middle, and an end.

The debt crisis that developed during the 1920s was a result of the easy money policies of the young Federal Reserve that ended in a collapse and led to the Great Depression. The debt crisis that has occurred over the last decade looks eerily similar to what the world faced then. The following five signs are an identical replica of the signs leading to that painful economic recession of the 1930s. They serve as a harbinger of what's coming next.

This chapter looks at five signs that we are at the end of the super-cycle and are headed for a new beginning. Each section includes its own "28 Trading Days Later" addendum.

#1 The Wealth Gap

The uber-rich at the turn of the nineteenth century, led by the banking cartel of the House of Morgan, included the Carnegies, the Vanderbilts, and the Rockefellers. The families were wealthier than the former monarchs of Europe. Their concentration of wealth should have forewarned the risks. When all of the money is controlled by the few, and the main pillar supporting the structure is increasingly higher asset prices, the entire mountain of paper is in jeopardy of collapsing like a house of cards. The stock market crash is remembered by many as the *cause* of The Great Depression, rather than a symptom. But the actual disease that had infected the world was *debt*. It was a malady America had considered itself immune to until the stock market collapsed. Soon thereafter, though, Americans suffered the same fate plaguing much of the world, *unemployment* and *poverty*.

Three years after the market collapsed in 1929, the American economy hit bottom. The Depression was so intense that even the affluent suffered. Doctors and lawyers saw their incomes drop by *40 percent*. More than *25 percent* of the US population couldn't find work at all.

While the roaring twenties were a time of American prosperity, it was an unequal abundance. According to Gabriel Zucman, an economics professor at the University of California Berkeley, in 1929 the top *one-tenth of 1 percent* of the richest adults owned a share of household wealth, which represented nearly 25 percent of the overall wealth of the country. According to statistics, the number of millionaires participating in the stock market in 1929 was between 25,000 and 35,000. Less than 1 percent of Americans owned any stocks at all.

The divide between the wealthy and the poor became a primary focus of vitriol and anger after the economy collapsed. Wall Street would eventually be identified as the culprit for the situation and sweeping regulatory change soon followed.

The wealth gap hit its highest point in history in 2020. The top 0.1 percent today own 25 percent of American wealth. The top 1 percent of Americans own 50 percent of the wealth in America. Today, it's not

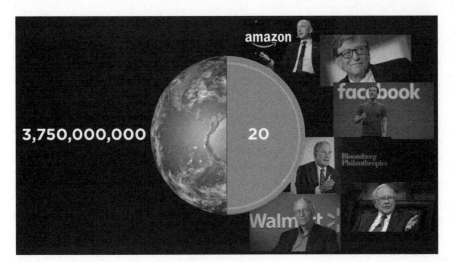

Figure 14.1

families but individuals: Jeff Bezos, Bill Gates, Mark Zuckerberg, Michael Bloomberg, Rob Walton, Warren Buffett, and others (see Figure 14.1).

28 Trading Days Later (More or Less)

This disparity between the wealthy and poor has never been more obvious than it is today. The Federal Reserve's extreme actions due to the coronavirus crisis have put their policies front and center. From March 23 to the time of this writing on May 10, and as a result of the Federal Reserve stepping in with what amounts to over $3 trillion in emergency liquidity, the Dow Jones has risen 5800 points and increased a total of 31 percent. During this exact time frame, 33 million Americans filed for unemployment benefits, reaching levels greater than seen during the Great Depression.

The lowest-earning workers have been hit the hardest. According to Axios, the jobs that have suffered the greatest layoffs have come on the low-income side of the spectrum. The estimate is that 77 percent of all employees making less than $25,000 have been laid off due to coronavirus. On the flip side, Axios estimates that only 2.5 percent of all employees earning over $70,000 have lost their jobs. Guess which group owns stock? The coronavirus crisis has, at warp speed, directly exposed the issue of income inequality.

#2 Populism

Prosperity and *stability* are prerequisites for democracy. When shared these become the fundamental values of the capitalist system. When these values are unequally held, the capitalist system is at risk. While America was enjoying her newfound wealth on the global stage after World War One, the remainder of the world was mostly suffering. The 1920s witnessed a deep and growing chasm among traditional political mindsets. The war had caused the downfall of four monarchies: Russia, Turkey, Austro-Hungary, and Germany. The uneven handling of the reconstruction by the British and French led to tremendous resentment and anger. As famine and poverty became the norm for many in Europe, populist political movements were born. *Communism, fascism, socialism,* and *nationalism* spread abroad. The lack of prosperity was the breeding ground. Wealth inequality spurred radical political movements that grew in size and momentum after the war.

The Paris Peace Conference held between the leaders of the globe in 1919, documented through a series of treaties called the *Paris Peace Treaties*, were intended to restore peace throughout the world. The city of Paris became the city of the newly formed headquarters of the world government. Bankrupted empires were *reconstructed* into new countries by the Allied winners. The results of these conferences included harsh penalties against the Germans who had been declared guilty and required Germany to pay for *all of the costs of the war* to the winners. Germany was not permitted to attend the meetings that would decide their fate.

The ensuing fall of these once-wealthy empires and the wobbly governments that replaced them caused tremendous strife for their citizens. The Great Russian Famine of 1921 led to the death of five million Russians. It was the result of a failed government unable to deliver food to its starving people.

The fate of the German people after World War I was not much better. France and Belgium's military occupation of the industrialized Ruhr Valley in 1923, in response to missed reparation payments, caused the German citizens to bond together in civil disobedience. Radical right-wing movements flourished. The Weimar Republic ruled Germany from 1919 to 1933, until the Nazi Party seized control. As German coffers were bled dry by war debt and reparation payments, the German currency suffered hyperinflation.

Populism is best defined as anger caused by *inequality*. The anger of the German people and the disparate populist factions formed as a result allowed Hitler to seize power in 1933 with less than a majority of support for the extreme views of Nazism. Hitler fanned the flames of anger directed toward the Jewish banking elite who had fared far better as a class than the average German after World War I. The income of a middle-class Jew was three times that of the average Berliner. As the crisis continued, six million unemployed Germans either directly supported or silently acquiesced to Hitler's demonization of the Jewish people, who were held as responsible for their plight.

28 Trading Days Later (More or Less)

Populism has spread alongside wealth inequality over the last few decades. In the last few years we have witnessed Brexit, the election of Donald Trump, and the election of Boris Johnson. Riots have broken out in Hong Kong and France, and populist leaders have come into power in Catalonia, Mexico, and Brazil. Anger, populism, and nationalism are spreading globally.

Sadly, it appears as if the coronavirus pandemic will send China and the United States on a path to deeper escalation. The Trump administration has taken the aggressive position by labeling the pandemic a "Wuhan virus" created in a Chinese lab. Chinese officials have denied the US allegations and have accused US officials of attempting "to shift their own responsibility for their poor handling of the epidemic to others."

While China bashing may seem expedient, especially during an election year, it can push the world ever closer to the extremes of nationalism and could very well lead to a new cold war between China and the US.

#3 Tariffs

Populist leaders throughout history have often turned to the policy of tariffs. Tariffs are a nationalistic approach that encourages domestic consumption over that of foreign goods. With the American currency strong relative to its European counterparts in the 1920s, American consumers were able to import cheaper goods. The strong dollar became a terrible drag on exports. In an effort to direct agricultural product sales nationally versus internationally, Hoover, in his campaign for the presidency in 1928, promised the American farmer he would put tariffs on imported agricultural goods from overseas. After the stock market collapsed in 1929, protectionism gained momentum.

Legislation was proposed by Senator Reed Smoot of Utah that placed tariffs on more than 125,000 imported goods. The legislation became known as the *Smoot-Hawley tariffs*. It was passed against the recommendation of more than 1,000 economists. Hoover disregarded their advice, and in a show of support to his base, signed the Foreign Goods Tax into law on June 17, 1930.

The reasons provided for the implementation of tariffs was that the American farmer was at a disadvantage to foreign agriculture due to the strength of the US currency. A strong dollar made exports more expensive and imports cheaper. The strength of the dollar would later play a role in Roosevelt's decision to devalue the dollar against gold.

Donald Trump has become known around the world as "Tariff Man Trump" for his imposition of tariffs on consumer goods from China and Europe. This has been enacted in defense of the American worker. Trump has also been at war with the Federal Reserve to weaken the dollar. Tariffs are a policy that has grown in usage and are currently employed by China, Europe, and virtually all emerging markets.

28 Trading Days Later (More or Less)

The collapse in the price of oil, a result of the oil wars between Saudi Arabia and Russia, could lead to additional nationalist policies as the Trump administration takes measures to protect the American oil companies and production. Tariffs are a logical next step, especially given that Trump has touted American oil independence as one of the main drivers of our new "booming" economy. Populism leads to nationalism—which leads to tariffs.

#4 Asset Bubbles

When central banks lower interest rates, commodities and tangible assets fall in price at the expense of financial assets, which become inflated as a result. This is a function of the *flow* of capital. As more money is printed and more credit is created, it flows to those who have access, and then where it can find the greatest return. In times of lower rates and *easy credit*, money flows into financial assets. Easy credit leads to financial asset bubbles. The decade of the roaring twenties witnessed such a bubble, during which the stock market increased four times.

Give a *working man* a dollar and he is likely to spend it. Give a *wealthy man* a dollar and he is likely to invest it. The economy, and the velocity of money, are deeply impacted by where the money flows. The early Federal Reserve created money and lent it exclusively to the executive class, which then took that money and bought financial assets. This effectively created a self-replicating loop that drove more and more dollars into the paper financial markets at the expense of the real economy.

The crux of the Great Depression was that prices kept falling. As money becomes concentrated among the wealthy, like it did in the late 1920s, there isn't enough available to hold up the prices of tangible goods. There is only so much corn and wheat a wealthy person can consume. Once the paper markets collapsed, the credit attached to these paper assets also vanished. What years earlier had been too much money in the system, all flowing to financial assets, evaporated with the collapse in equities.

Over the course of the last decade, as the Federal Reserve has created trillions of dollars, stocks have inflated four times. This while commodities and tangible assets have stayed flat or declined. The price of oil was $70 per barrel in December 2009. Ten years later, in February 2020, the price of oil was down almost 30 percent at only $50 per barrel.

28 Trading Days Later (More or Less)

The price of oil fell to negative $40 in April 2020 while the Dow Jones increased 18 percent during the same span.

#5 The Warren Buffett Indicator

Mankind is bound to make the same mistakes over and over again. Each time we believe "this time is different." So the wisest investors follow indicators from the past that offer clues to the future. One measurement that has been historically proven for its ongoing accuracy is the *market cap to GDP ratio*. This compares the amount of dollars invested in the stock market and measures it against total GDP.

Warren Buffett made the ratio famous in 2001 during a *Fortune* magazine interview. Buffett explained he used the metric to avoid the market collapse of the dot-coms. The ratio has since popularly become known as the *Warren Buffett Indicator*. The metric is quite simple and allows for a better understanding of where capital has flowed. When more money is flowing to the financial economy versus the real economy, financial asset prices become inflated, and ultimately pose great risks. The imbalance can be measured by the ratio (Figure 14.2).

Those that remember the heat of the dot-com craze will remember that corporations were raising capital on *projected future results* and growth.

Ratio = Total Market Cap / GDP	Valuation
Ratio < 50%	Significantly Undervalued
50% < Ratio < 75%	Modestly Undervalued
75% < Ratio < 90%	Fair Valued
90% < Ratio < 115%	Modestly Overvalued
Ratio > 115%	Significantly Overvalued

Where is it now?

CALCULATE

As of 01/13/2020

154.85%

Significantly Overvalued

Figure 14.2

These were firms that had virtually no revenues. This is eerily similar to the tech firms of today, who raise capital on growth-potential rather than on actual revenues. When capital chases unproductive returns, asset bubbles form. When these assets sell off, their declines can be rapid. As we know, Buffett had his best years after the collapse of the tech bubble. He had cash on the sidelines and was able to buy assets on the cheap thereafter. Today Buffett sits on the largest cash pile in history. The reason? He doesn't like the price of anything.

The historical average for the Warren Buffett Indicator is 90 percent. Just before the collapse of 1929, the market cap to GDP ratio hit 141 percent. The metric hit 151 percent before the dot-com's collapsed.

The market cap to GDP ratio hit an all-time highs in history of 154 percent in January 2020; this is an obvious indication of overvaluation and an ominous sign for equities moving forward.

For the last 40 years, one investment strategy has superseded all others. The all-powerful central bank has made financial assets the best place for investors to allocate their capital. During that time, the Federal Reserve has attained a God-like power that seemingly can always control the fate of financial markets.

These signs serve as warnings for those who remember history. As the famous saying goes, "If it looks like a duck, swims like a duck, and quacks like a duck—it's probably a duck." The signs are too similar to ignore. They foretell the turning of the cycle and of a new beginning.

The mindset shift of the imminent *Great Devaluation* represents a turning point in the future collective mindset. It is for this reason that I believe the 2020s will look and feel very similar to the Great Depression and cause the greatest transfer of wealth in human history.

28 Trading Days Later (More or Less)

Even after the coronavirus shock, the market cap to GDP ratio as of May 10 stood at a significantly overvalued 133 percent. This is a sign that far too much capital is chasing equity returns relative to actual real production.

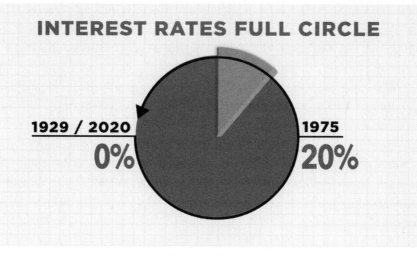

Figure 16.6

The swing from the 1930s through the 1970s witnessed a transition, from peak *ME* to peak *WE*. Not surprisingly, the wealth gap, which was the widest in 1929, swung all the way back to its most even in history by 1975. Risks are the greatest at the peak of the pendulum. During a *WE* peak, the problem is *inflation*. During a *ME* peak, the problem is *deflation*. As a result, interest rates rose from 0 percent in the 1930s to highs of 20 percent in the 1970s. Forty-five years later, interest rates have swung back to 0 percent (Figure 16.6).

The circle is complete. Millennials have been burdened with the unpayable debts of their grandparents. The US government spends *63 percent* of its annual budget on mandatory spending for the elderly in the form of Social Security, Medicare, and Medicaid. This lopsided flow of funds creates an inevitable evolution. Millennials will elect new leaders who will pass laws that will direct the flow of funds toward their agenda and away from wealthy boomers. In the 2020 Democratic primary campaign, several candidates promised student debt forgiveness, free healthcare, and ultimately, universal basic income.

The stock market collapse that began the Great Depression occurred 90 years ago in October 1929 and spawned a decade-long depression, the worst in modern history. It was preceded by a runup in the stock market that was fueled by a massive debt bubble propelled by the early Federal Reserve. The last decade has witnessed the same trajectory, as stocks and bonds have been inflated to extreme highs through monetary manipulation by the Federal Reserve.

When we recognize the world through the circle of the supercycle, and the two *180-degree* swings of the pendulums, change becomes a natural expectation and something to embrace. The 90-year cycle is coming to its organic end; a turning is now inevitable. The end of the saeculum's circle is complete. We are due for another crisis that will change the collective mindset. *The Great Devaluation* coming in the 2020s will bring with it a mindset shift—a new direction—and fiscal funding will flow from older to younger generations.

17 | Contagion

There is a flaw that is deeply ingrained in the human condition. This "programming error" mandates mankind will continue to make the same mistakes, over and over again. This blind spot can be explained in the mathematical curve called an *asymptote*.

An *asymptote* is a curve on an X and Y axis that at some point along the curve shoots upward toward infinity. These curves are the results of *unsustainable exponential growth*. When the growth curve hits the asymptote, the curve becomes a straight line. As we will learn, our brains do not easily comprehend *exponential growth* and the crises man continues to endure are simply asymptotes that can no longer be contained.

Identifying the asymptote allows us to *see* the conclusion *before* it occurs. It is the entire foundation for the saeculum, and the explanation for why mankind is destined to make the same mistakes over and over again, every 90 years. Mankind does not recognize exponential growth *as it's occurring*. Our brains do not readily process abstract ideas. It is this particular human limitation that causes crises to arise, and why black swans seem to come out of nowhere.

To best understand how asymptotes apply to our lives, imagine a man who has a massive coronary on his 75th birthday. He is told by his doctor that if he has one more french fry, one more cigarette, one more drink, it

147

could literally kill him. His heart attack wasn't caused by something he did the day before his birthday. The issue was something that had built up over decades of poor lifestyle choices. His arteries didn't go from being healthy to clogged overnight. It was a problem that continued to grow over time. Poor habits took place over decades.

The heart attack is the asymptote, it's the crisis moment. At this stage, he will need a dramatic lifestyle change if he wants to continue living. The crisis, therefore, is not a black swan from out of nowhere, but rather a predictable outcome. In this scenario, there are many things that could have been done to avert the crisis. This crisis is defined by the asymptote, and understanding its movement along the curve is critical for those wishing to predict the future.

Let's first recognize the functional limitations of our brain, which scientific research is still working to fully understand. We know that the brain is made up of specialized areas that work in complementary fashion and are responsible for both voluntary and involuntary reactions. To this point in human evolution, the average human brain is far better at calculating concrete concepts than imagining the abstract. Our brains more easily recognize tangible objects—people, places, objects, and things—than they do the theoretical, the spiritual, or the ephemeral. When problems are made concrete, it becomes far easier for the human brain to assimilate.

The idea of *exponential growth* is an abstract problem that the human brain doesn't instinctually recognize. This deficiency may be the number one reason mankind continues to fall victim to black swans that seem to come out of nowhere but that, in retrospect, seem so obvious. But understanding the reality of exponential growth will allow us to identify the coming crisis before it ruins us.

The following eighth-grade level math question, asked of 14-year-olds around the world, will highlight the natural limitation of the human brain to appreciate the concept of exponential growth: *If you take a penny and double it every day for one month, what is your quick guess as to how much money you will have at the end of the month?*

Most people confronted with this question immediately guess a number around $500.

Now do the actual math. A penny *doubled* every day for a month would result in *$1.35 million* in a standard 28-day February, over *$5 million* in a

30-day month, and over *$10 million* in a standard 31-day month. These numbers are mind-blowing to virtually everyone who contemplates the penny question.

The truth is unexpected, not because the concrete math is too challenging but because *instinctually* our gut reaction is to greatly *underestimate* the answer. The average man on the street won't recognize simple reality until they really focus on the facts they've known since they were kids. Even when told the correct choice, most people are *so disbelieving* of this answer that they insist on counting out the math on their fingers for themselves before accepting the answer. It just *feels* impossible. The doubling penny question is asked of eighth graders to illustrate the sneaky power of *exponential growth*. Our concrete-conditioned brains obscure the reality of exponential growth, even when it is happening right in front of us. It is this inherent weakness of man that is the root cause of why history repeats itself.

An interesting thing happens to the brains of test subjects who watch this played out in a sequence. As the numbers begin getting larger toward the last five days of the month, the size and scope of the answer start to become clearer. Our sixth sense typically kicks in by day 25, as the number hits $167,772.16. This is when most people recognize how wrong their initial expectations were and they get a foreboding sense that a much larger number is on the horizon. It is not until day 27, ninety percent of the way through the experiment, that the extrasensory awareness of something very big coming occurs to the human brain. At that point, our brains can suddenly see where we are headed (Figure 17.1).

The reality of the full scope of what is happening doesn't hit us until the very end. If it takes this long for a positive growth of a concrete object that we can actually see and hold in our hands, imagine how much worse this blind spot is for an unseen concept with no physical presence in our lives like debt. Exponential growth is a two-way street; it works both *positively* and *negatively*. If most people miss the positive effects of exponential growth, they most assuredly miss the negative, which are even more difficult for the human brain to imagine.

The near impossibility for our brains to appreciate exponential growth of things *unseen* is exemplified by another hypothetical. Consider a *deadly contagion* consisting of one bacterium placed inside an empty glass at 11 p.m.

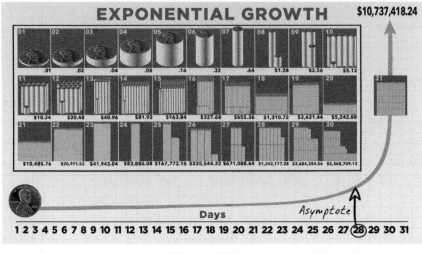

Figure 17.1

(Figure 17.2). The bacterium is undetectable by anything but the most powerful microscope. Suppose that once every minute after 11pm the number of bacteria in the glass doubles, so that by midnight the jar would be exactly full. Once full, the jar would overflow and the deadly contagion would no longer be containable.

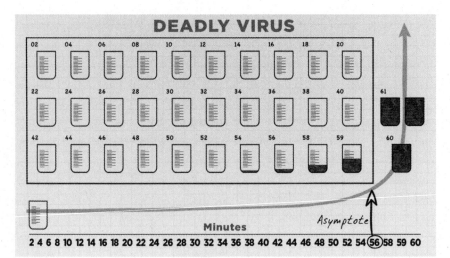

Figure 17.2

First let's consider what time it is when the glass is only *half full?* Most people, when asked this question, guess that the glass will be half-full at 11:30 p.m. But this is the exact same question of the penny doubled.

The naked human eye cannot see *one bacterium.* As we move through the doubling process, even though the deadly bacteria are growing exponentially, to the human eye it looks as if nothing at all is happening. While we can be told that the deadly contagion is growing, we don't recognize the problem because we cannot *see* it. Unlike the pennies, which we could envision growing before our eyes, the bacteria at 11:15 p.m. and 11:30 p.m. and 11:45 p.m. are still completely invisible.

Even at the 53rd minute of the bacteria process, the glass is only 1/238th full. Keep in mind that our pennies at this point were worth $41,943.04. With the pennies it was by then obvious that we had a number that was substantial and growing rapidly. With the bacteria, at this same moment in the equation of time, the bacteria are for the first time just becoming observable. The point is that the first 52 minutes that preceded this moment all felt the same, like nothing bad was happening.

At 11:57, the jar is *still* only one-eighth full. Based on the experience of the previous 56 minutes, we still don't compute that the next three minutes are going to look dramatically different. At the 58th minute, the jar is a quarter full and we remain unconcerned because, well, the jar is three-quarters empty.

It isn't until one minute to midnight that the glass becomes half full. But even at this final minute, we see no immediate problem because midnight is so close and the jar is half empty. Even though we've been told that the deadly contagion was growing exponentially, and were aware of the issue, we underestimate the urgency of the problem because we judge the current predicament based on our experience of the previous *59* minutes of tranquility.

This example represents the second challenge of man and why we continue to make the same mistakes again and again. Not only do we vastly underestimate exponential growth, we also have a *second limitation*: we base our *future expectations* on what we have experienced in the past. When looking at the deadly contagion growing before our very eyes, we don't calculate the doubling that is coming. We are thinking about the memory of the previous 56 minutes when nothing at all seemed to be happening inside the glass. We set our expectations for the future based on what we experienced for the first 93 percent of the experiment, not what is happening in the last 7 percent.

Our brains fool us into thinking that the future will look like the past. Even when we get to one minute to midnight when the glass is 50 percent full, our brains *still* think of the problem as 50 percent removed, and that we have far more time. Of course, by then it's too late.

This is the definition of man's blind spot. Black swans and the devastating impact aren't surprising after the fact. Quite the opposite. When we look back at the black swans of history, we wonder how on earth we missed them. The reason is, we don't *experience* exponential growth until it is too late. By the time we recognize the problem, it's one minute to midnight and no longer avoidable. Once we hit this stage, the game is over. The outcome is inevitable.

This phenomenon of exponential growth is why black swans have devastating results, seem to come out of nowhere, and always surprise us. The average person cannot even appreciate a problem until one minute to midnight, and by then it's far too late.

This math question of the bacteria is the exact same math question regarding the pennies. Both double in size for a specified period of time. With things we cannot see, like a deadly contagion, the unseen is so much harder for the human brain to assimilate. Of course, even in this experiment with the bacteria, we get a sense of foreboding before the final minute is up. Instinctually at this point we can feel the problem that's coming. This concrete example illustrates how and why mistakes of perception persist and repeat without the right perspective. We base our abstract expectations for the future on our personal experience over time. Our eyes trick our brains into ignoring the reality that is growing right in front of us. This cognitive limitation is best illustrated by a graph line of the bacteria as it becomes an asymptote.

Notice in Figure 17.2 how the curve of the line looks like it is traveling sideways on a slight incline for 90 percent of the time. However, as we near the end, the curve line shoots suddenly upward on what looks like a 90-degree angle. This curve is the *asymptote*, which is the point at which the chart line measured on an X and Y axis curves toward infinity. The key to predicting the asymptote is understanding when it will swerve upward toward a 90-degree angle.

A side-by-side comparison of the two curve lines highlights how the penny problem and the bacteria problem are exactly the same problem. Since the question proposed was identical, math calculated through *doubling*, the curve lines are identical. But once one identifies the dramatic upward swoop of the curve and we recognize the asymptote, it's already too late. The exponential growth is by then impossible to stop. Asymptotes, once they are found in nature, are impossible to derail. Once we recognize that an asymptote is coming, we can know for certain the inevitable conclusion. The growing US debt is charted on an X and Y axis in Figure 17.3. Can you see the asymptote?

Trump is on pace to double the debt of Obama, who doubled the debt of Bush, who doubled the debt of Clinton. Our national debt hit an asymptote years ago. Just like those witnessing the glass at one minute to midnight, we are living within this debt crisis expecting the future to resemble the past. We have convinced ourselves that debt is not a problem. In fact, many are convinced more debt is the solution. Howard Marks, in his book *Mastering The Market Cycle,* highlights that investment strategy is based on the idea that the future will look a lot like the past. It won't. The asymptote guarantees change is coming—like a roller coaster.

SEE IMAGE ON THE FOLLOWING PAGE

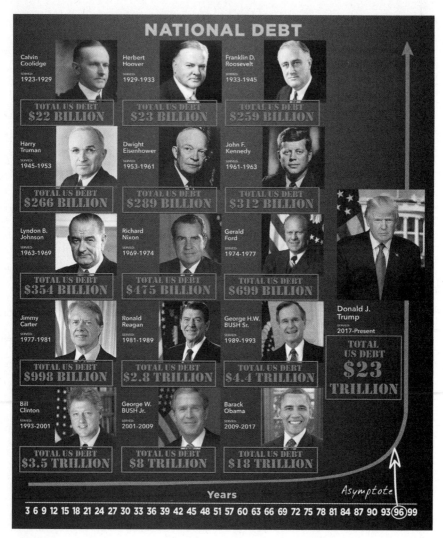

Figure 17.3

18 | The Big Short

As noted in Chapter 16, the word "crisis" comes from the Greek word *krisis,* which means "to decide." It can further be defined as "a crucial or decisive point, or stage in a sequence, involving an impending change from an unstable situation." The situation today is indeed unstable. The asymptote of debt is now a worldwide challenge. We are in crisis and the decision has been made for debt expansion. The supercycle is turning. Understanding that this *decision* has already been made is the key to winning at investing over the next decade.

Imagine swimming out into the ocean as far out as you can fathom. At some point you hit the exact moment where you must turn around in order to make it back to shore. One stroke further out and return becomes impossible. At this exact moment in the ocean, you are left with a choice: turn around or die. If you keep swimming, you've effectively sealed your fate.

Central banks have officially swum too far. There is no turning back. The only solution they have is to keep on swimming forward. While their heads may look like they're above water, central bankers are simply treading water. They will inevitably drown. Fed Chair Jerome Powell himself actually admitted as much at an October 2012 Fed meeting:

> I have concerns about more purchases. As others have pointed out, the dealer community is now assuming close to a $4 trillion balance

155

sheet. . .I am uncomfortable with it for a few reasons. The first question is, why stop at $4 trillion? The market in most cases will cheer us for doing more. It will never be enough for the market. . .When it is time for us to sell, or even to stop buying, the response could be quite strong. . . It seems to me that we seem to be way too confident that exit can be managed smoothly.

Powell's comments were prescient. After being appointed Fed chair, he attempted to normalize and reverse monetary policy. He raised interest rates and tightened the balance sheet, only to see stocks and bonds plummet thereafter. These were not big rate moves, but rather three small quarter-point hikes that almost collapsed the system. Powell learned his lesson. This is what happens when interest rates rise just a "little bit."

The key takeaway from this episode is that interest rates cannot go higher without collapsing the market. The only option from here is to keep swimming forward, and the Fed's arms are flailing wildly. From August 2019 to February 2020, the Fed was forced to add liquidity through the overnight repo market. The collapse in overnight rates had forced the Fed to print over $500 billion *before* Covid, all while Powell claimed, "This is not quantitative easing."

Those who forget history are doomed to repeat it. The world faced the exact same debt challenges 90 years ago. The result then was a decade-long depression that ended in war. Today, the entire world is sick. We are all dying of the same disease, one that comes from too much debt.

Every nation has taken on massive amounts of debt and runs large budget deficits. The results have led to a massive debt burden impossible to overcome. Unlike 90 years ago, no "healthy" nation can come to the rescue today. This distinction will speed up the timeline toward the next reset. Rather than endure a decade of depression, followed by a war, allowing for a reset timeline of 15 years after the crisis like in the depression years, the timeline for the next monetary reset will occur within the next four to five years and will come extremely quickly when it does.

The central banks have created a monster that will now consume them. By manipulating interest rates to the floor for so long, they have destroyed the natural ebb and flow of the business cycle. Any organic rise in interest

Figure 18.1

rates now becomes a massive headwind. The more *real growth*, the more our costs to service debt will grow (Figure 18.1).

My prediction is that the Federal Reserve will never willingly raise interest rates again. Debt has risen too high. From here we can expect that the Federal Reserve will only take steps to loosen. The Federal Reserve will create new tricks to continue manipulating the system. Pay attention to a plethora of new and unique complex words and policy tools. In the coming years we will see *negative rates, QE, dual interest rates, reverse repo operations, yield curve control and outright stock purchases.* These extreme policies are actively being discussed and will be employed during the next downturn. The savvy investor who anticipates the overwhelming monetary easing coming in the years ahead can position for maximum advantage.

This is a new paradigm that offers tremendous opportunities. Once we come to grips with the idea that the Federal Reserve has no solution other than to keep swimming, we can use that information to position ourselves for wealth as it occurs. There is no alternative from here other than for the US dollar to weaken. The Federal Reserve balance sheet will balloon to $20 trillion within the next five to seven years. The only real question is *how* exactly that will occur.

There are three routes that all lead to the same inevitable destination.

Around the Block to the Left

Traditionally, the Federal Reserve cuts interest rates 5 percent when faced with a downturn. When the next recession hits in earnest, though, the Federal Reserve will not have that option. This leads to an obvious question: How do you subtract 5 percent from zero? The answer is massive QE and negative rates. This is why Ben Bernanke recommended negative interest rates, why Janet Yellen suggested extreme policies, and why Jerome Powell took every move to be proactive and "keep the expansion going." They all understood that the next recession would be the nail in the coffin for the Federal Reserve. They will take every measure conceivable to stay ahead of this curve.

My estimate is that for every 1 percent away from 5 percent for the fed funds rate, the Federal Reserve will need to expand its balance sheets by $5 trillion. Unfortunately, zero percent rates will be followed by rates that go negative with trillions of dollars of QE to fend off the slowdown. With interest rates at current levels, the estimate is that the Fed will need to add $15 trillion to the balance sheet to avoid a recession. If this sounds outrageous, remember the Fed lowered rates 5 percent in 2008, and then still had to expand its balance sheet by $3.7 trillion. When faced with the next recession, just as in 2008, the balance sheet of the Fed will increase *five times*. Only this time around, the equity markets won't elevate to new incredible heights. In this scenario, the expansion of the balance sheet will have limited impact. While stocks and bonds may not collapse, they will have a hard time rising much higher from the current nosebleed valuations. An additional challenge for the Fed is that any downturn that occurs before the election in 2020 will make it more difficult for the Fed to operate at all.

The Fed has made an attempt to appear neutral in 2020 as it navigates both an upcoming election and the economic tidal wave related to government and business response to a viral pandemic. As asset prices sold off in early 2020, the Fed stepped in. Insufficient action by Powell will trigger aggressive tweets and accusations from president.

At this point only a massive input from fiscal policy could prevent markets from falling into the abyss. We can only avoid the pain for so long. At some point a serious reckoning will take place. Should monetary policy of the Federal Reserve continue to be the only game in town, they will be left with no choice but to increase their balance sheet to $20 trillion. This will be cheered as "necessary" by the market and politicians alike.

Around the Block to the Right

It is a popular opinion that the far-left socialistic policies proposed by Democrats in the runup to the 2020 presidential election are far too extreme to win the popular vote. While that may turn out to be true in 2020, be reminded of one thing: 90 years ago, the socialistic policies that Franklin Delano Roosevelt would enact in his first days in office were considered outrageous ideas to people three years earlier. The wave of socialism that overwhelmed the world in the 1930s was barely evident in the United States three years before. Policies that seem extreme in boom times have a way of turning into *necessary solutions* in times of crisis.

Elizabeth Warren and Bernie Sanders, whose policies today place them at the extreme left, are in many ways identical to FDR. If either is on the Democratic ticket, they will push for similar policies to FDR during the Great Depression. One need only look at *modern monetary theory* and the name of the green energy bill, the *Green New Deal*, to see the identical twin 90 years later. What the Fed would love more than anything else is for governments of the world to step up and add a huge dose of fiscal stimulus. The mindset is heading in that direction. Even the presupposed candidate Joe Biden has been pushed further to the left and will adopt policies that urge dramatic new fiscal expenditures.

The socialistic policies of free healthcare, wiping out student debt, and modern monetary theory are being promoted by the most extreme candidates on the left. At the same time Republicans, who at one time publicly stood for sound money, smaller government, and balanced budgets, have run a larger deficit than at any time in history. There are no "sound money" politicians left. So no matter which party wins, the deficits will keep growing and in greater flux than ever before. Regardless of political affiliation, debt is now considered a positive tool. By the year 2023, we will likely be running $2 trillion annual deficits. When a recession occurs, that number could rise to $4 trillion annually. The total national debt will skyrocket in the coming five years. The asymptote of exponential growth of the debt is unavoidable.

Spending more is the one thing that our tribal party system is actually in agreement on. Over the last several years, we have passed bipartisan agreements and spending bills that continue to drive higher deficits. When both parties agree on one thing, the discussion is no longer a political one, it's an inevitable one

When looking for the direction of global fiscal policy, pay particular attention to the German Central Bank. Germany's famously frugal approach has been criticized by the rest of Europe over the last decade. While the rest of Europe sought looser monetary policies, the Germans remained steadfast. That is, until now. Olaf Scholz, the German minister of finance, recently capitulated and said that a balanced budget should never become a "fetish." When the last man standing for sound money throws in the towel, the game is over. What comes next will be an avalanche of government spending and even larger deficits.

As fiscal faucets are turned on full blast, interest rates will surge uncontrollably. This will force central banks to purchase massive amounts of bonds and keep a lid on short-term rates. The result will be a combination of monetary and fiscal policy unlike the world has ever seen.

Jump across the Block: Negative Rates

The inevitable Great Devaluation doesn't have to occur over time with tremendous pain or long term erosion of currencies. It could happen at once. It happened this way four score and seven years ago, in 1933, when FDR devalued the dollar by executive order. It happened on the other side of the pendulum when Nixon closed the gold window in 1971. Twice in the last 87 years, each time at the peak of the pendulum and when facing an uncontrollable debt crisis, the dollar has been devalued. Each time by executive order. A weaker dollar is in the world's best interest. But how does a president weaken the dollar?

There are multiple options at a president's disposal to take action to weaken the currency. It actually wouldn't be difficult, and would likely come with little challenge. In fact, when Roosevelt and Nixon both accomplished this feat they were widely lauded for "doing what was necessary." This is where Donald Trump's battle with the Federal Reserve is likely headed.

For three years, Trump verbally abused the Central Bank and Jerome Powell for not allowing the dollar to weaken. He cited the unfair advantages of other countries who had allowed their currencies to devalue against the dollar. Trump understands that a strong dollar policy hurts exports, and offers foreign importers unfair advantages. When the next financial crisis occurs, Trump will be in position to force the hand of the Federal Reserve and take executive action to weaken the dollar directly. He has already set up the Federal Reserve as the fall guy for the economy, and has berated Powell for raising rates. When the next slowdown occurs, Trump will push for interest rates to be moved to negative. Should the Fed not comply, Trump could take emergency executive action to weaken the dollar directly.

Trump has been urging that the United States needs negative interest rates, "because governments get paid to borrow when interest rates are negative." Remember when Trump ran for president in 2016, he told the *Washington Post*, "I'll eliminate the US debt in eight years." Negative rates provide the solution. With interest rates that are negative, the central bank can buy up all the debt and then expunge it. Trump's plan is really not much different from that of the left. He wants to fund the deficit with devalued dollars. The left will do it through extreme fiscal policies, just as Japan has.

Japan has been "managing" its economy for nearly 30 years. Since the Nikkei collapsed in 1990, the Japanese Central Bank has been artificially propping up the dying economy. It began by manipulating interest rates to zero percent. When that didn't work, it bought government bonds in massive rounds of QE. When that didn't work, it lowered interest rates further and into negative territory. Today, it is openly buying shares of Japanese companies (the Japanese government is the number one owner of Japanese stocks) and has continued to adjust interest rates into negative territory for more than three years. The Central Bank of Japan continues to pump money into the system and today owns all of Japan's government debt.

Some are calling for America to copy Japan's *accomplishments* (Figure 18.2). Before getting too excited, keep in mind that the Japanese stock market collapsed 30 years ago and still hasn't gotten back to where it was then. These policies have failed. A central bank managed economy is nothing to leap for joy about. Through the manipulation, Japan has been able to steadily cancel out their own debt at an incredible rate of $720 billion per year. They are accomplishing this feat by selling their debt to

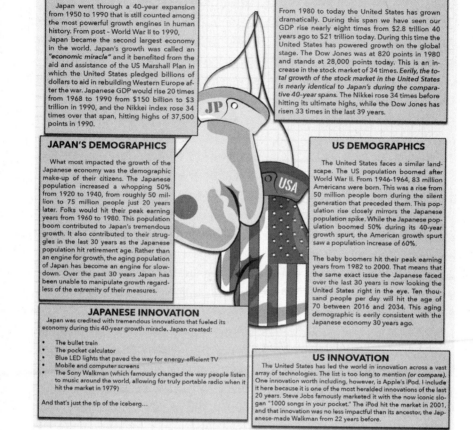

JAPAN'S GROWTH - 40 YEARS

Japan went through a 40-year expansion from 1950 to 1990 that is still counted among the most powerful growth engines in human history. From post - World War II to 1990, Japan became the second largest economy in the world. Japan's growth was called an *"economic miracle"* and it benefited from the aid and assistance of the US Marshall Plan in which the United States pledged billions of dollars to aid in rebuilding Western Europe after the war. Japanese GDP would rise 20 times from 1968 to 1990 from $150 billion to $3 trillion in 1990, and the Nikkei index rose 34 times over that span, hitting highs of 37,500 points in 1990.

US GROWTH - 40 YEARS

From 1980 to today the United States has grown dramatically. During this span we have seen our GDP rise nearly eight times from $2.8 trillion 40 years ago to $21 trillion today. During this time the United States has powered growth on the global stage. The Dow Jones was at 820 points in 1980 and stands at 28,000 points today. This is an increase in the stock market of 34 times. *Eerily, the total growth of the stock market in the United States is nearly identical to Japan's during the comparative 40-year spans. The Nikkei rose 34 times before hitting its ultimate highs, while the Dow Jones has risen 33 times in the last 39 years.*

JAPAN'S DEMOGRAPHICS

What most impacted the growth of the Japanese economy was the demographic make-up of their citizens. The Japanese population increased a whopping 50% from 1920 to 1940, from roughly 50 million to 75 million people just 20 years later. Folks would hit their peak earning years from 1960 to 1980. This population boom contributed to Japan's tremendous growth. It also contributed to their struggles in the last 30 years as the Japanese population hit retirement age. Rather than an engine for growth, the aging population of Japan has become an engine for slowdown. Over the past 30 years Japan has been unable to manipulate growth regardless of the extremity of their measures.

US DEMOGRAPHICS

The United States faces a similar landscape. The US population boomed after World War II. From 1946-1964, 83 million Americans were born. This is a rise from 50 million people born during the silent generation that preceded them. This population rise closely mirrors the Japanese population spike. While the Japanese population boomed 50% during its 40-year growth spurt, the American growth spurt saw a population increase of 60%.

The baby boomers hit their peak earning years from 1982 to 2000. That means that the same exact issue the Japanese faced over the last 30 years is now looking the United States right in the eye. Ten thousand people per day will hit the age of 70 between 2016 and 2034. This aging demographic is eerily consistent with the Japanese economy 30 years ago.

JAPANESE INNOVATION

Japan was credited with tremendous innovations that fueled its economy during this 40-year growth miracle. Japan created:

- The bullet train
- The pocket calculator
- Blue LED lights that paved the way for energy-efficient TV
- Mobile and computer screens
- The Sony Walkman (which famously changed the way people listen to music around the world, allowing for truly portable radio when it hit the market in 1979)

And that's just the tip of the iceberg...

US INNOVATION

The United States has led the world in innovation across a vast array of technologies. The list is too long to mention *(or compare)*. One innovation worth including, however, is Apple's iPod. I include it here because it is one of the most heralded innovations of the last 20 years. Steve Jobs famously marketed it with the now iconic slogan "1000 songs in your pocket." The iPod hit the market in 2001, and that innovation was no less impactful than its ancestor, the Japanese-made Walkman from 22 years before.

Figure 18.2

their own Central Bank. Negative rates allow the Japanese to roll over their debt at no cost, which allows the Central Bank of Japan to literally erase government debt. It also increases their balance sheets.

This is the third way that the Fed balance sheet gets to $20 trillion and one of the very best situations for an investor to be in. If we know the endgame is a weaker US dollar, we simply need to position our portfolios accordingly. According to legendary investor Jim Rogers, "The central banks will continue this madness as long as it is necessary. We are going to have a horrible time when this all comes to an end. . .the collapse will be the worst of my lifetime."

The United States could print the money to pay off our debt, and any other expenses for that matter. If interest rates were negative, we could do exactly what Japan is doing (Figure 18.3). If the Federal Reserve bought all of the US debt, it would need to expand the balance sheet from $4 trillion to $27 trillion. This is the exact place the balance sheet is headed, regardless. Sound crazy? In Trump's November 2019, speech to the Economic Club of New York, he stated, "We are actively competing with nations who openly cut interest rates, so now many are actually getting paid when they pay off their loan, known as negative interest.... Give me some of that free money."

The Great Devaluation is on its way, and Trump has laid out the exact handbook for how he would make it happen. When Trump made those comments, he gave us a glimpse into the future for his strategy to eliminate US debt. An expansion of the Fed's balance sheet is inevitable. The only real question is, can this occur *before* a financial collapse or only in *response* to

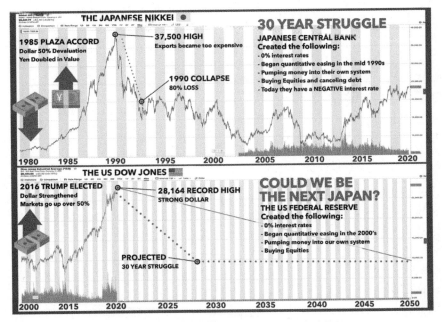

Figure 18.3

one? The biggest issue for Trump with this solution is that the only way to get rates into negative territory in America would be for the stock market to collapse. So in order for that plan to take effect, Trump would need to maintain power and preside over a crumbling equity market.

28 Trading Days Later (Thinking Ahead)

On January 29, 2020, I presented a webinar *The Black Swan* that was subscribed to by over 10,000 people and has since gone viral. During that event, I offered *The Decade Report*, where I predicted that the balance sheet of the Federal Reserve would increase to $20 trillion within the next five years. As I re-read the draft of the manuscript I turned in just 10 weeks ago, I am stunned by the early accuracy of my own predictions. The Covid-19 crisis has allowed for the central banks to proactively increase their balance sheets by 50 percent, and they are considered *heroes* for doing so. This has happened in a matter of weeks and is a certain sign that we can expect more to come. The arsonist has become the firefighter and is dousing the flames with an unlimited supply of more gasoline.

It is for this reason I ask you to consider the predictions for the future. I believe history repeats. Part Four offers a glimpse into the future.

PART IV

The Great
Revaluation and a
Look at the Future

19

The Mechanic

Rather than view the monetary system as a finely tuned machine that offers perfect pricing signals, we would be better suited to see it as an engine that is on its last legs and due for a sudden breakdown.

The existing monetary system reminds me of the car I had in college. It was a 1980 *Town and Country* model stationwagon, the kind with the wooden paneling on the sides. It was a 10-year-old family car I had inherited from my Mom and it needed a new transmission before it could be given to me as my junior year college gift. The new transmission seemed to do the trick and the car, which had sat idle collecting leaves in our driveway for two years, initially ran pretty smoothly.

When I first got the car, it leaked oil. This fact was impossible to ignore, because wherever the car was parked, an oil stain would appear. Fixing the oil would have required putting the car in the shop, investing a few dollars, and getting the oil pan and a few other things replaced. I was broke but went to my local *Manny Moe and Jack* to price it all out anyway. I was told by the mechanic that if I didn't get it fixed, the problem would only get worse. He advised that no matter what, I needed to be sure the car always had oil in it or the engine would seize up.

In the end, I decided I was better off just filling it with new oil every couple of weeks at a cost of $1.50 per can, rather than pay the $189 estimate and be without the car for a few days. My system worked for me, at least for a little while. After a few months, however, what had initially been one can of oil every few weeks had turned into a new can every seven days. A second spot evaluation by the mechanic told me more than I wanted to know. Not only was the oil leak causing the big problem he had predicted, but he also noticed that the transmission fluid was leaking. He recommended a complete transmission rebuild that would take about three weeks at a cost of $1200. Of course that was completely out of the question. What college kid has that kind of money?

There was an alternative short-term option I could choose. In addition to a new can of oil weekly, I could be sure to add a bottle of transmission fluid regularly. I soon became a junior mechanic, and every morning before school I would check the oil and the transmission fluid levels. If I was diligent, I could keep the thing going. As I did, the oil stains in the driveway went from dark black to a murky muddy blackish red.

Unfortunately, the oil and transmission fluids were just the beginning of the car's problems. The engine soon started to overheat anytime it was driven for more than 30 minutes at a time. I found myself filling it with antifreeze and water nearly every other day. I had a nice selection of oil cans, transmission fluid bottles, antifreeze jugs, and water bottles sloshing around in the back of the car at all times. These were the tools I would need to keep the machine chugging along. What I thought would be a cheap fix soon was running me up to $20 a week, and that didn't even include the gas. I had to work an extra five hours a week at McDonald's just to cover my "fluid" habit.

Just when I thought things couldn't get worse, the water hose cracked. In order to keep the car functioning at all, I had to use duct tape to hold it all together. My ongoing efforts to keep the car going even included having to fill each of the two front tires with *Fix o Flat* after I backed up over parking spikes.

The final end occurred when I put the car into reverse, and rather than moving backward and the direction my head was turned, the car lurched forward and I rammed through the garage door. I would spend the next six months taking the bus to work, and all of my earnings would go toward paying off the damage I caused.

The car was supposed to represent my freedom. Rather than spend the time and money to get the car fixed in the beginning, or have the wisdom to junk the car altogether, I tried to survive with a machine that wasn't capable of handling my needs. All I had to show for it in the end was a massive amount of debt and my monthly SEPTA bus pass.

I believe this experience is a good analogy for our economic system. Ray Dalio says the economy and the monetary system should be viewed as a machine. When the new economic engine was created in 1944 at Bretton Woods, the car was brand new and worked at peak performance. No leaky gaskets, no slipped gears, just a finely tuned economic machine. This was the golden age, and the world had an economic boom that lasted nearly 25 years.

Efficiencies eroded over time. By 1971, the manual transmission kept slipping and needed an overhaul. As a fix, Nixon closed the gold window. Detangling the dollar from gold and turning it into a fiat currency was the new transmission the world economy needed. The new transmission allowed for the car to go way faster. Detangling the dollar from gold was like supercharging the economic engine. It allowed for the world to use debt and money creation to increase performance. Debt was the "new oil" for the economic machine. In the 25 years before the US dollar became a fiat currency, the national debt of the country had only risen from $259 billion to $354 billion.

By the 1980s, the machine had been driven so hard that the economic engine guzzled massive amounts of new "debt oil." The national debt of the country rose from $354 billion to $2.4 trillion. The debt expansion was tremendous. The car flew down the freeway at incredible speeds. *Debt oil* was the magic potion that allowed everything to fly faster. It permitted governments to spend far more money than they brought in tax revenue. The world's economic engine became one giant *debt machine*.

And then it all collapsed. On Black Monday in 1987, the economic engine seized. Greenspan, the newly appointed Fed mechanic, realized that the engine had failed and sprung a massive oil leak. The machine had been run too hard and too fast but repairing it was not an option. The quick fix was to add more oil. Greenspan got out the funnel and poured in a can of lower interest rates.

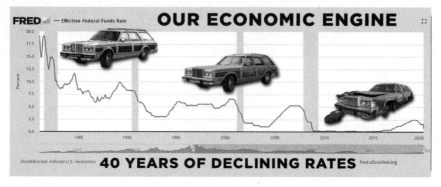

Figure 19.1

Since that moment in time, anytime the car would slow down, the mechanics at the Fed would simply add more oil by lowering interest rates. The engine has never stopped leaking oil since. Even though it has had a few good moments, the oil leaks continue to grow. The car nearly broke down in 1992, in 1998, and then again 2000 (Figure 19.1).

Each time the engine failed, more and more damage was done, and more and more lower interest rate oil was added to keep the machine running. Rather than fix the problem and put the economy in the shop for a complete overhaul, the decision was made to add more oil and offset whatever was leaking out the bottom. The mechanics understood the engine was broken. But fixing it would require investment and putting the car in the shop. Instead, they just added more oil.

So long as Greenspan was diligent, he could keep the engine running by adding more and more oil. Regardless of the obvious signs, and the necessary time and investment that should have been taken to simply fix the engine, the central bank resorted to the easier solution. Keep the engine running by adding more and more debt oil in the form of lower and lower and lower rates. It's all left a massive stain on the driveway of the real-world economy.

By the time Greenspan handed over the keys to Bernanke in 2006, the US national debt had reached $8 trillion. For two decades, we added oil we didn't have the money to pay for. As expected, the engine finally blew and the transmission of the economic machine stopped functioning altogether. The economy seized and the car wouldn't start.

This time, adding oil wasn't enough. No matter how much debt oil was dumped into the engine, the car wouldn't move. Rates were lowered to 0 percent and nothing happened. The stain on the driveway at the Federal Reserve was pitch black and over 30 years had expanded from a few drops to a massive puddle of debt oil. Just like the station wagon I inherited from my mom, Fed mechanic Bernanke had inherited a real lemon of an economic engine.

However, rather than put the engine into the "extended recession garage," Ben Bernanke decided to use a new trick. He decided that in addition to the debt oil, we should fill the broken transmission with a new type of transmission fluid. He called it *quantitative easing*. The fluid worked, and when added in combination with maximum doses of debt oil, the engine picked up speed. The new fluid was amazing. Bernanke was the savior. His new invention had made him famous, and his face was on the cover of every *Car and Driver* economic magazine in the world. Greenspan had always been considered "the Maestro" mechanic. Every Fed mechanic after him would become more and more famous simply for keeping the car flying down the road.

But the engine really wasn't functioning properly. It was leaking fluid from everywhere. Anytime Bernanke attempted to reduce the amount of new transmission fluid, the car would stall out and overheat. The only answer when the car slowed down was to add more fluids. QE1 turned into QE2, turned into QE3. Maximum debt oil was added as interest rates were held at 0 percent. At this point, the Fed mechanics knew they needed to always have fluids at the ready. The engine could blow at any moment, and the only way to ensure the car continued to run was to constantly fill it with liquidity.

Soon, Yellen took over as driver, and she made sure that every day she filled the fluids to the top. She was diligent and was going to make sure the car never broke down on her watch. More debt oil and more special QE transmission fluid was all she ever demanded. She didn't want anyone to know how bad a shape the engine was in. Nobody could ever know how bad the leaks were. The puddle on the driveway under the economic engine at the Federal Reserve turned into a murky reddish black lake. We were literally swimming in oil as the national debt grew *two and a half times* to $20 trillion.

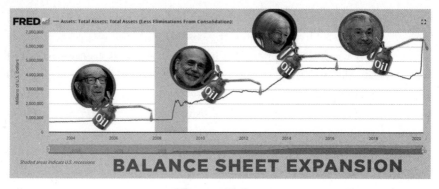

Figure 19.2

Then in 2018, Powell became the mechanic (Figure 19.2). For some reason, he was convinced the engine of the car was in better shape than his predecessors. He was against all the daily oil and transmission fluid injections. Powell began removing the excess oil. He stopped adding transmission fluid altogether. He allowed interest rates to rise. Despite warnings from Trump, investment gurus, and other Fed governors, Powell believed the broken engine would function on its own strength. He believed the engine was in much better shape than anyone.

He wasn't a very good mechanic. Powell's moves caused the broken economic engine to seize up. Powell was pressured by the president and immediately reversed course. Rather than raise rates as promised, he began lowering them again. He secretly added new QE back into the machine. Because Powell had promised "no more QE," he renamed his new transmission fluid. He called it *reverse repo operations* and continued to add to the Fed's balance sheet. Soon the engine began coughing and stalling out, forcing Powell to add more and more "not QE' fluid. Powell frantically added $50 billion a month in reverse repos. The balance sheet ballooned back over $4 trillion. Few noticed. They were too focused on the Dow Jones hitting all-time highs.

Stocks loved all the new liquidity and had shot to the moon. Bonds loved it as their yields turned south and back toward 0 percent. Trump touted the engine as "the greatest economy in history." Despite all the positive rhetoric, Powell had learned his lesson and knew the economic engine could blow at any moment. When it did, there would be little he could do other than recommend putting the whole thing in the junkyard. His only option was to never allow the car to break down again.

And then Covid-19 happened. The entire transmission dropped out of the car. This was akin to breaking down in the middle of the desert in 120 degree temperatures. Fluids began leaking and spouting from everywhere. The car overheated, antifreeze leaked out, and the water hose cracked. The economic engine literally collapsed. Leverage everywhere against a broken-down system had literally collapsed what had become a lemon of the world's financial system.

Powell didn't even need to call the tow truck. This was an opportunity to do the only thing that was ever going to work. The crisis gives the mechanics at the Fed all the excuse they need to take *radical* measures. Before the crisis, the mechanics did their liquidity injections in secret. Now Powell is publicly standing naked in front of the car with a massive oil tanker being pumped into the engine. Dollars must continue to be printed! There could be no shutdown or slowdown of these fiscal and monetary faucets. An unlimited amount of oil was promised.

In the first six weeks after coronavirus, the Fed has added maximum debt oil and lowered interest rates to 0 percent, dumped in another $2.6 trillion in QE transmission fluid, added new unlimited antifreeze by opening swap lines with other countries to allow more dollars to flow, and dumped water into the radiator in the form subprime corporate debt through outright asset purchases of junk bonds. The Fed has created new rules and granted $500 billion to the Treasury as duct tape for the cracked water hose.

And what do we have to show for all of the efforts? The economic engine that was designed to be our freedom has now become our shackles. We've lost all of the jobs that were created by the Fed's manipulations in the course of six weeks. The national debt will now fly over $25 trillion this year and likely exceed $30 trillion by the end of 2021, well ahead of previous CBO estimates of that not happening until 2025.

Now the more debt oil they need to add, the higher the price of gold will rise. It's why gold is up nearly 50 percent in the last 18 months. The "smart money" car enthusiasts have been able to see this coming, and well before the coronavirus crisis began investing heavily in gold. The price of gold was $1194 an ounce. Today it's near $1700. More liquidity than ever will be necessary to keep this engine running.

"I recommend you invest in oil. Prices
are down now, but auto oil leaks are up."

CartoonStock.com

Figure 19.3

As that unlimited flow continues, gold prices will soar higher. Ultimately, the engine will collapse and gold will explode to unthinkable levels.

The new direction and mindset is not hard to see. The new strategy is to *print more money*. But the economy is obviously broken. While the stock market speedometer is firing higher on a taste of new liquidity, the real world is a desert and 33 million people have lost their jobs (Figure 19.3). Millions more job losses are on the way, which naturally means more and more money printing can be expected as well.

The only solution now is to keep filling up the lemon engine with more and more liquidity. More debt oil, more QE transmission fluid, more swap line antifreeze, more junk bond water for the radiator, and more duct tape to hold it all together. The good news is we know they will never run out of liquids to inject. The bad news is, it's literally a matter of time before the entire engine seizes for good.

While everyone else is focused on the stock market engine that's gasping for air as it speeds higher, we are focused on the amount of oil being added. We don't know when the engine will seize up for good. We only know the entire thing is a lemon. The only way to keep it running is to keep adding more fluid. The costs in the end will turn out to be far greater than they would have been had we simply fixed the engine at any point along the way. The problem now is that it's too late to fix. We've passed the point of no return. The only way forward is to add more money forever. As we do, *the Great Devaluation* will occur. While the stock market may stay afloat for a period of time, the uncontrollable debt will shackle us forever. The only way out will be to add more oil. Someday soon, while we're looking behind us at how the Fed has our back, the car will lurch forward and wipe out the garage.

20 | White Men Can't Jump

Canaries are sent into coal mines as a warning signal. The little yellow birds are more sensitive to carbon monoxide and other poisonous gases than humans. Around the year 1911, coal miners began carrying canaries into the coal mines. They quickly became a metaphor for warning signs. When the canary keels over, it's time to get out, lest you be the next to keel over.

Figurative yellow birds are dying everywhere. Negative rates? Stocks surge on massive declines in corporate earnings? Thirty million people file for unemployment and stocks surge into a bull market? Oil drops to *negative $40*? The Fed buys junk bonds? These are just a handful of the dozens of canaries in the coal mine that have been left for dead. We continue to look the other way so long as the Fed is buying. What are dozens of dead canaries relative to a Federal Reserve bazooka anyway? What is the canary in the coal mine telling us? The system is full of deadly gases that can kill us at any moment.

But who's paying attention anymore? Do we even have the aptitude to recognize impending disaster? We've become so programmed to watching and following the Fed that we've lost sight of all the warning signs literally dying around us. The economic engine is completely busted. The mine is about to blow. The only question is, what will that explosion look like?

177

The explosion in debt will have an impact on everything. Printing more money is the only solution. Now that we understand what's coming, we must ask ourselves new questions. It's why I have created an informal survey that I now ask every stock investor I speak with. The survey is not complicated and only has three questions. Please take this survey for yourself.

Question #1: *"Do you want to win?"* This is the easy question. It'll be no surprise that the universal and immediate answer is yes. Everyone knows that they want to win. The second question is a little more difficult and requires more thought and consideration.

Question #2: *"Great, when do you want to win by?"* While everyone knows off the top of their head that they want to win, only some people know *when* they want to win by. People's answers ultimately vary. Question #2, while more challenging, is not impossible. Most people can find their answer as they think it through. It's the third question that stumps almost everyone.

Question #3: *"OK, great! How will you know you are winning?"* This question has been met with silence and confusion. Most people I have asked say, "I don't understand; what do you mean?" In response, I then quote one of my very favorite movie lines:

Sometimes when you win, you lose. Sometimes when you lose, you win. Sometimes when you win or lose, you actually tie, and sometimes when you tie, you actually win or lose.

The line was spoken by Rosie Perez in the movies *White Men Can't Jump*. It's wisdom has stayed with me. How do we know if we are winning? It may be the most important concept to understand regarding the coming *Great Devaluation*. Fortunes will be made over the course of the next decade by those who master the answer to this one question. *The Great Devaluation* will assuredly push stocks to all-time highs over the next decade. The masses will be focused on the *height of the tree*. The smart money will instead be focused on the *depth of the root*.

We've all heard it said that stocks always go higher over time. It's the reason we are told to hold forever. Technically, Wall Street is right; stocks do seem to go higher over time. Figure 20.1 is a chart of the stock market since 1929. The stock market is up 69 times over the last 90 years. This

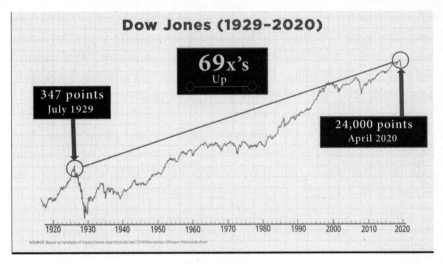

Figure 20.1

is incredible long-term performance and serves the argument from Wall Street well.

Or does it? Maybe the better question is, if the Dow Jones goes higher and you stay invested, does it also mean *you* win? Figure 20.2 is an inflation-adjusted chart of the Dow Jones. Notice that on an

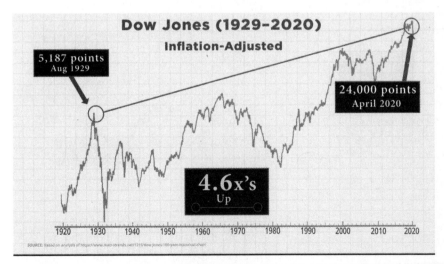

Figure 20.2

inflation-adjusted basis, the Dow Jones was at 5,300 points in 1929 and today is at 24,000 points. The massive 69 times nominal performance is really only 4.6 times higher on inflation-adjusted charts. That equals a compounded return of just over 1.7 percent per year over the last 90 years. The Federal Reserve is trying for 2 percent inflation per year. Hmmmmm. *Sometimes when you win—you lose.*

Figure 20.3 really identifies the problem. In the 60 years from 1929 to 1989, the Dow Jones began and ended at 5180 points on an inflation-adjusted basis. While on a nominal level the Dow increased from 350 points to 3000 points for what *appears to be* an increase of 8.5 times, on a *real basis* the stock market did not increase in value at all for 60 years! How do you feel about Wall Street's always staying invested advice now? *Sometimes when you win—you tie (but really, after 60 years you lose.)*

Pay close attention to what happens in Figure 20.4. There are three major points to understand in this chart. The first is that stocks doubled during the Great Depression. The Dow Jones rose from 52 points to 104 points during this span. The second thing to notice is that there were *six* different bull market moves during the Great Depression. The third, and the most surprising to most investors, is that the Great Depression was not a

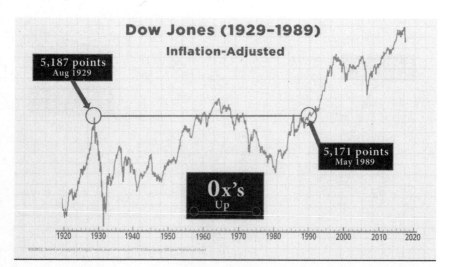

Figure 20.3

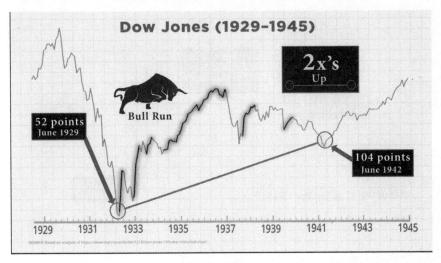

Figure 20.4

deflationary period for the value of money. The Great Depression witnessed massive money inflation.

Looking at the doubling of the Dow Jones over that 10-year span and concluding stocks were a big winner is akin to looking at the height of the tree without measuring the depth of the root. An example will help as we understand the concept.

Suppose portfolio A were to have invested $100,000 in the market in 1932. By the year 1942, that portfolio would have doubled to $200,000. That sounds great, especially during a massive depression, right? If you asked 100 people on the street whether portfolio A "won" or "lost," 99 out of 100 people would say that it was a big winner.

But was it really? No. In reality, it was a 10 percent loser. The reason was that the dollar was devalued by Franklin Delano Roosevelt in 1934. The price of the dollar was changed *overnight* from $20 to $36. This equaled a tremendous reduction in value of dollars and thus a massive overnight inflation. So even though portfolio "A" rose from $100,000 to $200,000, it was only worth 45 percent of that in *real* terms, for an actual real total purchasing power of $90,000 a decade later. Under this scenario, those who stayed invested in the stock market during the Great Depression lost 10 percent of their wealth over the next decade. *Sometimes when you win, you lose.*

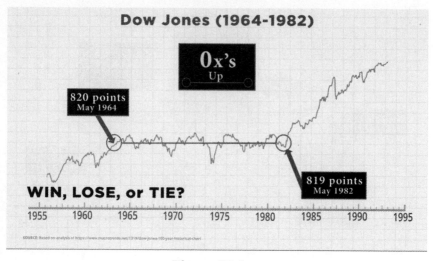

Figure 20.5

This is a very challenging concept for investors to get their minds around. So let's dive deeper. Now that we are aware that we need to look at the depth of the root, the underlying value of the currency, in order to really understand true value, let's see if Wall Street's premise that "the market always goes higher over time" also means that investors always win over time.

Figures 20.5 and 20.6 highlight the period between 1964 and 1982. This was a *tremendously* inflationary period. Interest rates would rise from 3.5 percent in 1964 to highs of 20 percent nearly two decades later. Notice that the stock market bounced around sideways for 18 years while inflation raged. I've read countless articles claiming that stocks do well in inflationary periods. That argument is presented as an alternative option to holding bonds, which certainly lose value as interest rates surge higher. Don't be fooled into believing that is the case for stocks.

Notice that on a nominal level, stocks were flat for 18 years. They returned 0 percent during this 18-year period. In May of 1964, the Dow Jones was trading at 820 points. Eighteen years later, in May 1982, it was trading basically the same at 819 points. If you asked the average investor on the street if they won, lost, or tied over this span, "tied" would be the answer from 99 percent of the people. Now that you are enlightened, you

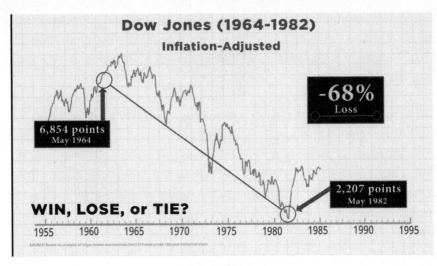

Figure 20.6

should be saying, "Hold on, we need to look at the depth of the root, too." What happened with the underlying value of the dollar during this 18-year span? This is the critical question.

Notice that on an inflation-adjusted basis, the Dow Jones was at 6854 points in May 1964. Eighteen years later in May 1982 the Dow Jones was at 2207 points. This is a real decline of roughly 70 percent. So while on a nominal basis $100,000 in 1964 was still $100,000 in 1982, on a *real basis* it only had purchasing power of roughly $30,000. Investors in the stock market lost 70 percent of their wealth over this 18-year span.

An easier way to think about it is, the price of a postage stamp in 1964 was $.05. In 1982, a postage stamp cost $.20. In 1982, you could only afford one quarter of the postage stamps you could 18 years earlier. *Sometimes when you tie, you actually lose.*

Why is all of this so critical to understanding? Once we come to grips with the reality that the Federal Reserve's entire directive is to devalue the dollar; once we wake up to the forward guidance that the Fed has an unlimited bazooka and intends to use it; once we recognize that all of the money printing will lead to significant inflation—we must be aware of what that will do to investments. On a nominal basis, we could see the Dow Jones surge to historic all-time highs. I believe we could see the Dow Jones hit 50,000 points over the next decade. That, however, doesn't make it a great place to invest.

If the Dow Jones moves to 50,000 points over the next decade, that would be an increase of 7 percent per year over the next decade on a nominal basis. But will the Dow Jones going up 7 percent a year between now and 2030 mean the Dow Jones is a great place to invest? Not if the value of the dollar drops by 60 percent, like it did during the Great Depression. If the *Great Devaluation* of the 2020s plays out the same way, $100,000 invested in the Dow Jones today would only have the purchasing power of $80,000 in 2030.

In Figure 20.7, we look at what's really going on. It's critical to recognize that for 40 years, from 1935 to 1980, as interest rates rose over that span, financial assets struggled. Interest rates do not move in a straight line in the short term. They move higher and lower in 45-year cycles. Forty-five years higher over time, then 45 years lower over time. Fiscal policies pushed interest rates higher from 1935 to 1980. They moved from 0 percent during the Great Depression to 20 percent 45 years later.

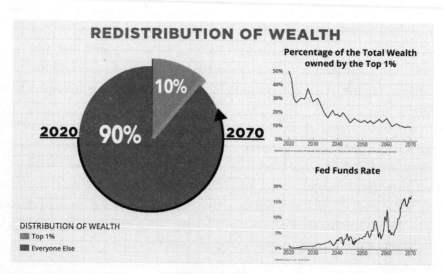

Figure 20.7

Over the last 45 years, as interest rates have continually been manipulated lower, and more and more debt oil has been added to the financial engine, financial assets have increased in value. The 40-year deflationary period from 1980 to today followed a 45-year inflationary period from 1935–1980.

Interest rates that go higher over time are bad for financial assets and good for gold. Interest rates that go lower over time are great for financial assets and not as good for gold. This is why long-term investors today must move away from financial assets and into gold. The next 45 years will see a massive devaluation of currencies as interest rates rise. The next decade, therefore, will look a lot like the Great Depression. Stocks will look like they are rising. While everyone is focused on the height of that tree, smart investors will be looking at the depth of the root. *For those that do, sometimes when you win, you win.*

It's also why the system is in such deep jeopardy. If central banks force the flow of rates lower still, they could cause the whole system to collapse. What the Fed really wants is for a long and steady dollar devaluation that is not rapid but occurs *over time*. If they get their way, we'll see interest rates rise over time. I believe it will look very much like the years from 1932 to 1942, and the years from 1964 to 1982. Each time witnessed stocks that were nominally positive, but in real terms, due to the devaluation of the currency, were very big losers.

21 | The Matrix

The *Collective Mind* is the most powerful of forces in all of nature. Just as the waves of the ocean are determined by the underlying current, the waves of investment are determined by a collective mindset. It's a force that can be impossible to overcome when swimming against. Its power can drive our spirit to euphoric highs when we catch the wave's momentum at the perfect time.

The strategy for investors has long been to own a portfolio of stocks and bonds. But what would happen if you learned that stocks and bonds were the exact *wrong way* to invest? Would you have the courage to step away from the herd? Imagine if everything you thought you knew about investing and everything you've learned over the past 40 years was completely turned on its head? For example, if you knew today that the Dow Jones would return 0 percent over the next decade, would you change your strategy?

Hindsight is 20/20; it's predicting the future that's challenging. It's why we continue to remind our readers of the scoreboard. The book *Gold Is A Better Way* was published on August 14, 2018. Since that time, gold has outperformed the Dow Jones massively. Gold is up 45 percent. The Dow Jones is down 5 percent.

We are among the very first to argue that gold should be considered a bullish asset—one that investors should transition into as a *growth* strategy.

Our premise is that rising debts and deficits will cause dollars to devalue relative to gold, and that investors would do far better buying and holding gold than they would following the Wall Street way and owning stocks and bonds. The scoreboard comparing gold to the Dow Jones, while looking pretty good in the short term, is nowhere near the good look it is going to have over time.

The idea represents a cultural shift. If the concept holds water, it means risk *and* opportunity have never been greater than at this moment in history. It's therefore impossible to appreciate one without recognizing the other. New mindsets wipe out old strategies. The long-term investors who are able to identify the change are rewarded. Those that don't suffer greatly.

It's all about the collective investment mind. Mindset shifts are generational. They take years to gather support, more years to gain momentum, and then even more years for the idea to become the accepted norm. Only after all of that, in the final years where the momentum becomes so great that it becomes universally accepted as truth, is it time for a new direction to overcome the old. By that time, it's time to exit. These mindset shifts happen roughly every 40 to 50 years.

Figure 21.1 highlights the ratio between equities and commodities. Notice that the ratio has only been this stretched a few times in history.

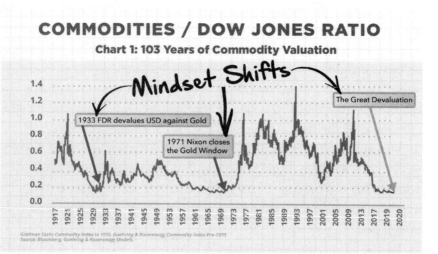

Figure 21.1

This ratio tells us it's a great time to buy commodities relative to equities. Each time this has happened in the past, gold was used to reset the value of the dollar. That mindset shift is occurring in real time before our eyes.

The CBO now predicts we will have a $4 trillion deficit in 2020. Should that continue, our national debt could hit $50 trillion in the next five years. Now a Fed balance sheet of $20 trillion doesn't seem crazy; it seems inevitable. It's probably why the *Decade Report* has since gone viral. Now the questions I'm getting aren't, "How could you ever predict such a crazy thing?" but, "How did you know?"

I don't have a crystal ball. I didn't predict the coronavirus. I simply predicted the *response*. A crisis always occurs. Recessions are *inevitable*. It was the response to the crisis that I believed was predictable. With interest rates on the floor, there was always only one solution to the next recession. It's the same solution that always occurs at the end of a debt crisis. The only way out of a debt crisis is a devaluation of the currency. A restructuring has indeed begun. The money-printing machines have been turned on and are in overdrive. The crisis simply makes it all more politically feasible for the Federal Reserve to sell it to the people.

The Covid-19 crisis has played out as a recession at mach speed. Market pundits everywhere have been quick to applaud the rapid response of the Federal Reserve to step in and backstop the world economy. Really? The arsonist and the firefighter are the exact same people. Rather than prosecute the people who started the fire, we applaud them for acting so quickly with their response. We are so programmed to believe in the Fed that we ignore the truth facing us straight in the eye.

We ignore collapsing credit markets. We overlook hedge funds that blow up when their models built on leverage implode due to a lack of liquidity. We applaud the Fed for buying junk bonds. We witness oil going to *negative* $40, something that at one time was considered impossible, and rather than recognize it as a sign that the whole system is about to implode, we continue to believe in the almighty Fed. Its only predictable response has been to print more money. Our predictable response has been to buy stocks and bonds.

The eight weeks from March 2020 through April 2020 were among the most volatile in stock market history. They witnessed a bear collapse that saw stocks drop 35 percent from peak to trough, only to be whipsawed higher by

30 percent due to an onslaught of government and central bank liquidity. Change is happening at a more rapid pace than at any time in financial history. That change has everyone asking questions. When will life return to normal? Is this the new normal? Will this be a V-shaped recovery? U? W? A swoosh?

Trump, Mnuchin, and company have been arguing that the economy will come roaring back when we reopen. They point to the pent-up demand and the desires of Americans to return to normal. Others, like Bill Gates, argue that we are in for a long road as the testing rolls out more slowly than we wish, vaccines are at least a year away, and people will change their habits to fit a new normal. So who is right?

Are we talking about the *economy* or the *stock market*? The reality is that the stock market is *not* the economy. Too many people have mistaken this essential fundamental. For over a decade, the Fed's goal has been to reflate the economy through asset purchases. It has worked for investors. The mindset shift that we've been sold is that the Fed *has our backs*. Stay invested in the markets because the central bank will support them. This mindset has allowed investors to confuse the stock market with the real economy.

But are stocks the economy? Logic suggests that since the markets are meant to represent our businesses and their level of production, that one could look to them as the main indicator of the economy. Trump's presidential victory and subsequent relentless tweets and boasts pointing to the stock market as the scoreboard for the first three years of his administration have only further branded the two one in the same. Assets are all higher. Therefore, the economy is better, right? And it's all because of Trump. "The best economy ever!" Stocks have risen over four times from their lows in 2009 through February 2020. The Dow Jones traveled from 6,500 points to 28,500 points. Those numbers mean we must have a great economy, right?

But are stocks the economy? Over the course of the past six weeks, 30 million Americans have become unemployed. This amounts to the largest six-week total in the history of our nation and eliminates all of the jobs that were created over the last decade. Ten years of central bank manipulation, and we are right back where we were a decade ago. All we have to show for it are a $24 trillion national debt, $4 trillion annual deficits, a massive divide between the haves and the have-nots, and an angry and polarized world. Oh, and stocks that are dramatically higher.

This recent spike in unemployment has likely pushed the jobless rate to 15 –20 percent, economists estimate. The only other time in American history when unemployment was that high was in the early stages of the Great Depression ninety years ago. And yet, despite that horrific reality, during this same recent span where 30 million lost their jobs, stocks are up 30 percent. Does this sound like the economy and the stock market are one and the same?

So are stocks the economy? Never before has it been more obvious that investors are living in a vastly different world than the real citizens. One of the main arguments of *Gold Is A Better Way* was that the stock market does *not* represent the economy. It's this massive divide that has created a dangerous wealth gap and has set the stage for a battle between millennials and baby boomers over the next few years that will ensure dramatic change.

There will be no *return* to normal. Life will be about *reimagining* where we go from here. It's about going forward. When you have the rug pulled out from under you, it requires a new thinking process about the future.

What most people will soon recognize is that we were due for a radical mindset shift already. The Covid-19 crisis only guarantees that that shift will occur at an even faster pace.

The divergence happening in real time is too great for anyone to miss. Stocks that are 30 percent higher are representative of one thing, manipulation. Do you think the 30 million people that just lost their jobs are feeling better that the stock market is higher? Or do you think that maybe that reality will only further increase the anger and vitriol between the haves and the have-nots? The magic tricks of the Fed are now obvious to everyone, and that's a really bad sign.

Is the economy headed in a better direction? The obvious answer is no. Things are headed to a much worse place. The entire way in which we approach the world will forever need to be reimagined. The exponential growth of and interconnectedness of this pandemic and how it's attacking our entire credit structure is being overlooked by optimistic investors who have been trained to follow the Fed. Their Pavlovian response? The Fed is buying, so we should too!

What matters to investors today is that central banks and governments around the world have turned on their massive and never-ending monetary and fiscal stimulus. The money-printing machines have been working in overdrive. Unemployment will soon surpass levels seen during the Great

Depression, but stocks and bonds have reason for optimism because of the Fed bailing out the world. We've all become conditioned that stimulus is good. Even when the world is falling apart around us, we prefer to stick our heads in the sand and trust the Fed's unlimited bazooka.

And why not? Only the dummies fight the Fed, right? The smart people who don't sell are the always winners that are rewarded as the Fed backstops every financial market regardless of underlying strength or weakness. The question for the future is, will what has worked so well until now still work moving forward?

Can the Fed continue to liquidate the world indefinitely? This is the question that demands consideration. My argument is yes, it can. And it will do so. That is near a guarantee because it's the Fed's only option. So if you are looking for a surefire bet, bet on one thing. *The Fed will print more money. It will add trillions and trillions of dollars to the system.*

This is why every investor must own gold. The Fed is now trying with all its might to weaken the dollar. Many investors hear the word "weak" and assume it's bad. The opposite is true. The strong dollar is killing the world economy. The Fed knows it and is trying to reverse it.

Will all of this money printing have the desired effect and weaken the dollar? So far, so bad on that front. Although the Fed has been pumping in liquidity, the dollar index hasn't budged. The Fed is openly trying to devalue the dollar but is facing a self-replicating feedback loop that makes that journey more challenging. When you are the trading currency of the world and everyone is rushing for safety, the safety they run to is the reserve currency of the world. We will need to print far more money than this in order to keep the dollar from rising higher. But in the end, investors will learn: Don't fight the Fed. I believe the Fed will win. The dollar will devalue and gold will soar.

Some people view the stock and bond markets as a highly efficient engine that are always sending perfect signals, where buyers and sellers match up and there is evidence of perfect value and price. A thing is worth what someone is willing to pay for it after all, right? Wrong. Capitalism is dead. It's been dead for over a decade. Our markets haven't been perfect price signals for decades. Now they are just evidence of central bank management. The evidence can be seen in the divide between the bank accounts of the haves and the have-nots.

Unfortunately, the jig is up. When the market ignores the reality of tens of millions of unemployed people *because* the Fed is buying, it is verifiable evidence that the machine is broken. How can we call it capitalism when the only buyer is the central bank? Does the efficient market theory hold water when demand is entirely managed? When the Fed is the *only* buyer, do the laws of supply and demand still apply? Have we become so brainwashed to the idea that the Fed has our back that we won't ever look forward again?

Keep in mind that mindset shifts start small. Those who employ new strategies are often questioned as they do. It's painful to break away from the herd mentality, especially when the herd is massive. Those who do attempt it do so quietly. The more quiet, the more the strategy can work. The key is to get maximum positioned before the real momentum comes along. Once "the play" becomes widely accepted, the momentum is beautiful, so one needs to get loaded up in advance to get maximum returns. Over the last three years, a new mindset has been growing. The transitions from old to new take time and occur through massive volatility and pain for those employing the old strategy. They come with validation and positive returns for those with the foresight to have moved in advance.

What creates a mindset shift? It's the combination of the avoidance of pain and the desire for pleasure. We all want to avoid pain and loss. Pain hurts. Loss takes time to overcome. We all want to experience victory. Investors who buy low are buying when no one else wants to. That's hard. Investors who sell high are selling when everyone else is buying. That's hard. For these reasons, pain and pleasure are essential emotions to the process of filtering. But what happens when we become numb to pain? When our sensors are distorted and our measurement tools provide false indications? What happens when we think we are winning and we are not?

22

Back to the Future—Part II

The reality is that we are *trying* to learn from history. Ben Bernanke was chosen to be the Fed chairman in 2006 for this very reason. Bernanke was one of the foremost experts in the world on the Great Depression. He has gone on record as stating that the Fed actually had learned from the mistakes of their past and would not make the same mistakes again. I believe he was wrong.

While the mechanism was different then, the problems remain the same. We sit inside an even bigger debt bubble today. Populism and wealth inequality are raging at the extremes, and rather than argue about how we got here and who's to blame, it makes far more sense to think through what's coming next. Central bankers in the 1930s tried to remain true to some semblance of sound money. Being responsible hurts. The problem then was exactly the same as today. Back then, the world was suffering through a massive debt crisis. Back then, the United States was the only solvent nation. The gold holdings of the Treasury equaled over 20,000 tonnes, and roughly 85 percent of the world's gold supply.

So while the 2020s will play out differently than the 1930s, there will be a few incredibly important similar takeaways that investors can learn from. Back then, markets suffered deep pain as institutions failed, leverage imploded, prices dropped dramatically, and the dollar depreciated against the real money of gold. The solution that allowed for things to reflate only came after FDR was elected and was able to shut down the banks, recall all of the gold, and then promise that every bank account would be covered by Federal Deposit Insurance.

The main "mistake" then, according to Bernanke, was that the Fed did not act fast enough or with enough force to fight off the Depression. The idea then was that insolvent banks that took on too much risk needed to be allowed to fail. Bernanke believed that failure of the central banks to act was what led to deeper recession. It's exactly why we witnessed the Fed step in after the housing crisis with such aggressive money policy, and why we can be certain that is about to be turned into overdrive. Unfortunately, the Fed's move in 2009 and beyond has created consequences that have driven an even deeper disconnect. Not allowing banks to fail is not capitalism, it's socialism. Necessary perhaps, but socialism nonetheless. Remember, "Capitalism without default is like Catholicism without hell."

Central bankers today are trying to avoid pain and are going to throw the kitchen sink at the problem in order to avoid experiencing the necessary pain. The lesson that Bernanke "learned" was that it is far better to avoid a recession than suffer through one. The only problem with that idea is that as dollars are devalued, a deeper type of recession occurs. It's a recession that comes from the devaluation of currencies. Don't worry, the Federal Reserve has "learned." For long-term investors, the news couldn't be more obvious. It will print more and more money. It's the only solution. That will happen over time and will continue to increase, and currencies will devalue as this occurs. *Don't fight the Fed* will still be the best strategy. Only now, the Federal Reserve *wants* the dollar devalued. It will get its way.

According to Newton's third law of physics, every action has an equal and opposite reaction. The actions of the central banks have led to a *reaction* of money and where it has flowed. That money flow over the last several decades has been directed toward the stock and bond markets. The Fed's policies have continued to bail out bankers that have taken on tremendous risks. Fed policies have allowed the paper markets to soar and led to asset bubbles that eventually pop. When they do, the Fed bails out the banks and real people suffer. All of it has led to a massive divide in the wealth gap as

www.zerohedge.com/news/2019-08-24/why-mark-carney-thinks-dollar-can-no-longer-be-worlds-reserve-currency.

_____. "Will The Drive To Devalue The Dollar Lead To A Plaza Accord 2.0?" Zero Hedge, October 4, 2019. https://www.zerohedge.com/geopolitical/will-drive-devalue-dollar-lead-plaza-accord-20.

_____. "'A Profound Shift Is Under Way Among Investors': Morgan Stanley Thinks 2020 Will Be The Year Of The Quants." Zero Hedge, December 15, 2019. https://www.zerohedge.com/markets/profound-shift-under-way-among-investors-morgan-stanley-thinks-2020-will-be-year-quants.

_____. "'Maybe The Rich See The Writing On The Wall': CEOs Stepping Down At Highest Levels Since 2008." Zero Hedge, November 9, 2019. https://www.zerohedge.com/personal-finance/maybe-rich-see-writing-wall-ceos-stepping-down-highest-levels-2008.

Index